Bill Evans

Everything Happens To Me – a musical biography

Bill Evans

Everything Happens To Me – a musical biography

KEITH SHADWICK

Bill Evans
Everything Happens To Me – a musical biography

Keith Shadwick

A BACKBEAT BOOK
First edition 2002

Published by Backbeat Books
600 Harrison Street,
San Francisco, CA 94107
www.backbeatbooks.com

An imprint of The Music Player Network
United Entertainment Media, Inc.

Produced for Backbeat Books by Outline Press Ltd,
115J Cleveland Street,
London W1T 6PU, England.
www.backbeatuk.com

ISBN 087930-708-0

Art Director: Nigel Osborne
Design: Sally Stockwell
Picture Research: Peter Symes
Editor: Tony Bacon

Origination by Global Colour (Malaysia)
Printed in Singapore by Tien Wah Press Pte Ltd

02 03 04 05 06 5 4 3 2 1

CONTENTS

Introduction:
Bill Evans
(1929-1980)

I t is virtually impossible to imagine the past 45 years of modern jazz without Bill Evans. The New Jersey-born pianist and composer's groundbreaking ideas were so widely absorbed by his peers and subsequently by every new generation of musicians that he ranks alongside the most influential figures in post-war jazz – Thelonious Monk, Charles Mingus, Miles Davis, John Coltrane, Charlie Parker and Dizzy Gillespie. Within that group, Evans (1929-1980) is often seen as someone whose initial contributions to jazz – around the late 1950s and early 1960s — were all that mattered. His style, runs the argument, hardly evolved over the following 20 years. Certainly it was during Evans's brief tenure with Miles Davis in 1958 that these early and enormously influential innovations were unveiled, followed by his work on Davis's *Kind Of Blue* album and the first version of Evans's working trio in 1960 and 1961. But the true picture is wider and much more interesting, as readers of this book will discover.

Until 1962 Evans was also a hard-working freelancer with a number of leaders, including Tony Scott, Oliver Nelson and George Russell. After he achieved wider jazz popularity through producer Creed Taylor's efforts at Verve, Evans continued to tackle large projects and to experiment occasionally with ensembles of various sizes. His increased popularity coincided with an explosion of avant-garde creativity in jazz tied closely to new social, cultural and political freedoms. But Evans was quickly left far behind the vanguard of the music. Most of his later experiments ran contrary to the musical trends of the day, making his efforts deeply unfashionable – but that hardly qualifies them for the neglect they have suffered. As we shall see, it is in these latter-day ventures as much as in his late trio work that the full musical harvest of Evans's early promise is to be found. It may not often seem commensurate with early expectations, but it is hardly Evans's fault if the fans and jazz critics who hailed him as a new jazz messiah later decided that he'd been no such thing.

Evans was a dedicated musician, very serious about his music and faithful to its continued evolution. It was never his ambition to keep up with jazz fashions and stylistic developments. This recalls the occasion when Charles Mingus badgered Duke Ellington to record "something really avant-garde" during a studio session, and the Duke replied: "Oh no, Charles, let's not go *that* far back." This book will deal with the merits and flaws in the music that Bill Evans actually produced rather than anything his critics felt he should have been playing, presenting a story that we hope will help readers to reinvestigate Evans's work for themselves and follow their own paths through it.

CHAPTER 1

Jazz Piano Before Evans (1945-55)

"BUD POWELL HAD THE MOST COMPREHENSIVE COMPOSITION TALENT OF ANY JAZZ PLAYER I HAVE EVER HEARD PRESENTED ON THE JAZZ SCENE."

BILL EVANS TALKING ABOUT ONE OF HIS FAVOURITE PIANO PLAYERS

Considering the ubiquity of Bill Evans's stylistic influence in the past 40 years of jazz, it is worth pausing here to consider the state of contemporary jazz piano in the mid 1950s. This will give us a clearer idea of Evans's initial impact when he unveiled his mature style, and a means to uncover his own musical roots.

By 1955 the first wave of bop pianists – Bud Powell, Al Haig, Dodo Marmarosa, Thelonious Monk, Lennie Tristano and George Wallington – had been and more or less gone, for one reason or another. Bud Powell was experiencing a devastating sequence of personal events, including electric shock treatment, which would eventually drain him of most of his

The piano awaits ... Bell Sound studio in New York City

creativity. Dodo Marmarosa had literally disappeared (he'd returned to his native city, Pittsburgh); Al Haig had faded; Thelonious Monk was in eclipse, unable for legal reasons even to appear live in New York City. George Wallington, though running an efficient bop group, was a waning force and would soon drop out of full-time musical employment.

Lennie Tristano, having been closely associated with New York's 52nd Street bop revolution in the mid 1940s, progressively isolated himself from the ideas of Parker, Gillespie, Powell and Monk, preferring to concentrate on his own theories. Tristano was for the most part brought in front of the public by students and acolytes such as Lee Konitz and Warne Marsh. By the early 1950s, disgusted at what he saw as the "anti-music" policy of most nightclub owners, Tristano was actively withdrawing from public engagements and concentrating on teaching. His ascetic style and influence can be traced in few pianists of the time – though Bill Evans would be one – and his theories seemed more readily to appeal to saxophonists. The hugely influential Nat "King" Cole, a swing-era player who presaged many later jazz piano developments, was at the peak of his popular singing and entertainment career, and now rarely appeared professionally behind a piano. George Shearing, who had first made his presence felt internationally in the late 1940s, was still very active and had consolidated a popular musical formula which became progressively more effete as the 1950s progressed. Of the major stars from the 1940s, only mavericks such as Errol Garner and Oscar Peterson were still developing their music uncompromisingly in styles close to their original conceptions.

Milt Buckner, a player more truly allied to the pre-bop piano traditions, never gained widespread fame or praise, his style becoming passé before the advent of the 1950s, but his method of playing extended melodic passages using a "locked hands" technique would prove to be hugely influential on younger players. "Locked hands" means playing entirely chordally, with both hands in unison. It was a technique that Buckner had brought over from playing the organ, and one which organist Wild Bill Davis also helped to popularise. The style filtered through to a wider public and professional audience when pianists such as George Shearing, Erroll Garner and a young Philadelphian, Ahmad Jamal, expanded and adapted the idea. Jamal's emergence in the 1950s was an important part of the new ideas that were superseding the standard bebop arrangements, group interplay, harmony and form.

It has been pointed out by many commentators that Bud Powell was not the first pianist to abandon swing conventions. Players such as Al Haig, Clyde Hart, Argonne Thornton, Dodo Marmarosa and (for one memorable Savoy session) Dizzy Gillespie had developed the rhythmic punctuations, from either hand or in unison, which rode over the rhythm of bass and drums and, during accompaniment of other soloists, provided harmonic fodder for the improviser. In addition to these players, Elmo Hope, a friend of Powell's since their youth, persistently claimed later in his career to have been playing bop contemporaneously with Powell, while Thelonious Monk has often been quoted as saying that all other pianists learned bop harmony from his own example at Minton's and Monroe's clubs in the early 1940s. While this may be true, Monk's recordings from 1943/44 betray a strong reliance on swing phraseology and a stride left hand: stylistic traits to which he would regularly resort when playing solo or trio dates in his years of triumph. From the mid 1950s onwards, Monk's mischievous sense of humour, as well as a rare irony, would have kept any accusations of anachronism at bay.

At medium and slow tempos, these pianists were also comfortable with a single-line melodic style of improvising largely taken from Parker and Gillespie and which avoided regular left-hand rhythmic accompaniment. Only at speed did their swing roots become evident, where stride variants and other perpetuum mobile techniques came to the fore in order to sustain momentum, both in solos and accompaniments. (Perpetuum mobile means repetitive note patterns throughout a fast piece.) They made plain the formulaic chord substitutions made to the "standard" underlying changes of most bop tunes. Even Dodo Marmarosa – on 'Dodo's Dance' in 1946, a 'Cherokee' variant taken at a Parker-like ultra-fast tempo – reverts to stride figures in his left hand for both the theme statement and improvisation. Marmarosa had not yet grasped the fact that, at such a tempo in bop, the degree of invention displayed in the right-hand passages was paramount; the bass and drums could keep everything else underpinned. None of the first-generation pianists with swing in their veins had been able to take all these elements and create a new and distinct musical personality which spoke for the younger generation of musicians. This was Bud Powell's achievement in the mid to late 1940s. Powell is habitually described as the pianistic equivalent of Charlie Parker, and to a certain extent this is a reasonable parallel. His harmonic language, rhythmic drive and complex, long-phrased melodies – as well as his complete mastery of the blues – are facilities all shared with Parker. Powell had a phenomenal technique through which he communicated a white-hot emotional landscape. He could gambol through conventional popular-song changes, as well as the bop generation's Parker-inspired inversions and substitutions on those changes, at any tempo and in a style guaranteed to terrify any other young turk. Indeed, at his best and most fluent, Powell was only surpassed technically at the keyboard by Art Tatum, the unrivalled pre-war giant. However, Powell's roots lay with the pianistic approximation of melodic instruments and their improvisatory lines, as developed in the 1930s by Earl Hines in particular. Hines's personal repertoire of long, asymmetrical and often dramatic melodic arabesques, combined with a spare and frequently explosive use of the left hand (picked up and developed by Teddy Wilson and Nat Cole), was taken to a very different level of expression by Powell during his early successes.

Powell, like Marmarosa and few other jazz pianists of the time, had formal piano training which allowed him to use his harmonic and rhythmic imagination in fresh ways. Using the low-register left-hand punctuations first heard in Al Haig's playing, Powell heightened their importance by employing them to more dramatic effect in his solos and accompaniments. He used them almost as a running commentary on his right-hand flourishes, rather than, like most other players, simply as a root-position chordal signpost, usually delivered on the first beat of a bar, through whatever set of chord changes were being negotiated.

As his style matured and he reached his late-1940s peak, Powell introduced other elements into his left-hand repertory, including ostinato patterns, rhythmic devices taken from Latin American and Caribbean music, and an occasional but strong blues flavour. He would also use left-hand chordal accompaniment only when he felt that it would add another element to the overall fabric of the performance. In his 1949 trio recording for Norman Granz of 'Tea For Two' he lovingly caresses the out-of-tempo introduction before launching into the theme itself. It is only ever picked out by the lower register notes of the piano, in an obsessive reiterative pattern, while his right hand rips through three minutes of searing chord-based single-line improvisation. The ensuing contrast and tension is part of the success of this classic recording.

Perhaps Powell's greatest improvisational legacy was his evolution of a piano style which could comfortably fit with the small-group solo excursions of the new bop generation as well as the freshly evolved role for drums perfected by Kenny Clarke, Max Roach and others. This type of playing mesmerised other pianists, few of whom could hope to compete with Powell either technically or temperamentally, but who were determined to emulate their idol. He remained the dominant influence among younger players well into the 1950s: as is so often the case when confronted with overwhelming genius, most younger pianists took parts of Powell's style and developed them into a sub-style of their own. Horace Silver, for example, took the darkly driving first and second-position triad figures of Powell's left hand and added a more unabashedly blues-drenched and rhythmically ebullient character, closer to his own musical personality. His right-hand melodicism initially echoed the long-limbed, unpredictable manner of which Powell was a master, but Silver, a highly gifted melodist, gradually evolved an improvising style which relied more on repetition of shorter phrases and motifs, and on rhythmic playfulness. Together these became cornerstones of the 1950s hard bop style. Ironically, Powell in his later years resorted to this shorter-phrased style of playing when his impaired inventiveness could no longer sustain the long-phrased patterns of his youth.

Powell was an original and arresting composer with a much wider stylistic palette than Charlie Parker. As such he exerted an influence on the next generation in jazz, through his own records and the recordings of his works made by others. A compositional experimenter in strange harmonic waters, Powell was influenced both by his friend Thelonious Monk and by his classical studies, as well as the long, sinuous melodies of Parker's bop works and the exotic Afro-Cuban rhythms brought to jazz by, among others, Dizzy Gillespie. Powell was also adept at working up memorable phrases into complete tunes, as ballads and mid-tempo swingers. 'Celia', for example, exhibits pleasantly crisp melodic contours and a peppy rhythm, while 'I'll Keep Loving You' demonstrates not only Powell's deep reverence for Tatum both harmonically and rhythmically but also his penchant for overtly romantic melodic lines.

An older man than Powell, Nat Cole was no revolutionary, but he knew few rivals in his own field. His style was more overtly an extension of certain rhythmic and melodic elements of Tatum's playing, especially the forceful left hand and the richly melodic right-hand variations. Cole rarely used the stride, which was a fundamental part of Tatum's style and technique, preferring to kick his rhythm along with adroit off-beat left-hand accents in the lower registers. This proved a boon when he was accompanying or soloing, and was a major factor in the mid-1940s evolution of bop piano, Cole being one of the first to use and dramatise space. His improvisatory phraseology remained at its core swing-based, both harmonically and rhythmically – he rarely ventured past 8th-notes, in duple or triple time, in his extemporisations. But his liberal use of harmonised right-hand passages presages much 1950s piano work.

The other aspect of Cole's approach which proved immensely influential during the 1940s and early 1950s was the idea of a piano-guitar-bass trio, of which his was the first; even Tatum had followed him in this development. Cole was not a significant composer, but his simplification of Tatum's formidably ornate approach and his application of that reduction showed the way ahead for many pianists, both pre and post-Parker. Oscar Peterson and Ahmad Jamal are perhaps the most famous and influential beneficiaries. They both made use of drummerless trios for a number of years, but drew on different aspects of Cole's techniques: Peterson the rhythmic drive and the trio's collective improvisation; Jamal the clear, well-structured arrangements and effective use of space.

A second wave of pianists came to prominence in the early 1950s, for the most part offering refinements and extensions of Powell and his contemporaries (especially Parker) and emphasising one or more aspects of Powell's creativity, in a way that suited the musical personality of each. Young players such as Hank Jones, Red Garland and John Lewis refined their touch and harmonically reworked standard changes on well-known songs and classic blues patterns, reflecting the progressive elements in the music of the time.

Hank Jones was a pianist in the Teddy Wilson tradition, widely admired by 1955 for his harmonic resourcefulness within standard repertoire and his lightness of touch. He did not extend modern jazz piano's repertoire, but found ways of bringing subtle and ingenious inversions and harmonic substitutions to well-known chord changes and musical forms, thereby freshening the impact of any group in which he appeared. His near-contemporary Red Garland combined the uncluttered rhythmic dynamism of Nat Cole with bop harmonies. A sideman during the 1940s and early 1950s with Coleman Hawkins, Lester Young and Charlie Parker among others, Garland made a considerable impact during his years with Miles Davis's quintet, immediately prior to Bill Evans joining that band.

John Lewis, who had spent time with the Dizzy Gillespie band in the late 1940s and with Lester Young at the opening of the 1950s, was a pianist whose main interests lay outside the area of piano-led trio invention on common themes. A supreme accompanist with a special gift for concision and telling understatement, Lewis was also a brilliant arranger and composer. Throughout the 1950s he used The Modern Jazz Quartet as an ideal vehicle for his musical expression. His piano style is more deeply rooted in pre-Powell players such as Tatum, Jess Stacey and Teddy Wilson, both in the way he would conceive a treatment of a particular tune and in his harmonic and rhythmic variety.

As Lewis's style matured these roots became less easy to distinguish. He became notably adept at producing the maximum effect through the fewest notes – more effectively even than Count Basie or Thelonious Monk because he shunned musical routines that, with Basie and Monk, eventually became so predictable that anticipating them became part of the pleasure of listening. Lewis attempted always to make his musical thinking and the development of his solos a rigorous process that took him and his audience to fresh musical fields. That he did this through subtlety rather than bombast is an even more remarkable measure of his achievement. Lewis had a particular love of European culture and music and was constant in his efforts to bring European music's sense of form and proportion to jazz performances. He went so far as to overtly import devices including fugues, simple counterpoint, and the suite form. Lewis had a deep appreciation for and love of the blues, but the models for many of his cross-cultural ventures were the great baroque and classical period composers, Vivaldi, Bach, Mozart, Haydn and the like. His grand and often highly successful experiments with the MJQ and larger, more disparate groups, including symphony orchestras, were lauded at the time but remained curiously isolated as a phenomenon within the jazz world. There were precious few independent contemporary attempts to develop his lines of thought.

Dave Brubeck was another pianist with a thorough knowledge of and interest in European music. He too touched few other pianists of the time – although curiously the young and avant-garde Cecil Taylor, usually caustic about his contemporaries, would later grudgingly admit to an early appreciation of Brubeck's methods. Arguably, Bill Evans was another isolated example: he was especially drawn to Brubeck's refreshing and comprehensive use of harmony and his often overlooked gift for melody.

Brubeck showed little direct affinity with the New York bop phraseology which in the 1950s metamorphosed into hard-bop routines. His jazz roots more typically spread through such self-professed influences as Nat Cole and George Shearing to Tatum, Fats Waller and blues and boogie players such as Jimmy Yancey, Albert Ammons and James P. Johnson. This seemed to fit naturally with the jazz roots of Brubeck's greatest single non-jazz influence, Darius Milhaud, whose early and most famous works show a love of the ragtime and classic jazz forms that arrived in Europe in the immediate aftermath of World War I rather than the styles of the 1930s and 1940s.

Brubeck's interest in form, time signatures and the application of advanced harmony found few kindred souls at the keyboard in the 1950s. But the methods he displayed in the 1956 solo recording of his own music, *Brubeck Plays Brubeck*, reveal a close link with what emerged as Bill Evans's main compositional and improvisational thinking and practice. Brubeck's feat in moving through all 12 keys in the opening theme statement of 'The Duke', for example, would have enthralled few contemporary jazz musicians, though such complex but effortless modulations and the musical reasoning behind them would be a source of fascination in Evans's art for the following 25 years.

The Philadelphia-born pianist Ahmad Jamal only began to emerge as an important national figure during the late 1950s. Initially he had combined the "cushioned chords" concept as perfected by Shearing with the drummerless trio used by players like Art Tatum and Nat Cole. By the late 1940s he'd taken this hybrid further with his drummerless trio The Three Strings, and then applied the techniques to an orthodox piano-bass-drums trio. His own pared-down, uncluttered style was judicious and hard-won, forging together elements of Cole and Powell, with a Shearing-like gift for organisation. Jamal's clearly articulated and evenly-weighted technique was closer to Tatum's than most, though rarely in a full set did he use his undeniable technical facility for more than a few moments of mind-popping display. He was much more interested in using the piano as the lead voice in his group's interplay, directing the audience's imagination through their careful articulation of light and shade. He used space in preference to bustle, and melodic and harmonic lucidity rather than jumble: these would prove valuable artistic pointers for Evans when he came to formulate ideas for his own trio.

Jamal's disinclination to follow Bud Powell in florid artistic display was also important. Like Evans, Jamal has often been accused of being an emotional lightweight. But as with Evans, Jamal certainly did bring emotional depth to his music – revealed, however, through restraint and implication. Jamal rarely dealt with the Dionysian artistic and emotional demons which drove Powell; his primary concerns were with peace and joy. Jamal's exquisite and often provocative trio arrangements of familiar songs, using bassist Israel Crosby and drummer Vernell Fournier, made a tremendous asset of the dramatic use of space, unexpected musical punctuation, ostinatos, and substantially slowed-down harmonic movement. All these devices quickly became models for many other leaders, including Miles Davis, who hired Red Garland in 1954 largely for his ability to imitate Jamal's spare but strongly rhythmic playing.

It may be argued that Thelonious Monk, the wellspring of many of the compositional and harmonic practices of early bop, remained a considerable influence during the early 1950s before his wider public acceptance in the second half of the decade. But between 1950 and 1956 his playing and his compositions were largely unappreciated by other jazzmen: there are virtually no recordings of his music outside his own work for Prestige, a session with Gigi Gryce where he played his own material, and the occasional treatment of his music by Powell. Then in 1956 Miles Davis helped bring attention to Monk by recording 'Round Midnight' on his debut LP for Columbia. Monk influenced few other pianists in terms of technique – though, curiously enough, Powell's latter-day recordings often show unmistakeable homage to Monk. Little of Monk's written music was investigated by other musicians, either live or on record, before his own much-publicised classic late-1950s recordings for the Riverside label which established him in the international spotlight.

During this period jazz did not exist in isolation from other musical genres. Many young pianists combined the complexities of Powell-driven bop styles with a simpler rhythmic and harmonic approach adopted from the more sophisticated end of the fast-fading R&B genre. Horace Silver and Hampton Hawes were both prominent and influential by the mid 1950s, driven on by the popular success of R&B-derived white acts spearheaded by Elvis Presley and the wide audience acclaim for the marrying of church and the vernacular in the playing of Ray Charles. Silver and Hawes became adept at expanding and amplifying the roots-based side of Powell and Parker's innovations, bringing more of the rough-hewn blues and gospel-tinged rhythms and harmonies into their playing than had hitherto been seen as acceptable in modern jazz. Silver also brought a genuine compositional talent to his own groups, forging a style of earthy melodicism widely admired and imitated during the decade from the mid 1950s to the mid 1960s.

During his period in tandem with drummer Art Blakey, Silver also began to explore musical devices more identifiably African, heard in his accompaniment to trumpeter Clark Terry on 'Swahili' from Terry's self-named 1954 LP for EmArcy. That track also features a stark ostinato from Oscar Pettiford's cello and almost primeval drumming from Blakey himself, some years prior to Blakey's Blue Note recordings featuring combinations of jazz and African drummers. But this type of playing, while often artistically successful, remained something of an exoticism – and was certainly not the methodical study of related musics that became fashionable in the 1980s and 1990s. Indeed, saxophonist Yusef Lateef's adoption of a great many reed and woodwind instruments from around the world – and between 1956 and 1961 his mild but intelligently eclectic incorporation into jazz of timbres, rhythms and melody from other cultures – was largely condemned by critics as "weird" and irrelevant to jazz as it was then construed.

Despite these extensions to the boundaries of bop, cool and what became known by the mid 1950s as progressive jazz, the essence of all these players – even Lateef, whose improvisation was never particularly harmonically adventurous – was a commitment to improvising (and composing) through the harmonic changes and shifts of each pre-existing structure on offer. The popularity of these players and the praise from colleagues was usually based on their technical facility and creative negotiation of the harmonic and rhythmic parameters, using a musical language for the most part adopted (and adapted) from Powell, Cole, Tatum and, to a lesser extent, Tristano. Given the need to articulate each passing chord, substitution and inversion, their playing was invariably dominated by the intricacy of their right-hand elaborations, most of which followed well-worn melodic paths and had hardened into convention. The left hand, meanwhile, would provide an occasional rhythmic and harmonic reference point. Apart from Tristano, who by the mid 1950s was virtually never heard in public, only Jamal, Brubeck and Lewis had deviated to any significant degree from the predominant bop guidelines established a decade earlier by Powell, Parker, Gillespie and their peers.

Bill Evans had deep roots in this particular jazz tradition, but he also added other crucial elements. His musical training included a relatively comprehensive study of the classical piano repertoire, then a standard component of advanced-level study of grade piano and theory. In addition, Evans was strongly attracted to the theories behind Tristano's distinctive musical practices, where the subtleties of melodic invention and rhythmic inflection were allied to harmonic thinking that broke free of bop conventions. Tristano was simply not interested in the standard harmonic substitutions and extensions of the bop pianists' stock underlying structures, such as 'I Got Rhythm', 'All The Things You Are', 'How High The Moon' or 'Cherokee'. Tristano's fascination with 'All The Things You Are', Jerome Kern's masterpiece which moves through all 12 key signatures, resulted in music that bore little resemblance to that which, say, Charlie Parker produced from the same harmonic steeplechase. Perhaps most decisive, however, was the study and work that Evans undertook in the mid 1950s with theorist George Russell. It was Russell who pointed the young pianist toward the study of scales and modes as an alternative to the obsessive negotiation of standard or expanded chord changes that drove most bop players.

This interest in using related scales to provide musical building-blocks and to redefine jazz form provided Evans's route into his distinctive modern jazz playing. He also benefited from an apparently straighforward fact: like Erroll Garner, Evans was left-handed. This gave him an unusually even natural balance in touch and weight between both hands. Regardless of the repertoire Evans could, through the medium of his unique touch and phrasing, apply his theories of harmonic reduction and the role of the leading harmonic voice to evoke his own distinctive sound and approach. In subsequent chapters we will investigate the progressive changes that Evans made to his initial style and to jazz in general as his conception grew to maturity at the close of the 1950s and into the early 1960s.

The young man as jazz pianist: a contemplative Bill Evans (1) at the start of the 1960s. New Jazz Conceptions (2) was his debut LP as leader, recorded in 1956. A few years later Everybody Digs Bill Evans (7) proved pivotal and widely influential, and Evans would frequently revisit the material. His popularity as a sideman in late-1950s New York is evident from the diverse leadership of the other sleeves pictured.

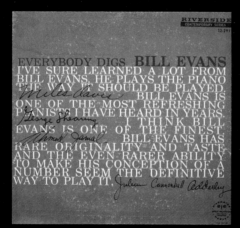

Kind of Blue
Sessions

Miles Davis's Kind Of Blue LP of 1959 (1) paved the way for many advances in modern jazz over the subsequent decades, and it remains influential to this day. Evans and Davis (2) were instrumental in organising the material. These shots taken in April at the second of Kind Of Blue's two studio sessions show (3) John Coltrane, Cannonball Adderley, Davis and Evans, and (4) Adderley, Davis, Paul Chambers and Evans.

19

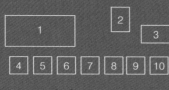

Evans with the Tony Scott quartet (1) in New York in July 1959: Scott on clarinet, Jimmy Garrison (2) on bass. Gunther Schuller (3) and the MJQ's John Lewis used Evans on Jazz Abstractions (9) and a number of live events. Schuller was an influential presence in progressive music in the late 1950s. The LPs here represent 18 productive months for Evans the sideman in 1959/60.

Know What I Mean?
Sessions

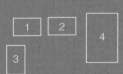

Cannonball Adderley and Evans were in the Miles Davis Sextet in 1958, later making two LPs together under Adderley's leadership. On 1961's Know What I Mean?, the second of the two, Adderley gave Evans a central role, making it a creative partnership between equals. These photos from the sessions show (4) producer Orrin Keepnews (left), with Adderley (seated) and Evans behind him, and (1,2) bassist Percy Heath.

Bill Evans

More photos from the LP made by Adderley and Evans (2) at Bell Sound in New York in early 1961 (see also previous pages). Completing the line-up on drums is Connie Kaye (4). The identity of the strategically placed pair of legs on the resulting album's original sleeve (5) remains a mystery to this day.

Know What I Mean ?
Sessions

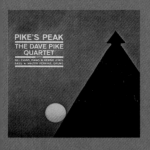

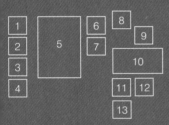

Four seminal albums (1-4) by the first Bill Evans Trio were released by Riverside in 1960 and 1961. The trio's bassist Scott LaFaro (5) is pictured at New York's Village Vanguard club during a summer '61 residency where Sunday At The Village Vanguard (3) and Waltz For Debby (4) were recorded. LaFaro died tragically just weeks later. The Dave Pike (6) and Tadd Dameron (7) LPs were the last on which Evans would appear as a sideman. The first three albums from Evans's new trio (8,11,12) had Chuck Israels on bass, with Paul Motian continuing as drummer.

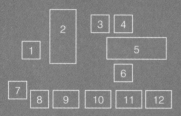

Drummer Shelly Manne (5) ran Shelly's Manne-Hole club in LA, where Evans recorded a live album (6) in 1963. Evans's groundbreaking multi-tracked 1963 solo LP, Conversations With Myself (3), won him his first Grammy. Bassist Gary Peacock (2) and drummer Paul Motian – pictured (1) in Boston in 1964 – together with Evans made Trio 64 (4) during a tense and difficult session. These and almost all Evans's recordings owned by Verve were collected on to 18 CDs in the late 1990s, accompanied by a lavish book (8-12) and encased in a progressively rusting metal box (7).

29

Bill Evans

By 1963 Evans had stabilised the line-up of his second Trio, featuring Chuck Israels on bass and Larry Bunker on drums. All three musicians are captured preparing for a concert in this set of photographs taken during their visit to Denmark in 1964.

Copenhagen
1964

Copenhagen
1964

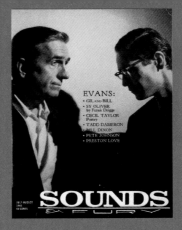

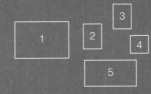

Photographs (1,5) from the Trio's Danish date in 1964 (see also previous pages). Evans's growing fame in the mid 1960s saw him on covers of jazz magazines (2,3) on both sides of the Atlantic. A trio-and-strings LP (4) made in '65 had a mixed welcome then, but has since gained wider respect.

Copenhagen
1966

Evans and Eddie Gomez (1,2), along with drummer Alex Riel, appeared on TV in Denmark in 1966 with the Swedish jazz singer Monica Zetterlund. Two years earlier Evans had appeared on an album with Zetterlund, the second LP to be titled Waltz For Debby.

Mid/late 1960s Evans LPs: with
drummer Shelly Manne (1);
live at New York Town Hall (2)
including a solo suite for
Evans's late father; second duet
with guitarist Jim Hall (3); and
second multi-tracked solo
record (5). This 1967 Trio (4)
in LA has Elliot Zigmund
(drums) and Eddie Gomez
(bass). One of Evans's favourite
drum partners, Philly Joe Jones
(6), returned to play with him
in New York in 1967.

Bill Evans

Montreux

1968

Evans's appearance at the
second Montreux Jazz Festival
in Switzerland in 1968 with
drummer Jack DeJohnette and
bassist Eddie Gomez (3,4) was
a career highlight, fortunately
recorded and released by Verve
(1). DeJohnette (2), who had
risen to fame with Charles
Lloyd, would soon be playing
with Miles Davis. Evans's
album titled Alone (5) was his
third solo record, made in
1968 and this time truly solo,
without the multi-tracking of
earlier projects.

Montreux
1970

Into the 1970s for the Bill Evans Trio, as the changing fashions of these photos demonstrate, with Eddie Gomez (2) in leather jacket at Montreux and drummer Marty Morrell moving from a snappy suit (1) to a Star Trek look in Denmark in 1970 (5). Fewer evident changes for Evans at Montreux that year (4), with a live record of the date (3) appearing on Creed Taylor's label, CTI.

Copenhagen
1970

Bill Evans

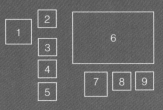

In 1970 Evans signed to Columbia Records, and was pictured at that time (1) with manager/producer Helen Keane and Columbia staff producer Teo Macero. Just two records resulted: The Bill Evans Album (2) and Living Time (3). Seventies fashion had now crept up on Evans, pictured in 1972 (6) at one of his favourite clubs, Ronnie Scott's. After a period when he was not signed exclusively to any company, Evans and Keane opted for the Milestone label in 1974 (4,5,7-9).

Bill Evans

Monterey
1975

Evans's appearance at the
Monterey festival in 1975 took
three forms: a duet with Eddie
Gomez (6); a piano workshop
with Patrice Rushen, John
Lewis or Marian McPartland,
and a set with the Oakland
Youth Symphony Orchestra.
In the mid 1970s he recorded
small-group and solo LPs for
Milestone – all but (9) here.
Evans left in '77 to record for
Warner; the first album was
You Must Believe In Spring (9).

Bill Evans

Molde
1980

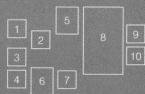

The last Trio, formed in 1979, had Joe LaBarbera (drums) and Marc Johnson (bass), pictured at Molde, Norway, in August 1980. Johnson was present on all post-'77 Warner LPs except the solo New Conversations (1). The recently released Last Waltz (10) caught the trio at Keystone Korner, San Francisco, in August and September 1980, just days before Evans's death.

Childhood, Youth, the Army & After (1929-1955)

"THE IDEA OF DOING SOMETHING IN MUSIC THAT SOMEBODY HADN'T THOUGHT OF OPENED A WHOLE NEW WORLD TO ME."

BILL EVANS ON AN IMPORTANT EARLY DISCOVERY

William John Evans was born in Plainfield, New Jersey, on August 16th 1929, the second son of a Welsh father and Russian mother. He grew up in a solidly middle-class family and in pleasant suburban surroundings, and later described his childhood as "very happy and secure".[1] His education too was untroubled, and when he moved from the family home in 1946 at the age of 17 to Southeastern Louisiana College in New Orleans it marked the start of the first sustained period he spent on his own. By the time this born-and-raised Northerner reached New Orleans, he had already been studying piano and music theory for a decade. Evans had been attracted to the piano as an infant after hearing his older brother, Harry,

Communing with the keys in Boston

taking elementary lessons: two years of Harry's efforts bouncing around the house finally led Bill to explore the instrument that so absorbed his brother. His parents decided that six-year-old Bill was sufficiently mature to begin piano lessons, and for the next five years he shared his brother's teacher, learning basic keyboard and reading techniques through the classical pieces and exercises popular in pre-war America. He worked on Bach, Haydn, Beethoven, Dvorak and Mozart, for "three hours a day"[2] according to his later testimony.

Evans's initial exposure to music was thus through classical music, reinforced by his parents' concern to give their child a rounded education; by his second year of keyboard studies he was introduced to the violin. During these early years he remained firmly in the shadow of his older brother, at least in his own eyes, and constantly attempted to match Harry's feats. This family competition gave Bill a relish for hard work and musical discipline that would remain with him for life. In combination with his natural intellectual curiosity and wide reading habits, it would eventually make Evans a more fully equipped musician than the vast majority of jazzmen of his generation.

He soon became a fast reader and highly proficient at the mechanical aspects of the keyboard. When he was 10, he recalled later, "I got medals for playing Mozart and Schubert, but I couldn't even play 'My Country Tis Of Thee' without the music."[3] He also learned the rudiments of good violin tone and fingering, although by the time he was 13, in 1942, he preferred the flute as a second instrument. By then he had discovered jazz through the excitement of boogie-woogie, and was quickly moved to emulate his new piano heroes. He later quipped to pianist Marian McPartland: "I used to be the fastest boogie-woogie player in central [New] Jersey. I have a cardboard disc someplace [that] I made when I was 12, playing boogie-woogie." Even a year before his death, when that interview took place, Evans was respectful of his first love in jazz. "I started playing boogie-woogie, which is good … it's the blues, and what better way to start playing jazz?"[4]

Not only was Evans immersed in classical music and literature, he was evidently becoming quickly proficient as a player increasingly familiar with popular music – enough to have depped at short notice for his unwell brother in a local dance band at the age of 12. He would make further appearances with this outfit, which dealt solely with stock arrangements of popular dance numbers and attempted no improvisation. (In the early 1940s dance bands and jazz bands were perceived as very different entities in terms of musical worth and entertainment potential: the jazz magazine *Down Beat*, for example, had two such distinct voting categories for many years in its annual popularity polls.)

During his gigs with the band Evans discovered the delights of harmonic substitution. In an oft-quoted anecdote which he told on a number of occasions much later in life, he recalled an unplanned moment of inspiration where he "put in a little blues thing". 'Tuxedo Junction', he would explain, is in B-flat. "I put in a little D-flat, D, F thing, bang!, in the right hand. It was such a thrill … The idea of doing something in music that somebody hadn't thought of opened a whole new world for me."[5] It was highly unusual in the 1940s for someone brought up with the idea of music as an interpretative art for the player and a creative art for the composer to find such delight in extemporisation. Few musicians of above-average calibre, black or white, passed happily between the two artistic and musical disciplines. Of those who did, fewer still had much to offer on either front.

Evans stayed on in Plainfield, New Jersey, until the completion of his high school education, developing his music with hard work and exacting self-discipline. He believed he was only moderately gifted and that he achieved what little he did through exhaustive training and the slow elimination of weaknesses or areas of ignorance. He developed an exceptionally broad taste in classical music, focusing on particular favourite composers who would forever have an effect on his feelings for harmony and form. Apart from more modernist romantics, aesthetes and symbolists such as Delius, Debussy, Satie and Ravel, Evans developed a considerable appreciation of more unashamedly popular composers such as Grieg, Rachmaninov and Chopin. All three were towering figures in American drawing-rooms, and Rachmaninov's US concerts were highly acclaimed during the whole of Evans's youth. Parallel to this passion, Evans was a member of a youthful semi-pro outfit nominally led by his brother. He also played with a band of professionals which occasionally featured trumpeter/mellophone player Don Elliott, a man like Evans destined for wider success later in the following decade. It was also in this band that the teenage Evans met his first important musical mentor in the jazz world, bassist George Platt. As Evans told interviewer Brian Hennessy, "George would call out the changes for me without ever suggesting that I should have learned them for myself. Finally, instead of thinking of them as isolated changes, I worked out a system upon which traditional theory is based [and I] gradually began to understand how the music was put together."[6]

In the fall of 1946 at the age of 17 Evans began the four-year undergraduate course at Southeastern Louisiana College (SLC) on the outskirts of New Orleans, where he majored in music education and piano studies. He had gained his place there through the Music Department head, Dr Ralph R. Pottle, with whom Evans would sustain a correspondence for years after his graduation (Pottle's son, Ralph Jr., was Evans's SLC room-mate). In the southern climate and relaxed feel of New Orleans – the famous "Big Easy" – Evans discovered a new approach to life. He found the town a perfect base for his musical and cultural excursions. "I had just turned 17, and it was the first time I was on my own," he said later. "It's an age when everything makes a big impression, and Louisiana impressed me big."[7] In particular, Evans responded well to the relaxed tempo of life in New Orleans and to the sheer amount of time he had to study and pursue parallel interests – and it was during this period that he began his lifelong interest in philosophy, both Western and Eastern.

New Orleans provided a fine mix of musical stimulation, leisure and hard work. As well as becoming a heavy-hitting "lefty" tennis player on campus, the young student was gigging regularly with a small-time collegiate trio, The Casuals, occasionally depping on flute too, in New Orleans as well as the surrounding areas. Evans revelled in the opportunities, opening up to the world and absorbing a new culture that was so unlike his own that it may as well have been in a foreign country. He came to love the locale and its special ambience, recalling years later that "there was a kind of freedom there, different from anything in the North. The intercourse between the Negro and white was friendly, even intimate. There was no hypocrisy, and that's important to me. I told this to Miles [Davis] when I was working with him and asked him if he understood what I meant. He said he did."[8]

If Evans had been unwilling to step over the divide between "legitimate" music and jazz during his early teens, preferring to gig occasionally around Plainfield but concentrate on classical repertoire and music theory, then New Orleans and its environs pushed him toward jazz. As his interpretative ability at the keyboard progressed and he studied composers who were to remain lifetime favourites – Delius, Ravel, Satie, Debussy, Scriabin, Brahms – Evans realised that a career in music education was not his ideal. All through his studies at SLC he had approached his work in a non-conformist fashion, often to the annoyance of his teachers. "But they couldn't flunk me, because I played the instrument so well,"[9] he once told Gene Lees. His enquiring mind and free spirit took him closer to jazz, as did his deepening determination to explore the depths of his own emotions and present them to his own public. He told Don Nelson in 1960: "This trumpet player in New Orleans … used to put down his horn and comp at the piano. When he did, he got that deep, moving feeling I've always wanted, and it dragged me because I couldn't reach it."[10]

Even at this early stage, Evans was trying to combine all the musical traditions in which he was involved. He wrote the first version of his sprightly waltz 'Very Early' while at SLC, though it had to wait until 1962 for its first recording. By that time Evans would add considerable polish and sophistication to what is essentially a study in modulations. It might have been considered unusual in the jazz of the late 1940s, even if the form is a simple ABA. With its triple metre, the piece is a refreshing and innocent early work, not dissimilar in character to the material Dave Brubeck was developing independently at the same time in the Bay area of San Francisco.

Evans was by his own admission listening carefully to the new lines of musical thought pursued at this time by pianist Lennie Tristano and his acolytes. Many years later he specifically recalled admiring the achievements of Tristano's 1949 recordings of 'Tautology' and 'Fishin' Around' with saxophonist Lee Konitz. In particular, said Evans, he liked the way the group were "building their lines with a design and general structure that was different from anything I'd ever heard in jazz".[11] Pointedly, however, in the same 1960 interview he said he had been more taken by Konitz and his tenor partner Warne Marsh than by Tristano himself. Though Evans's 'Very Early' in its later guise showed no allegiance to bop, it does reveal itself to be a not-so-distant cousin of Fats Waller's beautiful 'Jitterbug Waltz', written just half a decade earlier – although the older man's harmonic framework is simpler and perhaps more surefooted.

Yet it would be wrong to imply that Evans was under the excessive influence either of Waller or Tristano. He said repeatedly through his mature career when questioned about his formative influences that "a guy is influenced by hundreds of people and things, and they all show up in his work. To fasten on to any one is ridiculous."[12] It is also important to remember that at this time in his life Evans was still to embark upon a full-time career in music, let alone jazz. That was another half-decade away. Yet the ambition was there. In 1979, revisiting the SLC campus, he was asked if he'd started out there with a jazz career in mind. "I have probably precisely fulfilled what I had in mind, which was really to obtain a position in jazz which would allow me to play where I liked and to have a trio and to record without any pressure, to have the freedom to play the music I wanted to play. To that extent I did have it in my mind."[13]

Interestingly, his next tune that would survive to be recorded later was also a waltz – and perhaps his most famous piece of all, 'Waltz For Debby'. He wrote it soon after his national service in the army, which ran for three years from early 1951 to early 1954. He had graduated from SLC in April 1950 after enjoying what he later claimed to be "certainly in the last two years here, the happiest years of my life".[14] He came away convinced that one of his College teachers in particular, Gretchen Magee, "gave me a good background in musical theory and played a fundamental part in directing some of the inner workings of my music".[15] He stayed in touch with Magee by letter for many years after his departure from Louisiana. In 1959 he wrote to her: "I have always looked on your teaching as that rare and wonderful combination of exceptional knowledge and the ability to bring it to life in the student's heart and mind. I believe you were the greatest inspiration to me at college, and the seeds of insight and practical knowledge that you sowed have borne fruit many times already."[16] The pieces that Evans played in order to graduate with honours included a Prelude & Fugue from Bach's Well-Tempered Klavier, a Brahms Capriccio from Op.116, a Scherzo from Chopin, a Kabalevsky Prelude and, finally, a movement from Beethoven's Piano Concerto No.3 (in a two-piano arrangement, with a member of the teaching staff playing the orchestral reduction).

He gained his first professional experience after settling back in the New Jersey/New York State area. Guitarist Mundell Lowe had seen Evans play in Missouri and told him to look him up in New York, but a short-lived trio with Lowe and bassist Red Mitchell foundered on a lack of gigs. Evans supplemented the trio work with a number of other jobs, many falling outside jazz altogether – weddings, bar mitzvahs and the like. But he did play a memorable evening with the Buddy Valentino big band at the Renaissance Ballroom in Harlem, opposite Nat King Cole, an early hero of Evans. He later recalled: "I sat at the same piano and played the same keys that Nat Cole played! It was reverential."[17]

His most important job of this period was playing piano in the semi-R&B band of saxophonist Herbie Fields, a popular performer who had left Lionel Hampton's rip-roaring outfit in the post-war period in order to lead a band of similar inclinations. Working with Fields, Evans experienced much the same ambivalence toward R&B as many jazz musicians of the time. The swing big-bands were grinding to a commercial impasse while the small-group jump bands and R&B units took over the "race" charts. Musicians who before would have made a living touring constantly with the big-bands were having to move to the more commercially viable R&B outfits and swallow hard on their jazz convictions. Evans, like any open-minded serious musician, learned much from his tenure with Fields, who was, he said, "very patient with me".[18] Evans was pleased to discover the dynamics required for accompanying soloists and singers, but the technique most often required was to play loudly and with attack. He later commented that, with the Fields band, "I would come off the stand with split fingernails and sore arms."[19] So much for the fabled Evans touch!

Evans left Fields not because he was dissatisfied with the music or his role within it, but because he was called up for army service. "It looks as if I better brush up on piccolo," he wrote to Dr Pottle in October 1950, "because I received my selective-service physical examination notice last week, and it looks like I will leave Herbie [Fields] and go with Uncle Sam for a while."[20] His experiences in the military were similar to those of many musicians of the period, and while he managed to avoid the more brutally prejudiced service camps and NCOs, he would later recall no pleasurable memories of the army. And he had no time for organised violence. When his musical ability and expertise were made known to the authorities he was allowed to play flute in his company's marching band, stationed near Chicago. He spent his off-duty hours listening to groups on the Chicago scene. These jaunts, and his friendships with musicians Earl Zindars and Bill Scott, were the only positive things to come from the period.

Evans had bitter feelings to express six years later. He told Don Nelson: "I took everything personally, because I thought I was wrong. I was attacked by some guys for what I believed in, and by musicians who claimed I should play like this pianist or that. Pretty soon I lost the confidence I had as a kid. I began to think that everything I did was wrong."[21] He also felt that he'd been left behind. "There was [the] three-year interruption of the Army. I used that as constructively as I could, but … I was just out there, on the road after school with a pretty good jazz band – Herbie Fields – and was just sopping it up and learning and learning and, you know: the army … So consequently I didn't really hit the scene in New York until I was 25."[22]

At the end of his three years in the military Evans returned home – now Florida, where his parents had moved upon his father's retirement. He still didn't know what he wanted to do, so spent a year working on his piano technique and reading widely. After the destructive army experience he wanted to rebuild his approach to music. He told Brian Hennessey years later, "It did not come easy. I did not have that natural fluidity, and was not the type of person who just looks at the scene and, through some intuitive process, immediately produces a finished product. I had to build my music very consciously, from the bottom up."[23] It was during this year that 'Waltz For Debby' was first conceived, as revealed many years later by Evans during a radio interview and musical demonstration with Marian McPartland. This sparkling solo piano waltz, a portrait of a young niece, has an underlying sense of calm joy. It shows a decided affinity with the rhythmic and stylistic flourishes of Chopin, in particular, and has very little of what may be termed jazz content.

A man of natural scholarly bent and with the necessary discipline to teach himself, Evans spent time at the family home reading a good deal of philosophy, as well as keeping up his interest in literature from all periods. His fondness for Eastern philosophy and especially Zen was often commented upon during his life by reviewers and interviewers, especially after the sleevenote to *Kind Of Blue* where he famously described the Japanese calligrapher's art as similar in spontaneity to Miles Davis's contemporary group. However, he regarded Zen ideas and lessons as only part of a larger philosophical firmament. Unlike contemporaries such as Beat writers Jack Kerouac and Allen Ginsberg, Evans had not launched into Eastern philosophy before taking any coherent interest in the Western variety. He had already read Plato, Kant, Wittgenstein, Voltaire and many others before being introduced to Zen by a friend (who had himself been steered to it by the great British intellectual and latter-day mystic Aldous Huxley). In 1954, however, Zen was a good five years or so from being part of everyday American college culture, so Evans had to search widely for books on the subject, at last finding what he wanted in the Philosophical Library in Manhattan. Having digested the message, Evans moved on. In 1960 he allowed that he was "not interested in Zen that much as a philosophy … I don't pretend to understand it. I just find it comforting. And very similar to jazz. Like jazz, you can't explain it to anyone without losing the experience. It's got to be experienced, because it's a feeling, not words."[24]

After the leisurely, low-key, broad-based preparation of this "research" year at home, it was logical for Evans to move to New York and, once settled there, to round off his formal music education. He began a stint at the Mannes School of Music in 1955, in particular exploring composition more fully. He also began looking for work playing jazz around the clubs, bars and other venues. His obvious competence and his rounded, flexible approach attracted the attention of musicians who heard him, although he remained a complete unknown to the jazz public. For some years to come Evans would, in his own words, play "all the jobs and the weddings … When I had started to record already, had won the New Jazz Critics' Poll, New Talent, or whatever it was … I still had my tuxedo regularly cleaned and pressed. And was playing the Friendship Club in Brooklyn three nights a week, in Roseland and all that kind of – y'know – 'society' gigs."[25] New York, as Evans would later note in an anagrammatic song title of his own, was no lark.

CHAPTER 3

A Professional in New York City (1955-1958)

"I HAPPEN TO FEEL VERY STRONGLY ABOUT BEING EQUIPPED, MUSICALLY, TO SPEAK FOR YOURSELF."

BILL EVANS, ALREADY IN SELF-RELIANT MODE

Evans settled into his tiny New York apartment and began his studies at Mannes, additionally chasing worthwhile jazz work, hooking up with any of his old contacts who might lead him to better things. So it was that he renewed his acquaintance with Don Elliott, the multi-instrumentalist he'd met when both men were New Jersey teenagers. Elliott now had a high-profile jazz career. Evans also got in touch again with Mundell Lowe, now the guitarist in clarinettist Tony Scott's group, and began sitting in, but his first regular work came from another clarinettist, Jerry Wald. Evans worked on an LP, *The Singing Reed*, late that same summer, under the leadership of double-bassist and singer Lucy Reed. Evans's friend of some years' standing, Reed was

Evans (opposite) finds his place among the instruments

originally from St Paul, Minnesota, and had worked with bandleaders Woody Herman and Charlie Ventura before settling down to long runs as a solo in Chicago and New York. For more than a year Reed had sung without management or profile in New York clubs, but was now making her way in the city and impressing fellow musicians, if not the general public. During the course of preparing for the LP date she also orchestrated a significant meeting between her two friends, Bill Evans and composer-theoretician George Russell. Although the record was not of great artistic moment – it was subsequently reviewed by *Down Beat* in their "Popular" section – it underlined Reed's own musical integrity. In a 1957 *Down Beat* interview she said, "I find songs that mean so much to me … because I've had experience, more than many of the younger chicks singing today. I'm 35. The tunes are meaningful to me because I've lived them."[1] Of the small circle of singers with whom Evans recorded, Reed is far from the least memorable. She invited Evans, George Russell and a few others to contribute arrangements for the LP, while Evans's piano accompaniment was greatly appreciated by the singer. Asked in that *Down Beat* interview about her current favourite groups, she replied unambiguously: "I'd love to have The Modern Jazz Quartet backing me … I dig Tony Scott's group, too. Bill Evans has never played better."[2]

Evans had become a regular with Tony Scott's group in the time between the completion of Reed's album and its release, and the job would be a mainstay in Evans's increasingly busy professional life. Scott had re-convened his small group earlier in 1955 after spending nine months as musical director to singer Harry Belafonte, then one of the hottest live acts around. Scott had already worked with such big names as Duke Ellington, Billie Holiday and Claude Thornhill. The formation of a new group was the start of a concerted effort on Scott's part to become a leader with a large public following, an effort rewarded by his success throughout the rest of the 1950s, when he won popularity polls over the likes of Benny Goodman, Jimmy Giuffre and Buddy DeFranco and regularly toured internationally. In January 1956 Scott landed a contract with RCA Victor, then a major company with a considerable investment in the "cool" end of modern jazz. While Evans was not present on Scott's initial RCA date, he worked regularly with the clarinettist throughout 1956 and '57, also fitting in a great deal of pick-up work with other leaders.

Meanwhile, Evans's summer-1955 introduction to George Russell through Lucy Reed soon proved pivotal in his early career. Russell had been sufficiently impressed by his grasp of theory, pianistics and jazz feel to offer him a recording date for the LP that Russell had been asked to make in a special series planned by RCA Victor and overseen by Hal McKusick. The series was intended to showcase the art of the modern jazz arranger/composer – others involved included John Carisi, Gil Evans and McKusick himself. Evans said later, "It was a wonderful thing for me, because there were many pianists around New York who could have done the job, but George gave me the opportunity."[3] Considering their backgrounds and aesthetic inclinations, the match was a natural one. Russell was (and still is) a rigorous and original music theorist. His father had been a professor of music at Oberlin University. Attracted to jazz as a teenager in the 1930s, Russell must have feared that his career was over before it started when he contracted TB in 1942. But his long recuperation at a sanatorium allowed for his first concerted music studies, at this time mastering the basics of orchestration. His health remained variable throughout the 1940s, with a relapse in 1945/46 providing time for him to begin work on the thesis which was to govern both his subsequent career and his long-term reputation in music. The book that evolved from this work, *The Lydian Concept Of Tonal Organization,* was published in its original form in 1953. Russell's was a highly individual approach to the organisation of musical harmony and form. He has often described it as his "life-work" and has continued to expand upon and deepen the theory. In the early 1950s, however, he was respected among modern jazz musicians as a composer and arranger, regardless of his indifferent showing as a pianist or drummer for various groups. His compositions first became widely known through 'Cubana Be' and 'Cubana Bop' which he wrote for Dizzy Gillespie in the 1940s. Russell was accepted as an outstanding talent even by such hard taskmasters as the group of musicians based around Lennie Tristano. They were the first to record his 'Ezz-thetic', a wonderfully disguised reworking of the harmonic underpinning of Cole Porter's 'Love For Sale'. Asked in 1986 about his role in the evolution of jazz, Russell said, "I think [the Lydian Concept] made contemporary music – and I don't just mean jazz –

conscious of modes. It introduced modal consciousness in terms that no one was thinking about, certainly not jazz musicians nor, as far as I know, symphonic musicians. The Concept simply codified the modes and introduced chord-scale unity. In other words, for every chord there's a scale of unity, and this gives the jazz musician greater resources … Miles [Davis] picked up on the idea first, and he popularised it."[4] Russell's elegant and far-reaching ideas brought untold riches to jazz and other contemporary musics, yet he would exist in precarious financial circumstances until moving to Europe in the 1960s to assume a parallel career in music education. Evans freely acknowledged Russell's impact on his musical thinking and his career. "I respect George to the utmost," he said many years later. "[He's] a pure musician with complete integrity." Evans would demonstrate that respect by commissioning a large-scale work from Russell on more than one occasion. Back in 1956, however, it was Russell who gave Evans the breaks.

Evans was invited to a March 1956 session for Russell's *Jazz Workshop* album in the RCA Workshop Series. The pianist proves himself an admirable accompanist on four tracks for the likes of trumpeter Art Farmer, guitarist Barry Galbraith and reedsman McKusick, and on Russell's 'Ezz-thetic' takes a solo which reveals a huge delight in the piece's unexpected harmonic resolutions and double-feints. He plays with a forceful touch reminiscent of Bud Powell, while his extreme melodic economy, spun out in unusually long cadences, indicates the ghost of Lennie Tristano. It is a cogent and arresting statement that more than justifies Russell's faith in using him on the date. Gerry Mulligan, hearing the performance in one of *Down Beat*'s Blindfold Tests in 1957, commented: "I don't know who it is but the tune is 'Ezz-Thetic'. It's a George Russell tune … The piano solo was good – good construction and nice momentum."[5]

Evans completed the Russell album during two further sessions in October and late December 1956. By then he had made his debut on record as a leader and completed two LPs with Tony Scott. His first recording with Scott was in July 1956 as part of a big-band showcase for the clarinettist, eventually titled *The Touch Of Tony Scott*. Evans managed a strong feature on 'Round Midnight', one of four quartet tracks made to round out the album. On 'Aeolian Drinking Song', where the relatively bare harmonic plan based on the Aeolian mode allowed him great melodic freedom, Evans used the single-note style he would extend on record for the rest of the year.

By this time Mundell Lowe was in the process of leaving Scott's group, which remained a quartet for live work. This line-up underpinned the big-band arrangements that dominated December's *The Complete Tony Scott* (also on RCA) to which Evans contributed piano accompaniment and an arrangement of his own, a resourceful reworking of Richard Carpenter's 'Walkin'. It sat rather uneasily with the rest of Scott's album, openly dedicated "to William Basie of Redbank, New Jersey" and which used virtually the entire Count Basie band (down to Freddie Green on guitar) as sessionmen.

In conception and method, Evans's work on 'Walkin' is strongly reminiscent of George Russell's thematic dissections and linear writing. Initially stressing the blues element of the melody's intervals, he quickly begins weaving counterpoint lines between band sections and intensifying the mood of the music by modulations and such typically Russell methods as contrary movement and imitation, even as accompaniment to the brief solos. A busy three minutes of music!

The Evans arrangement of 'Walkin' was played to pianist Teddy Wilson by Leonard Feather in another *Down Beat* Blindfold Test in 1957, Wilson unsurprisingly finding the arrangement of the simple riff-like tune the most attractive part of the performance. He said: "I found this arrangement interesting – the untying of the different sections and the things the instruments had to do that were written. Some of the figures I thought were a little too cute, but the arranger is definitely on the right track. He's trying to get a nice, flowing swing in the band and [is] making things happen that are intelligible to the listener."[6] Evans's only solo of note on the album is on the long medium-tempo blues which was its last track, 'Time To Go'. Sounding nothing like Basie in a setting which was an open imitation of the Basie blues style, Evans sticks to single-note right-hand lines that still retain rhythmic and harmonic interest in their own right.

Evans's first album as leader, *New Jazz Conceptions*, was recorded for Riverside in two sessions in September 1956 and released early the following year. It received good reviews, *Down Beat* calling Evans "a man to dig". Riverside A&R man Orrin Keepnews recalled many years later, "By the end of 1957, a full year after it was issued, total sales had barely reached 800 copies."[7] Considering the nature of the music and Evans's non-existent public profile, this is no surprise. Perhaps the surprise is that the album was made at all, given that Evans himself was at first diffident about the idea. Keepnews has told the story of Evans joining Riverside many times, with a number of differing details, but it is accepted that Evans's old colleague Mundell Lowe made the initial connection. Keepnews claimed in his liner notes to the original release that "it took some time for us to convince him that he was ready to record"[8] and that, once Evans had accepted the rationale for making the date, he prepared carefully, choosing his own musicians: drummer Paul Motian from the Tony Scott group, plus the able Teddy Kotick, also previously with Scott, on bass. This care and preparation would prove to be consistent with Evans's approach for the rest of his professional career.

The original LP release contained 11 carefully sequenced tracks displaying a concern for pacing and an attractively wide taste in standards, and no fewer than four Evans originals. (CD reissues have preserved this and include a first take of the Evans blues, 'No Cover, No Minimum', while the *Complete Riverside* boxed set disturbs the running order to group the tracks in trio, duo and solo sequence.) In his liner notes Keepnews quoted Evans discussing his feelings about originality and influences, as relevant today as they were then. "Too many young musicians, [Evans] feels, merely try to find *the* man they want to follow and then proceed to try to be exactly like him – not just musically, but even by seeking to 'live the same life'. But, not having really developed as themselves, such men are apt to be severely handicapped: having little or no 'musical vocabulary for expressing their own personality', they are forced to rely on 'someone else's vocabulary', making them much more likely to become imitators than creators. 'I don't mean to be lecturing on this subject,' Bill notes. 'It's a problem I'm certainly still wrestling with to an extent. But I happen to feel very strongly about this matter of being equipped, musically, to speak for yourself.'"[9]

From the first track of *New Jazz Conceptions*, a typically well-organised Evans arrangement of Cole Porter's 'I Love You', the freshness of his conception is evident. He presages the melody with a vamp over a series of pedal tones anticipating Porter's changes, then delivers the melody using the locked-hands technique he admired so much in Nat Cole and George Shearing. When it comes to improvisation, his concentration on long, Powell-like horn lines is complete, though the constant shifting of emphasis in the 8th-notes reveals what became a central concern for Evans: the creation of tension, unity and interest through rhythmic displacement within a relatively narrow range of notes.

This displacement is equally evident in the following track, the Evans original 'Five' (which he would record again the following year under Tony Scott's leadership). The theme itself is a careful study in staggered time in the manner of Monk, though Evans's own piano technique does not allow him to deliver it in quite the staccato fashion that a player such as Monk would have used. Yet Evans manages to convey a definite personality of his own, with the kind of jauntiness found in a similar figure used by Stan Kenton's band on 'Blues In Burlesque' around the same time. The harmonic underpinning strongly suggests 'I Got Rhythm', a Gershwin tune that has supplied the framework for more than its fair share of jazz "originals". In his solo, Evans uses right-hand flourishes closely identified with Powell and Horace Silver; in the next track, a brief unaccompanied run through 'I Got It Bad (And That Ain't Good)', Evans adopts the approach used by Tatum, Powell and Erroll Garner, using block-chord theme statements liberally embellished by long right-hand arabesques and ornate fills.

His unaccompanied, out-of-tempo opening for George Shearing's 'Conception' (also recorded in the 1950s by Powell) once again finds Evans attempting to shape the performance through a device favoured on occasion by Powell as well as Tatum and Shearing himself. The forward momentum generated during his accompanied solo, played at a bright but not fast tempo, comes from the rare pauses in his long melodic lines and a heavy use of syncopated 8th-notes struck with considerable force. None of this playing is far removed from what was being attempted by others of his generation, from Wynton Kelly to Sonny Clark, and only in the overtly romantic playing on the ballad 'Easy Living' do we get a clearer glimpse of the emerging Evans personality. Again, his touch is heavy in the improvisations, but there are hints of what is to come in the use of chord inversions unusual in jazz at the time, in progressions based on minor sevenths, and in a willingness to let the melody breathe.

With Evans's own 'Displacement' closing the first side of *New Jazz Conceptions* we find him in one of his favourite musical areas: using rhythmic displacement to generate interest, excitement and – eventually – improvisatory form. At a relatively fast canter he delivers a block-chord theme not far removed from the contemporary efforts of Dave Brubeck (and with similar absence of subtlety), while his solo is almost entirely dependent on Powell-like devices, including right-hand pauses as the left hand plays a little rhythmic octave vamp. At just over two minutes' duration the track is remarkably short compared to the long blowing sessions favoured by a number of New York record companies at this time.

'Speak Low' is littered with references to other players, from Cole (in the left hand) to Powell (the harshly dissonant re-voicing of the verse) and Shearing (the smoothness of the overall harmonic re-working). 'Waltz For Debby', another solo performance, brings us into a very different musical world, one which would become familiar to Evans lovers the world over within a few years. Again, the performance is short – not much more than a minute – and consists of a theme statement only. Here Evans seems to borrow stylistically from Brubeck, using ritardando and accelerando to accentuate the theme's winsome grace, and employing widely-spread chord voicings to achieve a "splashy", rather grand sound. The tune's classical roots seem submerged, the song sounding closer to a Disney confection – 'Someday My Prince Will Come', perhaps – with the waltz seeming pretty rather than sublime. Evans would do much more with this theme within a short space of time, but here, in the midst of a programme of conventional piano-trio modern jazz, it served to point the listener in new and enticing directions.

Tadd Dameron's 'Our Delight' brings out perhaps the most wholly bop-oriented performance on the record. 'My Romance', the third short solo piece, is given the out-of-tempo treatment borrowed from Powell, Tatum and Garner, but at least in its intense reworking of Richard Rogers's chords shows how passionately Evans was involved in the song's inner workings. He would return to this piece on more than one occasion. For now, he finishes up his debut LP with 'No Cover, No Minimum', a blues which at over seven minutes is a good two minutes longer than any other track. His immediate double-tempoing on this slow duple-time performance suggests a level of discomfort with the form, as do the echoes of Tristano and the number of stock pianistic blues phrases hammered out with no particular regard for the solo's shape or continuity.

New Jazz Conceptions conclusively demonstrated Evans to be a highly competent and sophisticated modern jazz pianist with a definite compositional gift, but also showed him to be considerably short of a unified musical personality. It would be no coincidence that he would not make another album as leader for close on two-and-a-half years. As he said to his producer, who was waiting rather bemusedly for the follow-up album: "[I] didn't have anything particularly different to say."[10] That may well have been the case for him as a leader, but as a sideman he would continue to grow and shape his style, and in the next 12 months made decisive moves towards maturity. The first steps had been taken in the two remaining recording sessions for George Russell's *Jazz Workshop* album for RCA, in October and December 1956. Some six months or so after the initial recordings, Russell's admiration for Evans's playing had grown to the point where Russell constructed a piece, 'Concerto For Billy The Kid', as a vehicle for Evans – much in the way that Ellington created cameo settings for his great soloists. Using counterpoint and a swirling rhythm, Russell initially sets up a dense and dissonant texture using a minor scale on top of a pedal point. This resolves into a fast-moving set of major-minor modulations over which Evans solos, to a stop-time rhythm from drums and bass, at a considerable rate and with the right hand only. Thus half the solo is given added drama while Evans spins out a series of long lines using phrases which would soon become characteristic. Tightly-revolving patterns and repetitions propel the solo into its second half, where a normal common-time pulse is once more established behind him. The performance is lean, dynamic and concentrated, a virtuosic display with immediate impact. It demonstrates Evans's ability to swing hard across unusual harmonic constructs and contrasting rhythmic conditions. Along with the atmospheric Ravel-like inversions of the slow and mysterious 'The Ballad Of Hix Blewett', it hints at a newly emerging artistic maturity. At this stage of his musical career, while still working as a sideman, Evans had neither the budget nor scope to go much further. But the advances he would make over the next 12 months, up to the point where he joined the Miles Davis band, would prove to be especially significant for his personal artistic growth.

As Evans entered 1957 he had completed the Russell project, recorded his first LP as a leader, and rounded off the work on Tony Scott's project for RCA, *The Complete Tony Scott*. Within a short while Scott left to go overseas, working as a solo, and Evans had to cast around for work while keeping up his practice schedule. In the back pages of *Down Beat* in January he was quoted – apropos of nothing at all – as saying that a critic is "a man who makes money telling musicians how not to".[11]

The connection with George Russell bore fruit again in the late spring of '57. Gunther Schuller's *Music For Brass* project for Columbia in 1956 had, along with Schuller and John Lewis's Jazz & Classical Music Society, brought Schuller's "Third Stream" of music to a listening audience. Schuller saw classical music as the First Stream and jazz as the Second, and wanted to create in the 1950s a hybrid Third Stream that combined the best and most characteristic creative energies and disciplines of both. Now a follow-up concert to *Music For Brass* was planned, with Evans invited to take part. It had been commissioned in April 1957 by Brandeis University, the performance taking place in late June, with Schuller and Russell sharing the conducting. For technical reasons the event was recreated for recording a few days later at Columbia's 30th Street studio in New York City, and released as *Modern Jazz Concert*. It called upon George Russell, Charles Mingus and Jimmy Giuffre from jazz, plus Milton Babbitt, Harold Shapero and Schuller from modern "legitimate" music.

For the new performance and album, Evans played on both the Mingus and Russell compositions, sticking to a written ensemble role in the Mingus piece, 'Revelations (First Movement)'. In the Russell work, however, he had a key ensemble position plus the solo spotlight in the third movement. 'All About Rosie' was based on a children's song, each section being a facet of a child's character as perceived by Russell. The piece alerted influential musicians and observers to the fact that Evans was emerging as a pianist of superior skills and capabilities. Schuller, in his notes to the original LP release, comments on the third section of 'Rosie'. "The fast, relentless pace of the opening is resumed, with the element of improvisation added. Outstanding in this respect is Bill Evans's remarkable piano solo. The ideas are imaginative and well related, but – more than that – Bill's muscular, blues-based playing here fits dramatically into the composition as a whole."[12]

What Evans achieves in this hard-driving and for the most part single-line, densely argued solo is not far removed from his efforts for Russell in the studio the previous December. But there is an added confidence underlining that, if nothing else, his absorption of the Tristano legacy was now complete. Dom Cerulli, reviewing the *Modern Jazz Concert* LP release for *Down Beat*, considered 'Rosie' as the record's most gripping and exciting composition. "In it, as noted by Schuller, pianist Evans contributes a remarkable piano solo, pulsing with life, and driving with stated and implied rhythms and accents. Evans's work, at the very least the most demanding of the entire set, should serve to establish him as a significant pianist on today's scene."[13] For many musicians, this was as important a musical statement as any that Evans would make prior to establishing his own trio. Gerry Mulligan, for example, said when his Concert Big Band made its own recording of Russell's chart in 1961, "I asked George to write something for the band, and when he turned in 'All About Rosie' I almost died. I was haunted by the recording he made of the piece with that fantastic piano solo by Bill Evans."[14] Jimmy Knepper and Charles Mingus, two of the musicians closely involved in the Brandeis performance and *Modern Jazz Concert* LP, would make some significant music on record with Evans before the year was out. But the pianist's next major job – leaving aside a routine studio date as a sideman in guitarist Joe Puma's quartet – was at the Newport Jazz Festival in July 1957.

Evans, as a member of the Don Elliott Quartet which played an afternoon session on July 6th, appeared on one of the Verve LPs of that year's festival that combined Elliott's set with performances by the Eddie Costa and Mat Mathews groups. Evans appeared on three numbers, including a trio version of 'I Love You' that reprised more or less unchanged the 1956 version he'd recorded for Riverside. His playing, in the gregarious and relaxed atmosphere generated by Elliott, is apposite and competent without seeking attention. His touch remains heavier than it became in his first maturity, and his attention to Bud Powell in particular is quite plain.

One critic who noticed his talent was *Down Beat* reviewer Don Gold. Given all 14 Verve albums released from the 1957 festival to review in one sitting, he said about the Elliott set: "Evans is the standout performer on the three tunes – 'Dancing In The Dark', 'I Love You' and 'S Wonderful' – contributing a quality performance on the second tune. Apart from Evans's contribution, however, the set is not memorable."[15]

In the month following the festival Evans got a call from bassist and composer Charles Mingus who wanted him to participate in a recording session for the Bethlehem label. Mingus had heard Evans to good advantage on the Schuller session, while his trombonist of the time, Jimmy Knepper, was working regularly on dates with Evans outside Mingus's band. Mingus was using up pianists in quick succession during the summer of 1957, recording with Hampton Hawes and Bill Triglia in July. According to an anecdote that Evans himself told,[16] in early August he received a telegram from Mingus requesting his presence at a recording session at 10am the following day. A seasoned professional by now, Evans made the session and added idiomatically correct music to the Mingus hot-pot. On 'West Coast Ghost' (its bridge presaging harmonically Mingus's 1964 composition 'Meditations On Integration') he uses the simple, prodding minor triads in the left hand much favoured by Mingus himself for accompaniment when the leader sat at the piano.

In the liner essay accompanying the original release of the LP, *East Coasting*, Nat Hentoff noted "the emotional accuracy with which young pianist Bill Evans, who sight-read most of the parts on this record date, fitted into Mingus's demands".[17] His solos, more restrained and clear than his work for other employers, show a deepening regard for pacing and colour, while his voicings for the quietly yearning ballad 'Celia' tease out a slightly different, more airy romanticism than Mingus usually allows. Evans's sensitivity and imagination allowed him to be a fine creative foil for Mingus's larger musical ambitions. The eventual *Down Beat* review was aware of this. "Evans is an excitingly fresh pianist," wrote Don Gold, "constantly in command of himself and his instrument. What impresses me here is his devotion to the material at hand … Knepper and Evans are perfect companions for Mingus in the venture."[18]

Soon after this Evans made two records he made with Mingus band members. First was trombonist Jimmy Knepper's September 1957 album for Bethlehem, *A Swinging Introduction*, and then a few months later an all-star date with altoist Sahib Shihab for the Savoy label with Knepper, Shihab, bassist Henry Grimes and drummer Paul Motian. Shihab and Knepper also joined Evans on a series of tracks released under the title *The Modern Art Of Jazz* and made under Tony Scott's aegis for the Seeco group of companies. The two sides of Evans's development were aptly illustrated on *The Modern Art Of Jazz*: Evans's own 'Five' was given a brisk and disciplined workout by Scott's group; while a long, discursive look at 'Lullaby Of The Leaves' (minus Scott, who drops out on this track) would not have seemed out of place on a Mingus album of the period, such is the spare, brooding but lyrical aura that Knepper, Shihab and Evans evoke. The uneven but interesting *Modern Art Of Jazz* received a lukewarm welcome from *Down Beat*'s Martin Williams on release in 1958. "There is a praiseworthy variety in the programming of this LP," he commented, "but there is also what seems to me an air of pressure on many of the tracks which only a few men escape … At any rate, I think that Tony Scott's problem is one of relaxation … The comparative ease of Shihab, Evans and Motian (although all, except Motian who is very good, have played better on records) seems undeniable."[19]

Evans remained busy in and around New York during the fall and winter of 1957. In November, *Down Beat* reported a three-night appearance by the Bill Evans quartet opposite Anita O'Day at the Cork & Bib club, immediately after the singer had wowed the Village Vanguard audience and set new attendance records there. As 1958 began, Evans saw more action as a sideman, including a quartet date with vibes player and pianist Eddie Costa (who had recently won a New Star Pianist award from *Down Beat* critics), a full studio album with his friend Don Elliott in February, and an appearance on half a Helen Merrill session for EmArcy. A session with Hal McKusick in April 1958 returned him to the repertoire and arrangements of George Russell (along with material from Ernie Wilkins, Jimmy Giuffre and others) and to most of the band that had made Russell's date for RCA in 1956. Evans responded in much the same way as he had before, showing unmistakeable mastery of his material and the arrangers' styles on standards and originals. But April 1958 would be most important to Evans as the month he was ushered into the Miles Davis Sextet.

CHAPTER 4

Meeting Miles (1958)

"THE SOUND BILL GOT WAS LIKE CRYSTAL NOTES OR SPARKLING WATER CASCADING DOWN FROM SOME CLEAR WATERFALL."

MILES DAVIS ON EVANS

Miles Davis was experiencing a period of unprecedented musical growth and audience appreciation. His big-band collaboration with arranger Gil Evans, *Miles Ahead*, had gathered critical and popular approval around the world, while his original quintet – with saxophonist John Coltrane, pianist Red Garland, bassist Paul Chambers and drummer Philly Joe Jones – had made a string of classic records and many revelatory personal appearances between 1955 and 1957.

Davis was hardly an innocent when it came to drug abuse, yet had disbanded this group in the late spring of 1957 because of his increasing exasperation with the erratic behaviour and unreliability of the heavy drug

With Miles Davis in New York for a Kind Of Blue session, 1959

users in the band, especially Coltrane. The saxophonist had been the first to go, right at the end of 1956, temporarily replaced by Sonny Rollins. During the summer and autumn of '57 Davis began to reconsider the musical requirements for his small group and his general artistic development. By the end of the year he had assembled a sextet which included his old rhythm section, a newly heroin-free Coltrane back from his famous stint at the Five Spot with Thelonious Monk, and the urbanely fiery, soulful alto of Cannonball Adderley. But there would be further musical changes as Miles sought out what he wanted to hear. In the meantime, the Sextet made *Milestones*, revealing the first results of Davis's new fascination with the application of modes to jazz. Until now, modern jazz had been based on "running the changes", in other words resolving harmonies and chord changes. Modal jazz replaced this with harmonies that were static, or moved very rarely, and was based on the use of scales.

By mid spring 1958 Garland and Jones were gone from Davis's group. Jones was replaced by Jimmy Cobb, while the 28-year-old Bill Evans came in for Garland. Evans's friend George Russell helped him get hired – by giving him a lift to the gig where he was to audition for Davis. In a later radio interview, Russell remembered going to a club at Bedford and Stuyvesant in Brooklyn. "After the intermission [Davis] asked Bill to come up and play," said Russell, "and that night he hired him on the spot. He said 'You're going to Philadelphia with us next Saturday.'"[1]

Evans himself said later, "I thought that Miles was the king of modern jazz at this time, but until his call I had never spoken to him … I made this date and he asked me to stay with the band."[2] In his autobiography Davis explained that "Red's playing had carried the rhythm, but Bill underplayed it and for what I was doing now with the modal thing, I liked what Bill was doing better. I still liked Red and brought him back on a few occasions, but I mostly liked him when we were going through that Ahmad [Jamal] thing. Bill could play a little like that Ahmad thing too, although when he did, he sounded a little wild."[3]

Evans did not introduce Davis to the notion of modal playing in jazz, but the pianist already knew about it, having responded brilliantly to George Russell's highly individual application of Lydian modality in jazz composition and arrangement. Davis claimed to have been impelled to modality by watching an African ballet troupe perform in New York, but perhaps he too got his initial jolt from Russell. Davis wrote later, "George Russell used to say that in modal music, C is where F should be. He says that the whole piano starts at F. What I had learned about the modal form is that when you play this way [and] go in this direction, you can go on forever."[4]

Evans's pianistic and musical attributes – unique at the time in jazz – made him uncannily receptive and responsive to Davis's ideas. He could also bring in his own musical imagination and develop these ideas past Davis's own starting points, even if at first he felt somewhat overawed by the idea of playing with a group full of what he considered "giants". Davis's greatness came from his capacity to inspire these imaginative leaps in others, at the same time becoming so excited by them himself that he would outreach what he had already achieved. Evans's rich harmonic knowledge, plus his ability to apply it to jazz improvisation and accompaniment, provided the band with the light and shade necessary to refresh the ear of a soloist working with scales rather than chords.

The inspiration was reciprocated, for there is no doubt that Davis's ideas provided the perfect context for Evans's harmonic sense. Years of practice and study had given Evans what he described as "a complete understanding of everything I was doing",[5] equipping the pianist with the knowledge to respond in fresh and exciting ways to the limitless substitutions, partial inversions, harmonic methods of form construction, and expanded inner voicings that Davis's new approach invited. Evans's intellect and his own artistic imagination could make connections between the harmonic practices of earlier 20th-century composers – from Debussy, Satie and Ravel through Scriabin to Bartok and Milhaud – and their application to improvised music. Particularly adept in his manipulation of minor-seventh progressions and in moving between tonalities, Evans learned from the ambiguities of tonality perfected by Debussy and Ravel. He also revelled in the implications of the wider chord intervals systematically employed by Bartok, who sometimes abandoned conventional tonality, and Milhaud, who consciously embraced bitonality. Evans would repeatedly shift implied tonality through chords where the resolving note, or tonic, is deliberately abandoned. This also allowed Evans to quickly and elegantly refashion the harmonic structures of conventional jazz and standards to create a more personalised, subjective approach to well-known repertoire – an approach that would come to its peak in the trio years still in front of him. He began systematically to employ what is known as quartal harmony. This means the articulating of a chord on the piano in a way that allows each interval in the chord to be a minimum of four steps apart on the given scale. This wider intervallic spread added greatly to the richness of the music's texture and led Evans to explore the beauty of a chord's upper parts. This is nowhere more dramatically illustrated than in his famous introduction to the Miles Davis Sextet's 1958 recording of 'On Green Dolphin Street'. At that recording session Davis had asked Evans for simple but vital harmonic shifts in the introductory passage. Evans later remembered this was "[on] the original changes of the chorus ... the vamp changes being a major seventh, up a minor third, down half a tone. That was ... when [Miles] leaned over and said 'I want this here.'"[6]

Davis's request for simplification led to a distillation of the song's essence by sideman Evans, equal to that which Davis would extract from John McLaughlin on Joe Zawinul's 'In A Silent Way' a decade later. Evans's harmonic substitutions on the newly simplified structure of the intro to 'Dolphin Street' bring a completely new emotional and intellectual dimension to the standard. Davis himself accurately described the effect of those progressions, so new and influential to modern jazz. "Bill brought a great knowledge of classical music," wrote Davis, "people like Rachmaninov and Ravel. He was the one who told me to listen to ... Arturo Michelangeli ... Bill had this quiet fire that I loved on piano. The way he approached it, the sound he got was like crystal notes or sparkling water cascading down from some clear waterfall."[7]

In his short tenure with Davis, Evans continued to develop a dual approach. His unobtrusive but ever-apposite harmonisations on standard Davis repertoire such as 'Walkin', 'Bye Bye Blackbird' and 'Ah-Leu-Cha' do not move far from what Garland would have supplied, although Evans's touch and use of space and the choice of rhythmic emphasis were very different to his predecessor. Meanwhile, on the fresh material Davis and Evans were developing for the studio, his spare style and unique system of chord substitutions had a profound effect. The first surviving recorded evidence of his work with Davis is a bootlegged radio broadcast of May 17th 1958 from New York's Café Bohemia, where only Coltrane of the two saxophonists is present. The repertoire is completely standard Davis fare for the time: 'Four', 'Bye Bye Blackbird', 'Walkin' and 'Two Bass Hit'. Evans's accompaniment is so close to what Garland gave Davis's soloists as to be easily mistaken for the earlier pianist. He solos on just two tunes, 'Blackbird' and 'Walkin'. The piano is cripplingly out of tune, and he concentrates on single-note lines with the emphasis on simplicity and economy, as if echoing his leader's attitude to improvisation, such is his desire to fit in.

On the material the Sextet was playing at the time that was more naturally suited to Evans's musical thinking – 'On Green Dolphin Street', 'Milestones' and 'Stella By Starlight', as well as the few Monk tunes Davis still called – Evans would deliver his freshest, most fully-formed playing and register the most telling evidence yet of his personal musical identity. In doing so he re-defined Davis's own music and provided a tremendous spur for the two saxophone soloists, Adderley and Coltrane. For Adderley, it was an unlooked-for but wholly welcome introduction to a more vertical, harmonically-based method of improvising. For Coltrane, the combination of Davis and Evans provided his first access to the ever-expanding scalar universe he would inhabit for the rest of his tragically short career. And for Evans himself, the material made such an impression that it stayed in his repertoire for years.

Adderley's appreciation of Evans was demonstrated immediately by the pianist's appearance on two albums that Adderley made in 1958. First was *Portrait Of Cannonball*, a fine early-July quintet date for Riverside and his debut for the label. Then in August came an odd if ambitious last date for Mercury, *Jump For Joy*, employing a chamber string section and jazz small-group in unidiomatic arrangements of Duke Ellington's score for the eponymous 1940s musical. Evans's contribution to this latter date is hardly worth noting; he is way down in the mix. On *Portrait Of Cannonball*, however, he deploys his modified bop style – soon in itself to be a part of Evans's past – in a driving, sensitive and entirely successful manner, even though his solo space is limited. Similar to his live work with the Davis group, Evans sticks to doing the simple things well, including an effective short three-chord pedal-point vamp at the beginning of Gigi Gryce's 'Minority' and a beautiful locked-hands one-chorus solo on the Adderley ballad 'Straight Life'.

More significantly, Evans and his colleagues were introduced by Miles Davis to a new composition written especially for Adderley's session. (Davis was close musically and personally to Adderley, and had played trumpet on the saxophonist's previous session, *Somethin' Else*, for Blue Note.) The new piece was 'Nardis', a tune with an unusual series of augmented chords in its verse that gave it a Near-East flavour; Davis was present at the session to oversee its recording. Taken at a leisurely clip, it would have been a fine vehicle for the Davis group of the time, but they never recorded it. On the Adderley recording Evans is the outstanding player, finding magic in the progression and a special elegance in his smooth transitions from section to section. "You could see that the other guys were struggling with it," Evans said later. "After the date [Miles] said I was the only one to play it the way he wanted."[8] Evans would later in his career make it a staple of his live sets, usually playing it at a considerably faster tempo.

Prior to his second album as a leader, Evans's most significant playing was with Davis (apart from an appealing record, *Modern Art*, made later in the year as a sideman for Art Farmer, his old George Russell colleague). Davis took his new line-up – with Evans, Coltrane, Adderley, Cobb and Chambers – into the Columbia studios for the first time in May 1958, recording four songs. The aforementioned 'Green Dolphin Street', plus 'Stella By Starlight' and 'Fran Dance', a Davis original based on an old standard, were carefully arranged prior to recording. The last song, 'Love For Sale', was an afterthought designed to give the band a more upbeat and spirited end to the session.

Evans comps superbly throughout, his sparse, probing substitutions fitting each soloist like a glove. He solos to good effect on 'Green Dolphin Street', ending in a long passage of gently ringing, rhythmic block chords, while his brief 'Stella' solo consciously echoes Red Garland's block-chord offbeats. Perhaps the group's approach to this song dated from Garland's time with Davis, and Evans was following his leader's instructions. Drummer Jimmy Cobb's observation bears this out: "[When piano players] first got with the band they were always confused, because [Davis] would tell them when to play and when not to play."[9]

Somewhat surprisingly for a man who preferred to be well rehearsed, Evans plays his most rewarding improvisation on 'Love For Sale', the track that Davis counted in with finger-snaps as a spontaneous gesture to a rhythm section that had been concentrating hard all session. Evans stretches out in a manner not heard on record since 'All About Rosie' almost a year earlier. In a solo not far short of three minutes, he begins with the single-line melodic style inherited from Tristano, Powell and others, but before the first verse concludes, the pianist is breaking up the rhythm, leaving pauses, using two and three-part chords, and generally keeping the listener guessing as to what he will do next. His motifs are complex and there are constant subtle changes of pace. Evans also employs an almost obsessive degree of rhythmic displacement set against an equally imaginative altering of the harmonic base across which he is playing. It's a completely absorbing solo, shaped beautifully by his gradual reduction of its elements to chords and space before Davis re-enters with the theme.

The Sextet that day failed to make quite enough music to fill a single LP. One more track would have been needed and it is probable that Davis considered 'Love For Sale' inappropriate anyway, for it did not appear on record until a 1980 compilation of out-takes. Thus a remarkable early Evans solo was left unheard for over 20 years. The other three pieces appeared in the US and Europe on *Jazz Track*, in Europe sharing half an LP with Art Blakey's efforts for the French film *Des Femmes Disparaissent*.

Another French connection, made a month later in June 1958, was the untypical participation by Davis and his entire group (minus Jimmy Cobb) with players such as flautist Herbie Mann, vibraphonist Eddie Costa and saxophonist Phil Woods in Michel Legrand's prestigious big-band project *Legrand Jazz*. Of the four tunes recorded under Legrand's direction, Evans is strongly featured on 'Jitterbug Waltz', including a short solo, while his comping role for Davis on 'Django' combines elements of MJQ pianist John Lewis's own sparse style and Evans's more romantic approach. On 'Round Midnight' and 'Wild Man Blues' he is wholly given over to playing scored passages, and in the former piece is required to play in the Shearing manner: not exactly a high-profile opportunity for Miles Davis's new pianist. Still, Evans was being heard live nightly with the Sextet, as demonstrated by a number of radio airshots from nightclubs in New York and Washington DC that have appeared on pirate CDs. They follow a similar repertoire and routine to the concerts detailed below. Evans's new approach was helping to bring further kudos to Davis, with his new "light" rhythm section, as well as much-needed appreciation of Evans by a public which until now had been largely unaware of his existence. Apart from their usual rounds of the jazz clubs, the group appeared at two major festivals in summer 1958, at Newport in July and Randall's Island in August. The Newport set fell on the first evening of the event as part of the 4th-of-July celebrations, and also as part of what seemed to be a Columbia Records day: Dave Brubeck and Duke Ellington, also Columbia artists then, appeared directly after Davis. In addition to being recorded for LP releases, all three groups were filmed by a crew directed by Bert Stern for what would eventually become the famous *Jazz On A Summer's Day* movie. But this first day's filming was junked. The feature's music director, George Avakian, commented: "The first night's filming turned out to be a fiasco. No one seemed to know what to do. Bert had never made a film before, and my brother [film editor Aram Avakian, also on the crew] got so upset that he ended up getting violently ill during the filming."[10]

Equally problematic was the dedication of the evening to Duke Ellington. The festival's MC Willis Conover introduced the Davis band, desperately attempting to tie them in with Ellington's music, but to no avail. Alone of the groups playing that night, Davis's played no Ellington material, sticking to its own routine and, for the most part, digging hard and deep into Davis's repertoire from the 1955 quintet. The recently-recorded 'Fran-Dance' and 'Straight No Chaser', from *Milestones*, were the only exceptions. Evans is low in the recorded mix and not heard to particular advantage in a number of short solos. This was also the case over the festival loudspeakers: the *Down Beat* reviewer complained of band members being "drowned often by [drummer Jimmy] Cobb's oppressive support".[11] Davis's feelings about the night's performance might be gauged by the fact that the recording of it only appeared more than six years later in truncated form as half an LP (along with portions of a 1963 Thelonious Monk set).

Evans would not be back to play at Newport for a decade. He had better luck at the Randall's Island festival the following month, August 1958. The group's Newport repertoire was repeated, but with little of the tension and imbalance which had marred that outing. Evans's sensitive accompaniment was particularly appreciated on 'Fran Dance', announced that night as 'Put Your Little Foot Right In'. Evans, Adderley and Coltrane also appeared later the same evening with the festival orchestra alongside such luminaries as Lee Morgan and Ray Copeland (trumpets), Bob Brookmeyer and Curtis Fuller (trombones), Jimmy Giuffre and Charlie Rouse (saxophones), Chico Hamilton (drums) and Gunther Schuller (French horn). Ernie Wilkins led and contributed arrangements, but according to *Down Beat* reviewer Dom Cerulli the under-rehearsed band "was highly touted as the world's greatest collection of jazz soloists [and] proved to be just that … but not much as an orchestra". Cerulli was even less enthusiastic by 2am, fighting off boredom when "every member of the band got to solo (except Schuller) on a long, long blues. Bill Evans almost had something interesting when the parade of soloists started."[12]

September found the Sextet at another unusual live recording, this time in a plush New York hotel as part of a Columbia Records jazz promotion, along with the Duke Ellington orchestra and a number of distinguished guests including Billie Holiday and Jimmy Rushing. The Davis set came first and suffered from terminal recording imbalances, with Davis often off-mike and Evans virtually inaudible for large periods of the performance, even during his solos. Clearly dismayed by what they heard on playback, Columbia shelved the efforts of both leaders until 1973 when two separate LPs were released as *Jazz At The Plaza*, volumes 1 and 2. Uncritical and unhelpful notes by long-time Columbia producer Irving Townsend included a mistaken identification of Monk's tune 'Straight No Chaser' as 'Jazz At The Plaza' on the sleeve, even though the record label itself had the correct title.

The later Ellington set, though hardly perfect, had better recording balances. Davis consistently claimed in later years that he and his group were unaware that their efforts were even being recorded. Once again an attempt to record the classic Davis Sextet had yielded poor results, this time through Columbia's sloppy preparation. Yet Evans himself, despite annoyance at Columbia's unilateral decision in 1973 to release these below-par takes, had fond memories of the afternoon. "We had no idea that it was being recorded," he commented years later. "But I'm happy about it simply because it's the only Miles recording with me and Philly Joe. See, we had a particular thing going with Paul and Philly and me together as the rhythm section. I play differently with Philly. You can hear the rhythmic thing that happened, the laidback feeling and all, that I didn't get with Jimmy Cobb because he's a different kind of drummer."[13] (The identity of the drummer on that date has in fact been the subject of years of confused speculation, but research carried out by Columbia for their boxed set of complete Miles Davis recordings in 1999 came down decisively on the side of Cobb, who insists he was behind the kit that afternoon. It remains to be seen if this is the last word on the subject.)

When Davis and band played an August club date in Washington DC, probably at the Spotlite, they were again unaware of being captured in action. The surviving music has been taken from a radio broadcast, this time in decidedly inferior sound. But although the recording quality is dim, the balance is better than the Columbia hotel date, with Evans audible throughout. He solos again on 'Walkin', and also on 'All Of You', but this time reveals much more of his personal style. He sounds relaxed in his phrasing and much more readily identifiable, rather than attempting an uneasy copy of Garland. His career-long affinity with Cole Porter's music shows through in his solo on 'All Of You', at the close of which the group pauses as on the original Davis quintet recording, and Davis re-enters. Evans copies the Garland off-beat comping for a few bars, then allows a subtly altered chord to hang through four beats. Davis is on to this in a flash, moulding new, beautifully extended phrasing to match. Evans may have occasionally felt unsure of himself in the Davis group, but his musical communication with the leader is total, and most definitely a two-way street.

By this time the pianist was being noticed wherever the group performed, underlined by his New Star award in the *Down Beat* Critics' Poll published in August 1958. He also registered for the first time in the December issue's Readers' Poll, just scraping in at number 20. Yet Evans had left Davis prior to this poll's appearance and before the recording of his second album as a leader, *Everybody Digs Bill Evans*.

Why did Evans leave Davis after so short a stay? A number of opinions have been offered by those involved, as well as by many onlookers, but perhaps the most straightforward explanation came from the pianist himself. He recalled later that it was down to the punishing schedule of being on the road every night, which "drained me in every respect".[14] Yet this is disingenuous, for Davis was always careful to pace his appearances, often scheduling rests between jobs and usually opting for week-long or fortnight-long residencies at clubs rather than strings of one-nighters. An observation by Adderley shifts the perspective. "Although he loves Bill's work, Miles felt that Bill didn't swing enough on things that weren't subdued. When Bill left, [Miles] later found Wynton Kelly, who does both the subdued things and the swingers very well."[15] Other band members mentioned that for a good part of his eight-month tenure Evans was insecure and unconfident of his own worth among such established jazz giants. Adderley's assertions are borne out by the recorded evidence. Davis's working repertoire and his recordings were for the most part quite separate. While Evans was ideal for the trumpeter's newer ideas, as tried out for Columbia in their New York studio, when it came to live dates, in a set still bop-and-standards heavy, Evans was often overpowered aurally by the others and given less room to display his special strengths. Evans may well have been "drained in every respect" – perhaps most crucially because of his use of heroin.

Since joining the Davis group (and through no fault of the leader) Evans had picked up a heroin habit. Perhaps he was using the drug because he felt professionally inadequate, or simply to join in with at least one other member of the rhythm section. Maybe he was searching for new experiences, or had a deeper, more personal need to escape private demons, but this is a matter for conjecture rather than conviction. Perhaps all or some of these elements combined during that intense period. After all, a great deal of mental strength was required to swim against the very swift-running flow of a working group for at least part of every night. The effect on Evans's self-confidence was profound, bringing him to question on his departure from the group whether he even wanted to continue playing professionally. One thing was clear: by

November 1958 Evans was a regular heroin user who'd contracted the habitual junkies' ailment, hepatitis, and needed a break from his career to decide how to tackle a spiralling list of personal and professional problems. That Davis was sympathetic to the decision to leave is borne out by his help in finding Evans work in early 1959 and in the pianist's close involvement in the creation that spring of the *Kind Of Blue* LP. Evans and Davis had enjoyed a good working relationship from the outset, Evans soon becoming used to Davis's caustic nature and put-ons. But Davis was well aware that, as he put it later, "Bill was a very sensitive person and it didn't take much to set him off."[16]

Another stumbling block concerned race. Evans had witnessed Davis's own sardonic assessment of racial prejudice at the 1958 Newport Festival. As noted by onlooker Burt Goldblatt, Evans's old employer Tony Scott used the microphone repeatedly (and unsuccessfully) during his own set to complain to the crowd about having film-crews on stage. When Scott came off into the wings in a foul temper at the set's end, Davis commented to him in a stage whisper: "What's the matter, Tony? They call you a nigger?" Davis was convinced, both at the time and in hindsight, that Evans had left his band due to the resentment shown him by blacks outside the group. "Some of the things that caused Bill to leave the band hurt me, like that shit some black people put on him about being a white boy in our band," wrote Davis. "Many blacks felt that since I had the top small group in jazz and was paying the most money that I should have a black piano player. Now, I don't go for that kind of shit ... as long as they can play what I want, that's it."[17] Late in his career Evans recalled specifically that there was no racial tension in that band. "It was more of an issue with the fans," he said. "The guys in the band defended me staunchly."[18]

Contrary to some reports, Evans seems to have experienced little personal tension with other Davis group members (some of whom were reformed addicts themselves). This is underlined by Evans's work with Adderley in the studio, at the time and later, his use of Paul Chambers and Philly Joe Jones on his own recordings, and his discussions on Eastern philosophy with John Coltrane (it was Evans who recommended to Coltrane Krishnamurti's influential book *Commentaries On Living*). Evans and Coltrane also swapped stories about their common backgrounds in R&B bands back in the early 1950s. Coltrane joked about a guitarist in one such undistinguished band – Dorothy Mae & The Hepcats – who had discovered the lost chord: "It sounded as if he'd found the one chord that fitted everything: a chromatic crunch."[19]

Evans was confronting a personal and professional crunch of his own. He returned once again to his parents' house in Florida, where his father was also in bad health. According to Davis, Evans also stayed with his brother in Baton Rouge. Taking close to a month off from New York and his professional life, Evans contemplated his future path, determining that he had reached the point where he had to run his own group in order to fully express his musical ideas. His return to New York in December 1958 saw him not only appearing as a sideman on high-profile dates for others, but ready with material for his second Riverside album as a leader. As he related years later, "I'd had hepatitis, and I went to stay with my parents in Florida to get over it. When I came back, I felt exceptionally rested and well. I made [*Everybody Digs Bill Evans*] at that time. And I knew I was communicating the way I'd like to communicate ... I find that when I'm feeling my best, spiritually and physically, I project."[20]

CHAPTER 5

Finding the First Trio (1959)

"ALL GROUP MEMBERS NEED TO BEND FOR THE COMMON RESULT. AS THE PAINTER NEEDS HIS FRAMEWORK OF PARCHMENT, SO THE IMPROVISING MUSICAL GROUP NEEDS ITS FRAMEWORK IN TIME."

BILL EVANS IN HIS LINER NOTES TO THE *KIND OF BLUE* ALBUM

T his book is primarily concerned with music, delving into Evans's private life only where it had a direct effect on his career, but it is impossible to examine Evans's work at this stage without some discussion of his heroin habit. His use of heroin had an immediate and profound effect on his life and working habits. Hard drugs have a marked physical impact on the body – and if they shape how one looks on the outside, think what they are doing to the inside. Of course, this dependency takes a high financial and emotional toll as well. It also dictates the mode and rhythm of everyday life, as the need to score for the longed-for fix and the need for the money to pay for it become overriding imperatives. In the

At the Showplace club in New York in July 1959

year after leaving Miles, Evans slid further into an addiction which would tyrannise his life for over a decade. For some time, in a protracted flirtation with the drug, he avoided using needles, but by the end of that year he was injecting. Peri Cousins, with whom he had been living throughout this period, watched him slide down. "He knew what he was doing, and part of him felt that was something he had to do – and that when he was finished he'd stop. I suppose lots of people felt that way … He knew it was destructive, but it was almost as if he didn't want to stop."[1] The effect was to set back the development of his career through circumstantial complications and the continual short-term need for more money to pay for increasing amounts of heroin. This alone made it hard for the fledgling trio he was trying to establish to pay its own way, and he became a less than attractive proposition for first-rate managers and agents. It would take years to resolve these matters satisfactorily and for Evans's career to flourish internationally in the way it should have done much earlier.

Still, drug dependencies have rarely kept jazz musicians from making records. Back in New York City in late November 1958, Evans immediately became part of the all-star orchestra re-convened by George Russell in order to advance an ambitious recording project started for Decca three months earlier, *New York, NY*. Evans had given beautifully weighted support to a John Coltrane solo on the one track, 'Manhattan', to stem from the September session. Now at the November 24th date he accompanied adroitly throughout and solo'd on all but two compositions, playing with grace and imagination – including an assured outing on the Latin-beat 'Manhattan-Rico'. A final session, in March 1959, would complete this album; on it, Evans's arresting accompaniment to vocalist Jon Hendricks's lyrics on 'Big City Blues' and his subsequent solo, plus Russell's shaping of virtually all of 'East Side Medley' as a sparkling feature for his pianist friend, showed the poise and presence he could now bring to any recording session.

Within two weeks of that November studio date for Russell, Evans started on his second studio album, *Everybody Digs Bill Evans*. It was made in one session at Plaza Sound studio in New York, with Sam Jones on bass and Philly Joe Jones on drums. The album would give Evans a loyal record-buying audience of his own for the first time. Riverside's clever marketing campaign was important: after all, there was no doubting the implications of the record-cover art and the album's title, a literal reproduction of the high opinions expressed about Evans's playing by Miles Davis, George Shearing, Ahmad Jamal and Cannonball Adderley. (Evans, using Davis's sardonic wit, asked producer Orrin Keepnews when he saw the cover, "Why didn't you get [a quote] from my mother?"[2]) But even the cleverest marketing campaign cannot sell rubbish for more than an initial period, especially in the often cynical world of jazz. Fans heard in this music an important new statement from an artist who had evolved his own unique identity. The record sold on recommendations as much as smart campaigns.

Feeling ready to make his own mark, Evans had gone into the studio with renewed confidence about the maturity of his methods. Looking back in an interview two years after his departure from Davis, Evans remembered it as a very good period. "I think the time I worked with Miles was probably the most beneficial I've spent in years," he said, "not only musically but personally. It did me a lot of good."[3] This was curious, given what he would later say to interviewers about his all-pervading "exhaustion" on leaving Davis's band.

As with the first record, Evans planned a clear programme for this new project. He arrived at the studio with just one piece of original music, Epilogue'. It was Debussy-like in style and harmonic content, running diatonic fourths over a background of lower-register fifths. But he would underline the title of the piece by positioning it at the conclusion of each side of the LP. With just two exceptions, the rest of the tunes were standards played by the trio, from driving mid-tempo pieces such as 'Oleo' to lush, tender romanticism during Vernon Duke's 'What Is There To Say'. One of the two exceptions was a ravishing unaccompanied treatment of the Green-Bernstein ballad 'Lucky To Be Me'. The other started out as a solo-piano attempt at another Bernstein tune, 'Some Other Time', but evolved spontaneously into 'Peace Piece'. This was an inspired improvised investigation of the opening pedal-tone vamp of the Bernstein original, and called on Evans's detailed knowledge of the music of composers such as Satie, Ravel and – in parts – Scriabin. The trio performances stand in contrast to the exotic touches brought to the album by the solo piano pieces. Far from any hint of Evans asserting his independence from ex-boss Davis, they in fact make plain that link – from the choice of drummer Philly Joe Jones to the febrile drive of the medium-tempo numbers and the overt romanticism of the ballads. Thus on the opening track, Gigi Gryce's 'Minority', we hear Evans still using the firm touch and rhythmic urgency typical of his career to date. But here he paces himself more consciously, employing Davis's keen use of pauses and dramatic re-entries, carefully forming his phrases rather than running them on through harmonic change after harmonic change. All this contributes successfully to the way in which the group builds an improvising intensity and gives Evans a more fully focused musical persona, out at the front of his trio.

His most daring trio playing occurs on the triple-metre piece 'Tenderly' where he employs unusual rhythmic freedom to scatter 16th-note runs in unusual positions across bar-lines and through natural musical cadences. His ballad playing has also benefited from his work with Davis: his pacing is more deliberate, his touch lighter and more precise, especially in the more heavily scored sections where he is using chords in both hands, and he no longer lacks the confidence to let the music breathe. He allows notes to decay naturally as he relates his tale, ably demonstrated on his masterly statement of the theme to 'Young And Foolish'. It is on the ballads that we most nearly approach Evans's fully mature style and attitude to his material. His more up-tempo playing at this point retains enough of its bop-led drive and structure to leave the listener with the feeling that Evans is still attempting to propel the performance along, rather than to glide in, around and along with it, as he would do later. Evans himself remained pleased with *Everybody Digs* throughout his life, often specifically citing it when asked by interviewers or fans to name a record of his which he felt had been successful. Yet its most memorable moments come with Evans alone at the piano.

Even though jazz had been represented on long-playing records since the onset of the 1950s, very few albums attempted to use the physical properties of the vinyl record to help form the listening experience. Evans clearly signalled the end of one side's "recital" with his brief, enigmatic 'Epilogue' (same performance, by the way), in much the same way as a group's theme might end a set in a club or at a concert. A brief but ravishing moment also occurs at the end of the solo-piano rendition of Leonard Bernstein's 'Lucky To Be Me' (from the musical *On The Town*). Playing in the key of B, Evans uses a left-hand vamp alternating between seventh chords of the tonic and dominant, evoking not only the musical world of Erik Satie's *Gymnopedies* but that of Samuel Barber's *Knoxville, Summer Of 1915*. This would also appear as Evans's basic arrangement of the scales that would constitute 'Flamenco Sketches' on *Kind Of Blue* in three months' time. But this brief moment on 'Lucky To Be Me' would have an immediate effect on Evans's attempt at another Bernstein piece.

There was one track that Evans admirers would wear out long before the rest of the LP. 'Peace Piece', an on-the-spot improvisation on a portion of Bernstein's 'Some Other Time' (again from *On The Town*), employed rhythmic, harmonic and melodic devices long familiar to practitioners of this century's classical music but at the time virtually unknown to jazz. Indeed, many observers in 1959 would have been wary of allowing this as jazz at all. Using a simple 2/4 left-hand rhythm outlining variations on a C major 7th chord, Evans draws on his detailed knowledge of related harmonies to create narrative and emotional drama as his right-hand melody and chordal passages move progressively further away from the tonal "home" indicated by his left hand. Evans is drawing on much more than a single musical source here, approaching the mood suggested by his original vamp from a variety of different improvisatory angles rather than a single model.

Many years later Orrin Keepnews confirmed that Evans had originally intended to play 'Some Other Time' itself – and a previously unreleased solo piano version from the session did subsequently appear. But this is immaterial. Evans's inspired performance would be the starting-point for a generation of younger pianists in their own time, including Chick Corea, Keith Jarrett and Herbie Hancock. Their solo recitals would often reflect similar musical and philosophical concerns to those expressed here by Evans. To conclude our view of this remarkable piece, it is also worth noting a parallel with Evans's ballad 'Blue In Green', assembled with Davis for the upcoming sessions in spring 1959 for *Kind Of Blue*.

Everybody Digs was released in summer 1959 to a rapturous critical response. In the meantime, Evans had continued to look for suitable candidates with whom he could form a working trio of his own. He applied himself assiduously to the business of making a living, working at a furious rate as a sideman on stage as well as in the recording studio. Within a fortnight of completing *Everybody Digs*, Evans was a sideman on *Chet*, a Chet Baker date for Riverside featuring the trumpeter with a front line of baritone saxophonist Pepper Adams and flautist Herbie Mann. Had it been the Davis Sextet in the studio, the dominant mood would have been termed contemplative; for Baker it seems closer to somnolent. Even a flagwaver such as 'How High The Moon' checks in at little more than a funereal pace. The time is coolly measured out by drummer Connie Kay, bassist Paul Chambers and Evans, in sleepy anticipation of the minimalist but bewitchingly simple tautness that the same pianist and bassist would achieve for Davis just a few months later (with Jimmy Cobb on drums). The liner notes to the original issue of *Chet*, written by producer Orrin Keepnews, today read almost as an apologia for the general lassitude. "For Chet, home is clearly the world of ballads," wrote Keepnews, "of good, sound ballads that lend themselves to a leisurely tempo and to rich, melodic and often moody interpretation … 'How High The Moon', for example, even though it is included here to demonstrate that it can recapture its status as a romantic ballad despite years of high-speed workouts, is not taken *too* mournfully."[4]

Evans's beautifully-voiced unaccompanied intro to 'Alone Together' is terse, but thrillingly anticipates his introduction and coda to 'Blue In Green' for Davis. Baker's reading is so strung out on long, vibrato-less melodic lines as to touch on pathos. (The dead-slow treatment, which demands that each section of the melody stands on its own in virtual silence, might even have suggested the approach that Eric Dolphy and Richard Davis made to the same tune four years later in their justly famous duet for FM records – although their improvisations were of a very different character and construction.) Other songs on *Chet* receive further strung-out treatments: Kurt Weill's 'September Song' lasts for three minutes and is so slow that it is afforded only a simple melody statement, with Baker accompanied solely by Paul Chambers and, on this track, guitarist Kenny Burrell.

There was an unexpected bonus to *Chet*. On a mid January 1959 session booked to complete the allotted tracks, Evans and Chambers, plus Philly Joe Jones stayed on after Baker left, cutting five tracks together. These remained unissued until the 1970s, but they showed that it was the trumpeter and not his supporting band who had dictated the sluggish tempo of the earlier work. The trio came up with bright and spontaneously integrated performances of standards, such as 'Woody 'n' You' and 'You And The Night And The Music' (done just hours earlier with Baker at a much slower tempo). 'On Green Dolphin Street' receives a treatment already familiar to those who had heard the Davis Sextet version, with Evans's playing alert and imaginative. But there is little counterpoint between the players, giving the set a rather conventional sound compared with that which would soon evolve. It was this, plus the insurmountable fact that five relatively short songs do not an album make, that kept these transitional performances from being issued at the time.

A day or two before the *Chet* session, Evans had made another appearance as a sideman in a recording studio, this time as part of a big-band playing Bill Potts's arrangements of Gershwin's *Porgy And Bess* music. Called *The Jazz Soul Of Porgy And Bess* and cut for United Artists, it must have seemed something of a foolhardy venture so soon after the critically acclaimed Miles Davis/Gil Evans version for Columbia. But on release the record picked up a shortlived burst of praise, earning a top rating in *Down Beat* as an imaginative reworking of familiar material. Today it sounds like a competent cross between Gerry Mulligan and Quincy Jones. The big-band is stuffed with stars – its five-strong trumpet section includes Art Farmer, Harry Edison, Bernie Glow and Charlie Shavers – and the horns get most of the soloing, especially saxophonists Zoot Sims, Al Cohn, Phil Woods and Gene Quill. Evans is almost entirely buried in the arrangements, the occasional tinkle reminding the alert listener that he's on the job. But there is one significant event. He is given the theme statement on 'I Loves You Porgy' and plays it, single-note, with extreme eloquence and economy, his note-placement at its subtlest, exacting maximum feeling. Time stops while he plays and the listener enters another world. It is only marginally different from the way he would treat the melody when he recorded the song with his LaFaro/Motian trio at the Village Vanguard in summer 1961. The other Gershwin tune from this opera that he would play at the Vanguard date, 'My Man's Gone Now', is scored minus piano by Potts. While it is unlikely to have been Evans's first brush with this music, it seems that the *Porgy And Bess* session helped him define an approach to the tunes that would bear spectacular fruit in the context of his trio.

By early spring 1959 Evans was scouting for musicians for his own group. His heavy workload suggests that he was not simply accepting work that came in, but actively seeking it too. At the start of the year he had held down a regular supporting role for a few weeks at the Basin Street East club in New York City, running a trio that, thanks to the club's poor treatment of non-star musicians, had a constantly changing personnel. "They treated us as the intermission group, really rotten," Evans remembered many years later. "We couldn't even get a Coke without paying a buck and a quarter."[5] It was during this squalid time that Evans first brought together Paul Motian and Scott LaFaro. He knew drummer Motian from early days in New York; bassist LaFaro, fresh in from the West Coast and eager to play, dropped in at Basin Street regularly. But lack of opportunity to perform as a trio ensured that the group remained a dream for all three musicians.

A February gig at the Half Note with Evans substituting for an indisposed Lennie Tristano in a Lee Konitz/Warne Marsh quintet must have provided a considerable thrill, although his presence is not notable (recordings made of the gig by Verve were first released on CD in the early 1990s). Evans also recorded an odd record in mid-March 1959 with his old friend, trombonist-keyboardist Bob Brookmeyer, for the fledgling United Artists label which had used Evans on the Art Farmer and Bill Potts dates the previous winter. This session probably resulted from UA's extensive recording activity at the Half Note that spring. At that time Evans played the club with Konitz, while an Evans-Brookmeyer Quartet supported headline acts for part of March and April 1959 (as reported in *Down Beat*[6]). UA eventually announced two albums from the Half Note recording sessions – by Zoot Sims/Al Cohn and Phil Woods/Gene Quill, although the latter never appeared.

The Evans/Brookmeyer record, on which both men played piano, was called *The Ivory Hunters*, the self-deprecating irony of the title indicating its main strength as well as its weakness. Brookmeyer's credentials as a pianist had been established in person and on records for a number of years prior to this date, but the decision to drop trombone from the entire session still seems strange, given the match that his rounded sound and melodic approach would have made with Evans's lush, enticing harmonies. Still, the results are musically interesting and historically fascinating. With its Modern Jazz Quartet rhythm section of Percy Heath (bass) and Connie Kay (drums), the LP brings together many of the strands of progressive-jazz thinking as it stood in 1959. The musicians address the formal and interpretative challenges of a clutch of venerable standards – 'The Man I Love', 'The Way You Look Tonight', 'Honeysuckle Rose' and even 'I Got Rhythm' – in what would now be described as a post-modern manner, dissecting the harmonic implications of the pieces and looking for opportunities to establish interesting musical dialogues within the quartet.

The other significance of *The Ivory Hunters* was that by working in tandem with another pianist Evans foresaw his multi-tracked piano efforts of some four years later. Although Brookmeyer displays a more spare and less pianistic style than that of Evans, he deploys similar harmonic awareness, uses right-hand runs with economy and flair, and emphasises the ruminative nature of ballads and the playfulness of faster-tempo pieces. His ability to listen to Evans and for both pianists to keep out of each other's way is remarkable. Some of the theme arrangements are heavy-handed: 'The Way You Look Tonight' sounds particularly stilted as Evans's standard block-chord mid-tempo theme statement is decorated on the second verse by twinkling Brookmeyer arpeggios worthy of Liberace, or Garner at his most twee. But both players cross-fertilise to good effect during improvisation. Nonetheless, they are so close in their conceptions that for much of the time it feels as if the listener is intruding into a convivial conversation. The session does not sound like one greatly committed to the need to communicate to the outside world. Witnessed live, it would have been a lot of fun. On record it comes across as an only partially successful curio.

The other recording session involving Evans in March 1959 was anything but a partial success. It was the first of two dates – the other would take place in April – set aside to make what would become Miles Davis's *Kind Of Blue* LP. On the session of March 2nd three tracks were recorded: 'Freddie Freeloader', 'So What' and 'Blue In Green'. This was effectively the first side of the resulting album, save for 'Freeloader' and 'So What' having their order reversed. Evans appeared on two of these pieces. The second session, on April

22nd, would provide the second side of the LP: 'Flamenco Sketches' and 'All Blues', with Evans on both. Whole forests have been used up in retrospective homage to this record, so the comments here will be relatively brief, but there are some points that still need to be emphasised. First, there is the paradox of simplicity arising from sophistication. Davis had arrived at this stage in his development through a desire to reduce his music to its essentials and to rekindle his creative fire by playing to his own considerable strengths. He had spent much of 1958 re-investigating his own early musical inspirations as well as newer enthusiasms, some of which were introduced to him by another man named Evans. Gil Evans was the arranger and composer with whom Davis made a string of late-1950s big-band-plus-soloist masterpieces. Davis was determined to apply the lessons learned from all these sources to his working band. He voiced his thoughts on the subject in a 1958 interview, naming some of those who had helped push him in this direction. Commenting on the *Porgy And Bess* sessions just concluded in tandem with Gil Evans, he alluded to the arranger's use in one piece "of a scale for me to play. No chords … [there is] a long space where we don't change the chord at all. It doesn't have to be all cluttered up." He went on to add this prediction: "I think a movement is beginning in jazz away from the conventional string of chords … There will be fewer chords but infinite possibilities as to what to do with them."[7]

That spring, one part of Miles's new creativity was far removed from Bill Evans's natural musical world. "I added," claimed Davis in his autobiography, "some other kind of sound I remembered from being back in Arkansas, when we were walking home from church and they were playing those bad gospels … That feeling is what I was trying to get close to … that feeling I had when I was six years old, walking with my cousin along that dark Arkansas road."[8] Davis had determined some way in advance that Bill Evans was the ideal collaborator to bring to fruition these ideas for his small-group performances. He said he had planned the album "around the piano playing of Bill Evans".[9] Davis also commented in his autobiography: "Some people went around saying that Bill was co-composer of the music in *Kind Of Blue*. That isn't true; it's all mine and the concept was mine. What he did was turn me on to some classical composers and they influenced me. But the first time Bill saw any of that music was when I gave him a sketch to look at just like everyone else … Bill was the kind of player that when you played with him, if he started something, he would end it, but he would take it that little bit further. You subconsciously knew this, but it always put a little tension up in everyone's playing, which was good."[10]

Evans did not see the gestation of *Kind Of Blue* in quite the same way, though he freely acknowledged Davis as the catalyst. "He said he had some things sketched out and I should call round to his apartment on the morning of the date," Evans later told an interviewer. "I took a tune of mine called 'Blue In Green'. We talked over various tunes and I wrote out some parts for the other guys in the band … In a sense, we co-composed 'Flamenco Sketches', but 'Blue In Green' was entirely mine."[11] Evans has also said that 'Blue In Green' came from Davis's musical challenge to him to compose a tune using a series of scales which were difficult to integrate compositionally.

Each man's recollection naturally placed his own role in high relief, which is what most people do when they recall significant past events. Just as naturally, no one could foresee the impact the music would have. Evans said: "When we did the album we had no idea it would become that important. I have wondered for years just what was that special quality, but it is difficult for me as a contributor to be objective." However, in attempting to sum up his feelings about the date in the same interview he identified a crucial element in the record's artistic success: "It was one of the most comfortable times I had with that rhythm section."[12]

When he had been a regular member of the Davis Sextet the previous year, 1958, Evans experienced consistent difficulty trying to mesh perfectly with the bass and drums. Jimmy Cobb's dynamic playing was a particular problem, as had been demonstrated by his sometimes overpowering drumming at Newport that summer. Cobb had his own reasons for playing this way, not least his desire to show himself equally as capable of driving the band as his predecessor, Philly Joe Jones. During the *Kind Of Blue* sessions, however, Davis had given Cobb a very different role. Indeed, for much of the date he approximates the minimalism of the MJQ's Connie Kay, with barely more than ride and hi-hat cymbals deployed. The only time Cobb significantly departs from this approach is on the first tune recorded in March, 'Freddie Freeloader', where the pianist is Wynton Kelly. Listening to the tracks in the order that they were recorded draws attention to the fact that 'Freeloader', in essence a minor blues, is not far in style and conception from the point Davis had reached with *Milestones* 12 months earlier. The main indication of the track's later date is its further reduction of elements and a more measured, restrained rhythmic pulse. Kelly happily supplies minimalist funk lines with rhythmic panache; heard in isolation, the recording has a happy radiance at odds with the rest of the date and even the album's title, though the form sits perfectly with the record's overall aims.

When Evans takes over the piano chair, the mood shifts perceptibly. His intensity and intellect are immediately apparent from the evocative and enigmatic chords he uses to accompany Paul Chambers's graceful opening lines before the main theme of 'So What'. (There is a growing consensus that Gil Evans sketched out this mysterious, gripping introduction to the tune, underlined by the 1961 Carnegie Hall concert recording of this piece with Davis and Evans's orchestra, where this section is the only part fully scored for the assembled forces.) Once the Sextet is fully engaged, Cobb's timekeeping is the epitome of quiet discretion, while Chambers keeps the pulse beautifully alive and supple and Evans uses his piano in a sparse but highly dramatic and colourful way to feed the soloists. Evans's occasional contributions are powerfully effective within such a subdued context. Perfectly at home in the modal environment Davis was using, he could use his chordal and scalar knowledge with great imagination and to maximum effect, stimulating each soloist in succession and providing aural delights for the listener who simply wants to enjoy the fresh and almost sensual pleasures of his chord voicings. What Evans is doing here is not particularly complex, but comes as the result of a great deal of hard work and sophisticated musical thinking. It also has to do with such neglected musical attributes as taste and sensitivity, qualities Evans had in abundance. He knew just where and how to deploy his most telling touches.

Evans always insisted, to the astonishment of his admirers, that he was not in possession of a particularly good "ear", and that his comprehensive harmonic capabilities were the result of endless hard work and application. Martin Williams explained succinctly just where all that hard work was expended. "It was Evans's chord voicings that had the widest effect. They are not too difficult to explain: Bill voiced certain chords – that is, he chose the notes to go in those chords – leaving out the root notes that tie down the chord and its sound. Without them, a given chord can sometimes have several identities; it can lead easily and consonantly to a wider choice of other chords, and it can accommodate a wider choice of melody notes and phrases for the player on top of the chords."[13] Given that description, it is no wonder that Davis, concerned with opening up new avenues for melodic improvisation, built *Kind Of Blue* around Bill Evans. Listening to the almost miraculous beauties discovered by the group on 'Flamenco Sketches' during the April session, where each soloist seems to delve more deeply into a treasure-trove of eloquence and controlled passion, one can only be glad that Davis had such prescience. In pursuit of this theme, it is also worth noting just how appropriate for each player is Evans's accompaniment. He shifts his approach to provide the ideal cushion for Davis, Coltrane and Adderley in turn, in particular giving Coltrane as much room as he desires to explore the scalar possibilities opening up in front of him.

Another aspect of *Kind Of Blue* that had a more lasting effect on Evans, as well as on jazz in general, was the attempt to capture the freshness and excitement of a newly emerging musical idea or form. Evans had been out of the Davis group for a whole season or more when *Blue* was made, and although he was involved in the development of its concepts, he stressed in his liner notes for the original album's release that spontaneity was of the essence. "There is a Japanese visual art in which the artist is forced to be spontaneous," Evans wrote. "He must paint with a special brush and black water paint in such a way that an unnatural or interrupted stroke will destroy the line or break through the parchment. Erasures or changes are impossible. These artists must practice a certain discipline, that of allowing the idea to express itself in communication with their hands in such a direct way that deliberation cannot interfere. The resulting pictures lack the complex composition and textures of ordinary painting, but it is said that those who see will find something captured that escapes explanation."[14] Everything was new, and each player had to make a complete mental preparation in order to confront such unanticipated musical challenges. It made for exciting results with musicians of this calibre. Evans in particular revelled in this type of balancing act, and in the trio that he would shortly assemble he found a dynamism that allowed him to bring fresh concepts to the recording studio and create exciting new dialogues with his colleagues. As he wrote in the *Kind Of Blue* liner notes: "Group improvisation is a further challenge. Aside from the weighty technical problem of collective coherent thinking, there is the very human, even social need for sympathy from all members to bend for the common result … As the painter needs his framework of parchment, the improvising musical group needs its framework in time. Miles Davis presents here frameworks which are exquisite in their simplicity and yet contain all that is necessary to stimulate performance with a sure reference to the primary conception. Miles conceived these settings only hours before the recording date and arrived with sketches which indicated to the group what was to be played. Therefore, you will hear something like pure spontaneity in these performances."[15]

It is worth pointing out that this was the first LP on which Davis had jettisoned the usual sleeve blurb by a well-known critic or the album's producer, and that the notes by Evans were important to the idea – novel for jazz at the time – that the music could be considered intellectually. No one prior to this had publicly written on LP sleeves about jazz's legitimate connections to the artistic disciplines of other cultures. The short, formal interpretations of each piece by Evans were also rarities in jazz commentary at this time. Evans may have been keeping pace with George Russell and John Lewis, who were pursuing sophisticated and challenging musical paths of their own, but Davis's choice to highlight the intellectual approach in this way marked a new self-confidence in jazz as a significant contemporary musical force.

Years later, talking to Brian Hennessy, Evans would recall the spontaneity of the *Kind Of Blue* experience. "The first complete performance of each thing is what you're hearing … there are no complete outtakes," he said. "First-take feelings, if they're anywhere near right, [are] generally the best."[16] Four years later, John Coltrane would re-learn the same lesson first-hand from Duke Ellington on their small-group date together, according to producer Bob Thiele. Yet Evans, unlike Coltrane, would not make modality the central object of his musical investigations for the next few years. *Kind Of Blue* would remain one of many diverse projects in which he successfully participated and to which he made vital contributions.

The following month, May 1959, Lee Konitz and Jimmy Giuffre neglected to allow Evans the space to make any vital contribution to their date as twin leaders for Verve, *Lee Konitz Meets Jimmy Giuffre*, where the musical ideas of Lennie Tristano meet the orchestration of Woody Herman's Second Herd. The resulting improvisation sounds curiously pale, the players seemingly happy to stick to the ideas they had been exploring for some time. Konitz does manage to inject urgency and passion into his lines, and his oblique solos are by far the most rewarding music made on the date. Evans comps with taste and discretion, but seeks – and receives – no special highlighting of his talents. During the summer *Everybody Digs* was released and caused a flurry of publicity for a pianist still unable to get regular work for his putative trio. Evans continued to record for a variety of leaders and labels, including a return to Riverside's studios for another Chet Baker album, this time themed as *Plays The Best of Lerner & Loewe*, once again using Herbie Mann and Art Pepper but adding Zoot Sims to the mix. Mann supplied the arrangements while Evans appeared on just half of the tracks after making it to only one of the two July sessions. The degree to which he could affect a record date is pointed up here by comparing the tracks on which he appears with those where the competent but conventional pianisms of Bob Corwin provide Baker and the other horns with their harmonic fodder. Around the same time, Evans was drafted in as a member of the large orchestra used by John Lewis to supply the soundtrack for a Hollywood movie, *Odds Against Tomorrow*, starring Harry Belafonte and Frank Sinatra. The music calls for The Modern Jazz Quartet to be showcased within a larger ensemble and allows little room for Evans to do more than just a professional session job. (It was undoubtedly this exposure to Lewis's themes for the movie that would lead Evans to put forward 'Skating In Central Park' for *Undercurrent*, the 1962 duet album he made with Jim Hall for United Artists.)

Private tapes owned and subsequently issued by Tony Scott as *Golden Moments* revealed that in the first week of August 1959 Evans appeared with Scott's Quartet, alongside bassist Jimmy Garrison and drummer

Pete LaRoca, at the Showplace club in New York City. This was a return to old times for Evans as well as a continuation of his flourishing freelance career. On many tunes he managed to bring into his accompaniment and his solos some arresting ideas, working them up as he went along. Jazz critic Harvey Pekar was especially taken with 'Melancholy Baby' from this date. "Part of the way through his solo Evans does a highly unusual thing," wrote Pekar, "playing a counter line in octaves along with Tony and then continuing on to play his entire solo octave-unison style. What a display of freshness and continuity!"[17] But Evans was not breaking any new ground personally, despite the presence of so many high-quality players in the group.

He was, however, required to produce something a good deal beyond the status quo during his attendance at that August's School Of Jazz at Berkshire Music Inn in Lenox, Massachusetts. Organised by John Lewis and some close colleagues, the School had been started two years earlier as a nurturing ground for progressive ideas in jazz and new musical educational concepts with a particular relevance to jazz. Previous years had witnessed a number of successful workshops and concerts, especially those featuring John Lewis and The Modern Jazz Quartet, with guest stars such as Jimmy Giuffre and Sonny Rollins. The 1959 School was planned to fall within this general pattern but also to contain a number of lectures and workshops on widely differing subjects within what was then perceived as "contemporary" music. To this end, Gunther Schuller was present for the first time in a professional capacity, as were Tanglewood classicist Jack Duffy, bandleader Herb Pomeroy, and Bill Evans.

Schuller taught a course on *The Analytical History Of Jazz* and also led a group of students that included latter-day educator David Baker and clarinettist Perry Robinson (who would become a major player in the New York avant-garde scene in the 1960s). The School's regular faculty members, Bill Russo and George Russell, along with Schuller, took students for a composition class. Evans was one of a number of jazz professionals coaching student small-groups (others included trumpeter Kenny Dorham, Jimmy Giuffre, drummer Max Roach and John Lewis, Connie Kay and Jim Hall). Evans's group, a septet, featured such soon-to-be-notables as guitarist Attila Zoller and vibraphonist Gary McFarland. Two of McFarland's compositions were among those rehearsed and then performed at the final concert. Evans oversaw their activities and made the announcements for the band, according to *Down Beat.*[18]

But the most significant event at that summer's School was the debut of saxophonist Ornette Coleman and multi-instrumentalist Don Cherry as part of the student body (and on a scholarship from Atlantic Records, according to eyewitness Martin Williams). They were among the group overseen and sponsored by Roach and Lewis which also included pianist Steve Kuhn and bassist Larry Ridley. Coleman's playing at the group's concert – which performed three of his early compositions – caused a sensation among the musicians and observers present. Even within the confines of the big-band overseen by Herb Pomeroy, Coleman made an impression both with his ability to learn an ensemble style and with the sheer force and beauty of his music. He affected all who heard his playing, and was described in *Down Beat*'s unsigned report as having "a driving, exciting, highly individual style".[19] Had Evans but known it, he was witnessing the first moments of the eclipse of the progressive jazz movement with which he had been so closely involved for the past four years. As well as many of the teachers and professionals at that year's School, the movement included players such as Lee Konitz, Lennie Tristano, Miles Davis, John Coltrane, Sonny Rollins and Dave Brubeck. Some of these musicians would have to reinvent themselves or adjust their style to accommodate the ideas and freedoms that Coleman and his followers would introduce into jazz during the next handful of years. Evans had just months earlier been a force behind one of jazz's greatest records, yet he would never regain the musical initiative or be a member of the front-line innovators of jazz, even though one of the members of his first trio, Scott LaFaro, would play and record with Coleman. From this time on – even before his first great trio had recorded its debut LP together – Evans would be treading his own path and working increasingly further away from any new trends in jazz. This had its advantages, but also posed problems – and was another factor in the gradual ossification of Evans's mature style. It meant that he would no longer be willing to expand his musical horizons, but instead would consolidate and more fully explore musical territory that he had already marked out.

CHAPTER 6

The First Trio
(1959-1961)

"WE REACHED SUCH A PEAK WITH SCOTT LAFARO, SUCH FREEDOM. IT SEEMED THAT EVERYTHING WAS BECOMING POSSIBLE."

DRUMMER PAUL MOTIAN ON THE POTENTIAL OF THE FIRST EVANS TRIO

Evans had spent much of 1959 attempting to find sufficient work for a trio so that he could launch his career as a leader. As usual, he had put plenty of thought into the type of music he wanted to create within the confines of a trio, and was keen to put a firm emphasis on the three-way dialogue that he felt could be achieved between piano, bass and drums. In direct contrast to Lennie Tristano's method – and to that of most bop practitioners – Evans wanted the bass and drums to play an equal role in a three-way conversation. They were not, he contended, to be regarded purely as time-keeping machines which, in the case of the bass, also marked the passing of the harmonic signposts. As he told Brian Hennessey much

Scott LaFaro, Bill Evans and Paul Motian during a break at the Village Vanguard, New York, 1961

later, "I wanted to make room for the bass and try to leave some fundamental roles empty so that the bass could pick them up. If I am going to be sitting there playing roots, fifths and full voicings, the bass is relegated to a time machine ... Contrast is [also] important to me. I even thought that drums would be a problem and we might be better without them. It was remarkable that Paul Motian came along and identified with the concept so completely that drums were never a problem."[1]

As for the bassist, there is a sense of inevitability about the arrival of Scott LaFaro in the band. "I was astounded by his creativity, [he was] a virtuoso," said Evans. "There was so much music in him, he had a problem controlling it ... He certainly stimulated me to other areas, and perhaps I helped him contain some of his enthusiasm. It was a wonderful thing and worth all the effort that we made later to suppress the ego and work for a common result."[2]

Drummer Paul Motian's arrival in the trio was a logical one, given the amount of time that he and Evans had spent together as sidemen in a variety of settings, both live and in the studio, over the previous three years. Motian felt at ease with Evans's reserve and attention to detail, with his balance between careful rehearsal and spontaneity. Motian was rare among drummers of the day in his ability to concentrate for long periods of a performance on what the others were playing. Most drummers at that time tended to rely on a supply of licks and rhythmic gestures that would be deployed for the most part in a stereotypical way. It was as if the bop and hard-bop style of playing had reached a formula where each bar of theme statement or improvisation had its own rules and set patterns. Motian's ability to avoid these automatic responses and react instead to what he actually heard coming from the other two musicians added in no small degree to the unique quality of Evans's first working trio. Not the attention-grabbing type, he also had a light touch, a large range of dynamics, and a crisp, propulsive drive at medium and faster tempos.

Bassist Scott LaFaro was young, energetic, confidently outgoing and very ambitious. He was also extremely talented, as Charlie Haden – among many others – has consistently stressed. "I think one of the greatest losses to music – not just to jazz – was the loss of Scott LaFaro," Haden said in 1966, five years after LaFaro was killed in a car accident at the age of just 25. "He was one of my closest friends, and I'm not recovered from his death. He would have gone on to become one of the greatest musicians, greatest human beings, in the world ... It was my pleasure to record an album with Scotty, which I'll never forget – the double quartet album with Ornette [Coleman]."[3]

Born in Newark, New Jersey, in 1936, LaFaro studied a range of instruments as a child, moving on to bass after high school. By the mid 1950s he'd travelled to Los Angeles where he became active in the jazz scene, and was tutored by Red Mitchell. By 1959 LaFaro had come back to the East Coast and settled in New York City, quickly becoming a regular player in a range of groups from Benny Goodman to Stan Getz and, of course, Bill Evans. LaFaro had roomed with Charlie Haden for a while in LA. "We met and became very close," said Haden. "We shared an apartment for a while, and he went to New York about the time Ornette's group did."[4] During his time with the Evans trio, LaFaro would revolutionise modern-jazz bass playing, largely through what he played with Evans but also through a number of other appearances live and on records with various leaders, and most especially the two albums he made in the winter of 1960/61 with Ornette Coleman, *Free Jazz* and *Ornette!*. A regular freelancer with all manner of bands, LaFaro also ran his own occasional trio throughout his time with Evans.

The Evans trio worked where it could during the summer and autumn of 1959, often as support for better-known artists, and sometimes with other players depping where one member had previous commitments. By December, Evans felt ready to take his now settled group into the studio for the first time. "I found these two musicians were not only compatible, but would be willing to dedicate themselves to a musical goal, a trio goal," he said. "We made an agreement to put [aside] other work [in favour of] anything which might come up for the trio ... We could make records – not enough to live on, but enough to get a trio experienced and moving."[5]

The resulting album, recorded three days after Christmas 1959, delivers the blueprint for every subsequent working trio that Evans would run. *Portrait In Jazz* finds the pianist often using the more percussive keyboard attack associated with most of his previous playing, his ideas crowding in, his urgency all too apparent. His theme statement on the opening track, 'Come Rain Or Come Shine', is anything but reflective of the message carried by the song's lyrics. The pianistic asides and arabesques, the harmonic reworkings, all give his performance considerable edge and brittleness, with his rhythm choppy and uncharacteristically over-busy. LaFaro and Motian, in contrast, stroll through the song, the bassist in particular almost laconic in his easy lines, casual double-stops and occasional rhythmic pauses.

A more characteristic sound and approach is discernible after the hectic, George Russell-like intro to 'Autumn Leaves', the performance showing signs of being well rehearsed in every detail. Here Evans is busy and silent by turns; Motian constantly breaks up his timekeeping role, engaging in intelligent dialogue with his partners; and from the first verse LaFaro is creating the types of note cycles and little rhythmic motifs with which he would soon become closely identified and which would prove so influential throughout jazz. It is worth noting that it is LaFaro who takes the opening solo here. Only halfway through the performance do all three break out into a swinging medium tempo, all the more refreshing for its long-delayed entry.

Other standards have less stimulating arrangements. 'Witchcraft', for example, is pure George Shearing in its initial statement, but its musical focus comes unequivocally from the trio, with LaFaro's melodic gift and astonishing facility of phrasing constantly stealing the listener's ear from the lines or chords that Evans is delivering. This feature of LaFaro's playing would survive alongside such a strong improvisatory force as Ornette Coleman, and indeed it is possible to listen rewardingly to both Coleman's records featuring LaFaro by focusing entirely on the bass player(s). LaFaro is especially effective within the confines of the Evans trio, whose leader constantly stressed that the sharing of the music's spotlight was fundamental to what his band should be doing, so long as the musicians concerned were happy to share musical goals. As for Evans himself: "As a leader, it's my role to give direction to the group, and Paul and Scott have indicated that they are more comfortable in the trio than anywhere else. Does a group get stale? It all depends on whether there is continuing stimulation, whether all the musicians concerned want to share each other's progress."[6]

Just two Evans originals appeared on *Portrait In Jazz*, one being a new version of 'Blue In Green', the piece Evans had recorded earlier in 1959 with Davis. It now appeared on his Riverside LP co-credited to Davis and Evans. The second original was a sprightly mid-tempo tune, 'Peri's Scope', named after Evans's girlfriend of the time, Peri Cousins. It's delivered in the locked-hands approach which he was gradually inflecting with enough of his own musical personality to make it a signature sound. The performance on this track finds Evans at his most playful, toying with phrases and emphasising the major tonality of the piece in a way that gives no room for doubt about his feelings for the song's subject. Even the feeble pun of the title has a naïve charm of its own.

By contrast, some of Evans's most explorative, chance-taking playing of the date occurs on an old favourite, 'What Is This Thing Called Love', where crisp up-tempo stop-time passages allow him plenty of opportunity to display his talent for rhythmic displacement. LaFaro's solo on the same track is one of his most technically impressive of the session. 'Blue In Green', taken at a pace very similar to the version on *Kind Of Blue*, allows Evans to adopt the combined roles of that session's trumpeter and pianist. It also points the way to the more rarefied trio performances of the future. These would use gradations of touch and a "cushioning" of accents by all three players to create the trio's own special ballad language, communicating surprising levels of emotional depth though a music notable for its restraint and economy. These qualities are also evident on the version of the Disney song, 'Someday My Prince Will Come', brought to jazz by Dave Brubeck some three years earlier and, after Evans's version here, adopted by Miles Davis using a very similar arrangement. This language was now being recognised by other musicians as originating from Evans. In a Blindfold Test in *Down Beat* in January 1960 Ornette Coleman was played 'All Blues' from *Kind Of Blue*. "I believe Bill Evans was the most dominant figure on that side," said Coleman, "but Cannonball and Coltrane sound very wonderful … But Miles Davis seems to have had the closest execution and emotion to blend with the way Bill Evans was playing his chords for the instruments to play on."[7] Evans was thrilled and stimulated by the music his trio was making and looked forward to the promise of even better things to come as 1960 commenced. He cut down on the amount of freelancing he was doing, concentrating instead on rehearsing the group and finding regular work, aiming to make the trio financially self-sustaining. They managed a brief cross-country tour in January and February which took them as far as San Francisco's Jazz Workshop before returning to New York. Back home they appeared on the bill at a Town Hall concert that was headlined by The Modern Jazz Quartet and including groups led by Ornette Coleman, Art Blakey, Philly Joe Jones and Carmen McRae.

In late March *Down Beat*'s In Person column listed the trio as appearing "indefinitely" at New York's Hickory House restaurant and club, taking over from an extended "indefinite" stay by the Mitchell-Ruff duo. By mid March they were debuting at Birdland on Broadway. During this spring of 1960 Evans appeared as a sideman again, on three tracks contributed to a Warwick album, *The Soul Of Jazz Percussion* (later reissued, equally inaccurately, as *The Third World*). The session quintet, co-led by trumpeter Donald Byrd and baritone saxophonist Pepper Adams, would evolve – minus Evans and the rest of the rhythm section – into a working band under Byrd's leadership. The music contains an ersatz Eastern flavour and apes the contemporary work of Yusef Lateef, using vamps and scales which, in the case of 'Prophecy', sound more like the Hollywood version than the real thing, with occasional overtones of so-called "Red Indian" film-score identification music. 'Quiet Temple', a simple pseudo-Eastern ballad, is transformed by the harmonic interest that Evans provides with his trademark reworking of the simple minor progression's inner voicings. For the straightforward swinger 'Ping Pong Beer' Evans reverts to his pre-trio single-note style.

This single-note approach was also used, fittingly in a more avant-garde guise, on Evans's latest recording session with George Russell, *Jazz In The Space Age*, made in May 1960 (the sleeve describing Evans as "perhaps the most significant jazz pianist to come along in the past decade"[8]). Here he was paired on many tracks with pianist Paul Bley, newly arrived in New York from a long period in Los Angeles where he had, among other things, led a quintet briefly with the entire first Ornette Coleman Quartet.

The group writing on *Space Age* is typical of Russell's style of the time: dissonant, rhythmically ebullient and always ready to stress the contrapuntal in ways that were new and fresh to jazz. His use of Evans and Bley is equally arresting, calling on them to improvise spontaneous duets on the first number, 'Chromatic Universe Part 1'. Russell said in the sleevenote interview: "Bill and Paul were free to come close to the tonality – [the] sum total of the bass notes – [and] relate to the 5/2 gravitational pull or not. Tonally and rhythmically out in space, they are not victim to the tyranny of the chord or a particular metre. In essence, this is musical relativism. Everything can be right … This is panchromatic improvisation."[9] Evans and Bley were called upon to deliver comparable responses to various incarnations of similar musical ideas and frameworks during the rest of the record, including 'The Lydiot', a piece to which Russell would return frequently in his later career.

Russell was applying ever more sophisticated versions of his musical theories to his latest efforts. Quoted extensively in the album's liner notes, at one point he talked perceptively about the forms that the jazz of the future might take. "Specifically, it's going to be a pan-rhythmic, pan-tonal age," he said. "I think that jazz will bypass atonality, because jazz actually has roots in folk music, and folk music is scale-based music, and atonality negates the scale … The answer seems to lie in pantonality. The basic folk nature of the scales is preserved, and yet, because you can be in any number of tonalities at once and/or sequentially, it also creates a very chromatic kind of feeling, so that it's sort of like being atonal with a Big Bill Broonzy sound. *You can retain the funk.*"[10]

For Evans, this was a very different type of freedom to that which he was finding in the New York clubs with his trio. As he spelled it out to Dan Morgenstern four years later: "The only way I can work is to have some kind of restraint involved – the challenge of a certain craft or form – and then find the freedom in that … I have allowed myself the other kind of freedom occasionally. Paul Bley and I did a two-piano improvisation on a George Russell record which was completely unpremeditated. It was fun to do, but there was no direction involved. To do something that hadn't been rehearsed successfully, just like that, almost shows the lack of challenge involved in that type of freedom."[11] Evans was not entirely fair with that assessment. He and Bley had brought their formidable training, experience, knowledge and musical sensitivity to the two-piano session, ensuring the event had a good chance of success. As Russell revealed in those liner notes, he was conducting a controlled experiment, not a formless, open-ended free-for-all.

Namechecks in jazz magazines were increasing during the spring and summer of 1960 and the Evans trio, regularly appearing at Birdland, were announced as appearing at that summer's Newport Jazz Festival. Evans himself was publicly confirmed to repeat his consultancy at August's Music Inn Summer School in Lenox, Massachusetts, while his group gained an effusive entry in *Down Beat*'s nine-page Jazz Combo Directory of June 1960, organised "to help club operators and other buyers select groups to hire". It noted that "Evans has a fine sense of melodic and harmonic invention. LaFaro is one of the newer talents on bass and is receiving more and more attention from jazz listeners".[12]

The trio did not in fact appear at Newport because the festival closed prematurely after street riots by drunken teenagers. Evans did manage an appearance in May with Gunther Schuller's band in a concert in the Jazz Profiles series at New York's Circle In The Square. Dan Morgenstern described what he saw. "Schuller employed as the basic units of his ensemble a classical string quartet and a jazz trio (… Bill Evans, piano; Scott LaFaro, bass; and 'Sticks' Evans or Paul Cohen, drums). The two groups performed in all the seven compositions heard. Additional musicians joined them from time to time: Ornette Coleman, alto saxophone; Eric Dolphy, alto, clarinet, bass clarinet and flute; … Eddie Costa, vibes; Barry Galbraith, guitar; and Buell Neidlinger on bass."[13]

Morgenstern, not entirely enamoured with Schuller's efforts to meld jazz and classical, did not mention Evans again in the course of his two-page review. Instead he singled out just two musicians for praise: Ornette Coleman and Scott LaFaro. "The main event of 'Variations (On Django)' was a bass solo by Scott LaFaro," wrote Morgenstern, "a young bassist who here demonstrated that his ample and beautiful instrumental technique is matched by a musical imagination of the first order. But he could have, and has, played as well in a purely jazz environment."[14] Morgenstern concluded his review by commenting, "At the Circle In The Square, jazz, representing Dionysius, met a somewhat anaemic Apollo in the guise of Gunther Schuller. It wasn't even a close contest."[15] Whatever else, the concert did at least provide an important musical meeting between Coleman and LaFaro.

Portrait In Jazz was released by Riverside at this time and there were rave reviews from all directions. By the end of the summer Evans, already involved with a booking agency, signed a management deal with Monte Kay, proprietor of Birdland and husband to actress and singer Diahann Carroll. In the *Down Beat* International Critics' Poll announced in August 1960, Evans came third on piano (just two votes behind Oscar Peterson) while his group, still very much an emerging force, were placed equal fourth in the New Star section alongside Slide Hampton and Paul Horn (although, to keep things in perspective, Humphrey Lyttelton's group came fifth).

Everything seemed to be set for a quick take-off in his career, but then Evans suffered his latest bout of hepatitis, probably brought about through shared heroin needles and lax hygiene. It forced him to spend much of August and September recuperating and the trio's progress came to a complete, if temporary, halt. Bassist LaFaro took the opportunity afforded by this unwanted break to join Ornette Coleman's Quartet as a replacement for his friend Charlie Haden, another addict who, in order to rid himself of his habit, had checked into a sanatorium. LaFaro toured with the Quartet until the beginning of November, which took him to San Francisco and back via the Monterey Jazz Festival where they appeared as a trio.

Evans, meanwhile, had slipped back into New York by early October and taken a number of jobs as a sideman while re-establishing his health. He had his first dealings with the fledgling Impulse! label and its A&R man Creed Taylor, contributing neat, apposite and professional accompaniment to a date that involved trombonists Kai Winding and J.J. Johnson in tandem, *The Great Kai & JJ*. He also appeared in December on a Kai Winding Septet date for Impulse!, *The Incredible Kai Winding Trombones*, but his most important recording activity in October 1960 came on the 20th for Gunther Schuller. Evans reprised his role on some Schuller concert pieces from earlier that year, 'Variations On A Theme By Thelonious Monk (Criss Cross)' and 'Variations On A Theme By John Lewis (Django)'. Both would appear on a 1961 Atlantic record, *Jazz*

Abstractions. LaFaro was also present on this album, as were Eric Dolphy and Ornette Coleman, and all three would participate the very next day in recording Coleman's masterpiece, *Free Jazz*, for the same label. Dolphy too made a classic album on the 21st, cutting *Far Cry* for Prestige with Booker Little.

The Evans trio had still not resumed playing residencies together. In fact, LaFaro stayed with Coleman into 1961, recording his second (and last) album with the altoist on the last day of January. Two days later he would be back with Evans making the trio's second date for Riverside. Three days prior to that Evans had been in the Riverside studios with Cannonball Adderley for the first of three sessions that would spread across January, February and March to fit in with the saxophonist's hectic performing schedule with his own group. The session would result in *Know What I Mean?*, released under Adderley's name with Evans as featured guest, Percy Heath and Connie Kay completing the rhythm team. In contrast to the previous Adderley date featuring Evans – *Portrait Of*, from 1958 – this record was largely given over to Evans arrangements of original material ('Waltz For Debby', 'Know What I Mean?') and standards ('Goodbye' and 'Nancy With The Laughing Face'). It presented Adderley in an unusually lush and reserved but sympathetic setting that brings out most positively his deep appreciation of Benny Carter's playing, especially on the ballads. Evans's own playing across the three dates is relaxed and expansive.

Ironically, given the confused state of their own ambitions, Evans and his trio had featured prominently in the December 8th 1960 edition of *Down Beat*. Evans appeared on the cover and was interviewed in depth by Don Nelsen, while in the December 22nd issue Evans was listed fifth on piano in the Readers' Poll, one place up from the previous year, and LaFaro came 12th on bass.

The conditions under which the trio's *Explorations* LP was recorded on February 2nd 1961 were not ideal. Tension from the separations of the previous months still simmered, particularly between Evans and the abrasive LaFaro, who made no secret of his disgust at Evans's addiction. LaFaro played on a borrowed instrument, while the pianist was quickly complaining of a headache, probably brought on by the strain in the studio. There are moments on the album where the connections between the three men, and especially between pianist and bassist, seem momentarily to go dead. LaFaro, who has a darker, less focused tone than usual, is quite often to be heard playing lone whole notes as a tune's arrangement is dispensed with, or moving harmonically with Evans in minims on the tonic and dominant (for example on the Gordon-Warren ballad 'I Wish I Knew'). Meanwhile, Paul Motian holds down the time with the minimum of brushstrokes to cymbal and drum-head.

On other, more fully integrated pieces LaFaro is in top gear and playing all over the range of his instrument, as his solo on 'Nardis' demonstrates. His is the first, taking priority over Evans's – in itself a considerable departure from the jazz conventions of 1961. The piece exhibits a similar harmonic construction to the uncredited 'Quiet Temple' from the Donald Byrd/Pepper Adams *Soul Of Jazz Percussion* session of spring 1960, suggesting that Evans, a 'Nardis' fan, had dressed it up in new clothes for that quintet date. During 'Sweet And Lovely' the wonderful co-ordination of mind and effort between all three is perfectly judged, an indication perhaps that this tune, at least, had been thoroughly rehearsed in the recent past. Evans commented in retrospect about this set: "Scott was just an incredible guy about knowing where your next thought was going to be. I wondered, 'How did he know I was going there?' And he was probably feeling the same way."[16]

For an album that was to be so influential and remain the only studio recording of this trio at its mature peak, *Explorations* is singularly bare of Evans originals, relying for its effect on his perfected approach to familiar material and the unique interplay between the three musicians. This interplay can be most readily appreciated by comparing this music with that recorded the same month by Evans and Cannonball Adderley for *Know What I Mean?*. On the latter, each member of the rhythm section sticks strictly to the conventions of his instrument's role. By contrast, the effort to listen to everything being played and to simultaneously react to it is almost palpable on the *Explorations* sides. Yet it is fair to say that this record represents the trio at a relatively early phase of its evolution, even given LaFaro's vastly increased role. The piano leads from the front and is much more the dominant voice in the dialogue than it would be by the time the trio made its midsummer recordings at the Village Vanguard. Evans's piano is also a significant voice in an important record he made as a sideman soon after the *Explorations* date. This was a carefully considered programme of variations on the blues recorded in February 1961 and put together by the saxophonist, composer and arranger Oliver Nelson under the aegis of A&R man Creed Taylor at the fledgling Impulse! label. Called *The Blues And The Abstract Truth*, it is a justly famous and popular collection that brings together a stellar set of musicians, including Eric Dolphy, Freddie Hubbard and Evans, as well as Nelson himself on tenor. Evans plays impeccably, showing great sensitivity as an accompanist and with flashes of flair and inspiration as a soloist. The opening theme is 'Stolen Moments', which has long since become a modern jazz standard, performed and recorded by thousands of jazz musicians and even set to lyrics. Here it finds Nelson conjuring a brooding, pensive mood at medium tempo that, once the improvisations commence, carries distinct echoes of *Kind Of Blue*. Evans's position as accompanist is no small part of this perhaps unintentional evocation. Nelson's composition 'Cascades' uses a quickly moving set of chords beneath a cascade of arpeggios articulated by Nelson. It is set up as a solo vehicle for Hubbard and Evans, the pianist proving comfortable and highly inventive at a bright tempo with this particular variation of blues changes. A passage where Evans displays extreme rhythmic flexibility and unusually extended lines contrasts superbly with others where he trails minor-third triads in asymmetric patterns through the changes. This album alone dispels the notion that Evans was an undistinguished practitioner of the blues form.

Nelson's self-penned liner notes for the record are singularly insightful and informative. He knew this was a personal watershed: "It was not until this LP was recorded, on Thursday the 23rd of February 1961, that I finally had broken through and realised that I would have to be true to myself, to play and write what I think is vital and, most of all, to find my own personality and identity."[17] The result of this breakthrough was that rarest of events, a jazz classic that was also a bestseller. The line-up's solo power rivals *Kind Of Blue*. Dolphy and Hubbard are in brilliant form and Nelson is a revelation. *The Blues And The Abstract Truth* also brought Evans once more into significant direct contact with Creed Taylor, soon to move on from Impulse! and take over the reins at Verve. Within a year he would sign Evans to Verve and begin the star-making treatment with the pianist that had already benefited Nelson. During the 1960s Taylor would make Wes Montgomery, Jimmy Smith and Stan Getz into major "crossover" stars in contemporary popular music.

Meanwhile during the spring, work for the trio continued as a hit-and-miss affair. There was a week during February 1961 at the Cork & Bib club in Westbury, New York state; a March residency that extended to three weeks at the Sutherland Lounge in Chicago (sandwiched between a week of John Coltrane and a fortnight of Shirley Scott); and a week in April at The Showboat in Philadelphia – but still very little in the way of steady work in New York City. There were a number of interruptions, including Evans's participation in the Nelson record; the most significant was the regular absence of the in-demand Scott LaFaro.

The bassist's ex-boss, tenorist Stan Getz, had recently returned from an extended stay in Stockholm, and LaFaro was announced in *Down Beat* as part of Getz's "promising new group [which includes] Pete LaRoca, drums, Steve Kuhn, piano, Scott LaFaro, bass".[18] This group had preceded the John Coltrane Quartet into Chicago's Sutherland Lounge in February. The same report went on to give details of Getz's recording activity. "The first recording session for Getz since his return to this country two months ago was held in New York City with Bob Brookmeyer, trombone, Bill Evans, piano, Percy Heath, bass, Connie Kay, drums."[19] This recording seems not to have happened, although Getz did record two numbers (so far unissued) with Brookmeyer and a very similar group in New York in February, using Dick Katz on piano instead of Evans. Getz also made an album's worth of material in Chicago on February 21st with his new quartet, including LaFaro on bass. Just one track, 'Airegin', has been released to date, on a latter-day Getz CD compilation. By the time Getz hit The Showboat in April 1961 he had an ad-hoc rhythm team of Steve Kuhn on piano, Jimmy Garrison on bass and Roy Haynes on drums. LaFaro was back with Evans and Motian.

This sort of movement between bands and personnel may hardly seem ideal for pulling together the various threads of a group's musical development, but it is utterly typical of the life of the post-war working jazz musician. Still, it illustrates the distance Evans had to go to become a sufficiently big name with the public and maintain his band in the manner of leaders like Miles Davis and John Coltrane. Nonetheless, his group had developed an audience for itself at the Village Vanguard in Greenwich Village, New York City, during infrequent appearances over the past six months. When the trio was booked for a two-week stay there in mid June 1961 opposite Lambert, Hendricks & Ross, Riverside producer Orrin Keepnews decided that it would be the ideal venue for what had recently become a craze among jazz A&R men: an "on-the-spot" recording in a cosy jazz club.

The Evans group was more than ready for the challenge of recording in front of an audience, having rehearsed regularly over the months to build a large repertoire of carefully arranged tunes. As Evans observed later, "Scott, Paul and I would play the same tune over and over again. Rarely did everything fall into place, but when it did, we thought it was sensational."[20] They also welcomed the test of an audience's reaction to refine their interplay and approach. "The music developed as we performed and what you heard came through actual performance," Evans continued. "The objective was to achieve the result in a responsible way."[21] The new live recordings were to do that in full measure.

The trio was taped by Riverside during the last full day of their week at the Vanguard, on Sunday June 25th 1961. The extra time allowed by the Sunday matinée at the club was used to record multiple versions of the same repertoire, offering more chances to capture flawless, complete versions of each piece under consideration. Years later, producer Orrin Keepnews recalled a chance factor that added to the success of the recording. "Our staff engineer, Roy Fowler, was not on hand, perhaps on vacation. His replacement was Dave Jones, one of the best at 'live' location recordings in that two-track era. The sound of these selections remains as crisp and undated as the music…"[22] In fact, Jones's brilliant realisation of the group's sound is one of the major factors that makes this set of recordings so highly valued among Evans's overall output. It also helps that for once the piano is in tune. In a recording career spanning seven years, Evans had rarely been taped on a properly tuned instrument. Even on *Kind Of Blue* there are registers on his studio piano that betray the need of a professional tuner.

Clearly the group itself had no reason to think that this recording session would be any more special than others they had done together. The usual planning took place and the tunes were considered and selected. The playbacks heard later were a pleasant surprise. Evans: "I was very happy when after the Vanguard date we were listening through stereo headphones, and [LaFaro] said, 'You know, we didn't think too much of it while we were doing it, but these two weeks were exceptional.' He said something to the effect that, 'I've finally made a record that I'm happy with.'"[23] That contentment is understandable, given the peak of creativity the trio had attained unawares. Many years later, Keepnews wrote about the initial selections that he made with Evans for the two original LPs released from the material, *Sunday At The Village Vanguard* and *Waltz For Debby*. He claimed that "the necessary choices were quite arbitrary; it is clear that nothing played this day was without considerable merit".[24] This may well be a record-company man justifying a later issue of all the extant material; after all, he and Evans cleared just those two albums' worth for release in 1961/62, and the recording of multiple versions of the same piece had been based on the premise of choice. The group's drummer, Paul Motian, had his own thoughts on this, saying recently, "There's a record called *More From The Village Vanguard* which is an album of outtakes that we hated … and Orrin Keepnews put that out. Bill would have been freaking, man. Those are all the takes that were dismissed, and they put that out as a record. He would never have approved that."[25]

Approved or not, all but two takes – one technically marred beyond the point where it could have been coherently issued, the other irretrievably lost – have now been made publicly available. Thirteen different tunes were recorded. Apart from the felicities of the individual improvisations themselves, the differing takes of the six songs attempted more than once reveal a remarkably consistent conception in basic matters such as tempo, dynamics and playing order. Only details shift, as well as the take-to-take levels of precision and cohesion from the performers. It is this matter of cohesion – of making sense of the music and its challenges – which is most striking about the first-issued recordings. The dynamics that the group employed (especially on ballads such as 'My Foolish heart' or 'My Man's Gone Now') were extraordinary for the time, allowing

THE FIRST TRIO 1959-1961

levels of nuance and inflection rare then in jazz and found most often in jazz vocals such as those by Billie Holiday, Lee Wiley, Louis Armstrong or Ella Fitzgerald.

In the eyes of many contemporary observers, the major musical reason for this extraordinary level of group intercommunication and creativity was the ability of LaFaro to match and, certainly in rhythmic areas, outpace Evans in terms of the ideas fed in for counterpoint. Critic Harvey Pekar observed once that "even when accompanying, LaFaro didn't limit himself to one particular pattern: he might play two quarter-notes in one bar and superimpose a rhythmic figure containing 16th, dotted-8th, and quarter notes over the beat in the next one".[26] LaFaro also contributed significantly to the emotional content of the trio's music. Evans, a contemplative and often inward-looking player, found a counterfoil in LaFaro as perfect as that between himself and the other soloists in Miles Davis's group. As Pekar observed, "[LaFaro's] improvising is reminiscent of John Coltrane's because he was seemingly more concerned with harmonic and rhythmic exploration than with overall construction … At times his playing suggests the human voice, and the passion with which he played is almost overpowering."[27]

Not everyone shared this laudatory view of LaFaro's contribution to jazz bass. Pianist and composer Cecil Taylor, in a swingeing attack in 1965 on Evans's music, talent and musical philosophy, commented: "The weaker musicians have always benefited from the technical things engineers do. On the other hand, if you're powerful, the engineer usually feels he has to cut you down … Recording gives Evans's piano a scope of highs and lows that his original touch cannot achieve. This is particularly clear with bass players. Take … Scott LaFaro. He was thought to have a fantastic technique, but my definition of technique is not only the ability to play fast but the ability to be heard. To have a fat sound. LaFaro, however, had a minute sound. By contrast, Charlie Haden really had something going. But engineers made LaFaro sound big."[28]

It is true that LaFaro had lowered the bridge on his bass to give him a lower "action" between strings and fingerboard, and that this had altered the sound he was getting compared to that of conventional bass players – certainly different from Haden, Wilbur Ware and Paul Chambers of his contemporaries. But nobody else ever complained openly about LaFaro's tone and volume, not even other bass players. Taylor seems to be airing some of his own problems concerning the outside world in the guise of an attack on Evans, stretching the point about what may or may not be an acceptable sound or volume from any instrument in an ensemble. When Evans commented on LaFaro's tone, he said his instrument "had a marvelous sustaining and resonating quality",[29] while other musicians who played with LaFaro, including Ornette Coleman, Stan Getz and Charlie Haden, all paid tribute to his unique qualities. Coleman even named an outtake from the January 1961 *Ornette!* date on Atlantic as 'The Alchemy Of Scott LaFaro' when it appeared for the first time during the 1970s.

An engineer, no matter how brilliant, can only capture what is being produced by the musicians with as much fidelity and presence as possible. No engineer in the world can create a gradation of touch or any other inflection if it has not first been articulated by the musician. It is not the fault of Evans's group that they were so sympathetically recorded in the Village Vanguard in June 1961: they just got lucky. Cecil Taylor, by contrast, would have to wait until his 1966 records for Blue Note to be recorded to a high degree of technical fidelity. It is no accident that his music, too, benefited enormously from the clarity, full tone and careful mixing brought to bear on his albums *Unit Structures* and *Conquistador*.

The September 1961 release of *Sunday At The Village Vanguard*, the first selection of material from those June sessions, emphasised LaFaro's playing and composing: it even leads off with a medium-tempo LaFaro line called 'Gloria's Step'. The tune swings contentedly through a major-minor verse and bridge pattern and finds the bassist in mind-bogglingly creative mood during Evans's opening solo, constantly dragging the ear away from the piano which for the most part improvises chordally rather than with a single line. Gershwin's 'My Man's Gone Now', played as a slow waltz but by no means a dirge, is one of the trio's greatest spontaneous masterpieces, from Motian's swirling brush-stroked cymbal beats, through Evans's passionate improvised melodies, to LaFaro's separate but intimately connected musical commentary on both. The intensity, all the more potent for the restraint exercised by Evans and his trio, is overpowering by the end of the tune's recapitulation. 'Solar', by contrast, receives an adequate interpretation but only the bassist really shines, with some rhythmic problems occurring during the course of a long (nearly nine-minute) performance at a bright medium tempo.

'Alice In Wonderland' invokes the utter delight a child finds in fantasy, Evans's arrangement of the Disney song revealing a happy touch of innocent humour as the simple and appealing melody is allowed to dance across a light waltz beat – always a favourite Evans device. His first solo here is his best on the record and one of his best ever. It has a sense of form and dynamics and a seemingly artless (but highly subtle) development, effortlessly invoking a range of emotions associated with the song. A perfect cadential resolution into fresh whole-note chord voicings ushers in LaFaro's bass solo: a perfect exit. The pianist's second solo, after LaFaro, is less consequential and less well organised than the first, but the team still ends perfectly together on a pleasant modulation.

Cole Porter's 'All Of You' inspires a similar level of cohesion, but its common time seems to inspire Evans less. The original LP ended with another LaFaro composition, the contemplative 'Jade Visions', recorded according to Keepnews "almost as an afterthought"[30] but in two versions, both marred by a noisy crowd. Its deceptive simplicity hides considerable musical sophistication, and the piece harks back harmonically and rhythmically to the Debussy of the second book of *Images*, its pensive Oriental atmosphere having few precedents in jazz. This short piece has a minimum of improvisation, the bridge completely chorded with no leading voice, and is given interest by falling into 9/8 time throughout and by LaFaro's triple stops over a low bass pedal note. On the original LP it ends with no applause, but rings in the mind for a long time afterward, and helps give the trio's music a suggested dimension shared by no other piano trio in jazz at that time. 'Jade Visions', like 'Blue In Green' and 'Peace Piece', was to prove powerfully influential on pianists such as Herbie Hancock, Keith Jarrett and Chick Corea.

The second LP release from the live sessions, *Waltz For Debby*, followed in the spring of 1962. The new version of the title track is full of joy, lightness of rhythm and vitality of line, and alone would mark out this trio as a very special group. On this performance, as on 'Detour Ahead', on a heartbreakingly beautiful reading of 'My Foolish Heart', indeed on the whole collection, there are simply no stretches of playing where the musicians are vamping in wait for something to happen, never a feeling that one member of the trio is off on a musical quest of his own. Everything is integrated and has meaning as part of a greater whole. LaFaro's bass anchors Evans's chords beautifully in theme statements, Motian provides impetus and rhythmic colour, and Evans makes his instrument sing more often than not, avoiding his own improvisatory clichés much of the time due to the inspired level at which he is working.

Other standout renderings on this second disc include a sensitive and idiomatic investigation of Bernstein's 'Some Other Time' that avoids the sentimental through a combination of a relatively bright ballad tempo and an unembellished interpretation. 'Milestones' is less of a success: its alternative viewpoint on a Miles Davis exercise in scalar improvisation has little forward momentum and is no match for the trumpeter's approach, with Evans incapable of the staccato thrust given the theme by Davis, Coltrane and Adderley on their 1958 recording. Only LaFaro comes out of this well, his brilliantly conceived and executed rhythm patterns and variations – in and out of tempo – consistently captivating in their daring.

The only significant selection from all the "additional" material later made available from this session by Riverside is a warmly observed and perfectly controlled version of another Gershwin piece, 'I Loves You Porgy'. This initially appeared on a mid-1970s LP compilation of Vanguard material otherwise entirely made up of previously issued selections: possibly, then, Evans approved its appearance at the time. Presumably the intrusive level of audience chatter and glass clattering led to its initial rejection in 1962. The music itself, however, is as seamlessly integrated and perfectly realised as the other ballads from this date.

After the gig was finished and the playback tapes had been listened to, the three men went their separate ways, having no immediate work together. Evans was never to see LaFaro alive again. Just ten days later, after appearing at that year's jazz festival at Newport with Stan Getz, LaFaro and two companions were killed when the car the bassist was driving in upstate New York left the road and hit a tree. The news of this tragic event during the early hours of July 5th 1961 made a deep impact on the jazz world. Bassist Ray Brown told *Down Beat*: "This was one of the most talented youngsters I've seen come up in a long time. For his age, he really had it covered. He wasn't really a power bassist. He had something different going, something of his own. I got a chance to hear him at Newport only a few days before, and I was really amazed by his facility, his intonation, and his ideas … It's a shame, really a shame. It's going to set the instrument back ten years. It will be that long before anyone catches up with what he was doing."[31]

Gunther Schuller, who had used the bassist on various projects, dedicated the *Jazz Abstractions* album to LaFaro, who appears with Ornette Coleman and Eric Dolphy on the record. Schuller wrote in the liner notes to *Ornette!*, the Coleman quartet album featuring LaFaro and released after his death, that "LaFaro, had he lived, would certainly have become one of the great bass players (jazz and classical) in our century".[32] For Evans the loss was devastating, both personally and musically. LaFaro was, he said, "one of the most, if not *the* most outstanding talents in jazz".[33] All of which would, of course, make it especially hard for Evans to replace him.

As Paul Motian later confessed, "We didn't know what to do. We didn't know if we'd still have a trio. We'd reached such a peak with Scott, such freedom. It seemed that everything was becoming possible."[34] Part of the possible may have been a date with Miles Davis. Motian recalled in 1996: "We were supposed to make a record date with Miles: the trio, Bill, myself and Scott … We were talking to Miles about it, it was all set up, and then Scott got killed and the whole thing got forgotten."[35] Now, Evans and Motian had to decide how to move forward – and if it was worth the effort of starting again from scratch to create a new trio.

CHAPTER 7

A Second Trio Struggles to Emerge (1961-1963)

"IT'S A MELANCHOLY THING TO SAY, BUT IF SCOTT LAFARO HADN'T DIED, I'D BE STRUGGLING STILL TO FIND A SITUATION WHERE I COULD PLAY WHAT I WANT TO PLAY."

THE TRIO'S NEW BASSIST, CHUCK ISRAELS

T he death of Scott LaFaro had a debilitating effect on Bill Evans, both personally and professionally. For a while his grieving was so intense that he even lost all interest in playing the piano. Evans later told his friend Gene Lees that he felt "vaguely guilty" about it. Lees said, "He felt that, because of his heroin habit, he had made insufficient use of the time he and Scott had had together. LaFaro was always trying to talk him into quitting. After LaFaro's death, Bill was like a man with a lost love, always looking to find its replacement."[1]

It would take Evans six months to work again with his own trio, when he brought in bassist Chuck Israels alongside Paul Motian to fulfil a commitment

At work in the studio during 1961

in Syracuse, New York. With Israels on board, the music would grow in a different way to the previous trio, bringing Evans more to the fore. This would have advantages and disadvantages. LaFaro's death produced an effect that often occurs as a result of an early and tragic death: the departed bassist – and Evans – became larger figures in the jazz world. The romance of tragedy lingered around the demise of his old trio, brought to a piquancy by the release of their best recordings that had been made less than two weeks prior to LaFaro's death. It spurred people's interest in what Evans would do next, lending him a new aura beyond the musical.

Evans played a handful of recording dates in the autumn and early winter of 1961, also appearing as a solo act on a limited range of club gigs. His playing on a Dave Pike Quartet recording for Columbia, *Pike's Peak*, in November 1961 suggests that he was falling back on the practices and approaches that he'd crystallised during his stay with Davis. The lead track, 'Why Not?', credited to Pike, is in fact Coltrane's 'Impressions', itself inspired by *Kind Of Blue*'s 'So What' and by a Debussy piano piece, 'L'Isle Joyeuse' (hence Coltrane's title). Evans is entirely at home with the dual scales of the piece, but his approach is linear and loosely swinging, with no attempt to make dialogues with the entirely conventional 1961 rhythm section that follows the stylistic lead of the old Miles Davis Sextet. This is Evans the professional fulfilling his duty to an exemplary standard. The other interesting performance on a date otherwise made up of standards is an interpretation of Davis's 'Vierd Blues' which, with Pike's Milt Jackson-inspired vibes, could have been an outtake from a Prestige Davis session of the mid 1950s.

Soon after this date, in early December 1961, Evans began recording *Nirvana* with Pike's erstwhile employer, flautist Herbie Mann. The disc would be finished off by three extra selections from the same personnel in May 1962, and would lie unissued for over two years. The probable reason for its delay was the huge success Mann was about to experience with his live album *Herbie Mann At The Village Gate*, recorded just three months earlier and on the point of being released. It carried what was to be Mann's greatest hit, 'Comin' Home Baby', and defined what the public came to consider to be "the Mann sound" for the 1960s. When *Nirvana* did finally appear in 1964 it sounded rather anachronistic. Had it been issued at the time, it would have been a valuable pointer to where Mann and Evans were headed. It would also have introduced the new version of the Bill Evans trio, for the rhythm team here is Paul Motian and bassist Chuck Israels.

The title track, with its two alternating chords, is credited to Mann and sounds like a pared-down version of 'Blue In Green'. Evans's playing comes directly from the harmonic palette he had been employing with his own trio earlier in the year. The group's version of Erik Satie's 'Gymnopédie No.2' once again gives a strong pointer to an array of Evans's own musical interests and pursuits. It is the earliest jazz version of the piece that this author is aware of, and is unusual because it is 'Gymnopédie No.3' that has become the most popular over the years. This was some years before Satie was generally perceived as a charmingly eccentric precursor to many of the fashionable musical ideas of the post-World War I period – a view as partially accurate as the previously orthodox opinion that he was of limited worth.

The *Nirvana* album is only a qualified success, in part because Mann finds it difficult, without vibrato, to retain the listener's interest in his melodic line at slow tempos – and much of this album is very slow. Also, Evans's partners are so tentative in their contribution as to beg the question as to why the pianist chose to chance it with them in the first place. A decidedly anaemic recording quality doesn't help in this respect. It is no accident that the sprightly 'I Love You', a Cole Porter tune that Evans had already recorded on more than one occasion, is the most steadily cohesive and accomplished performance by the four men, Israels and Motian at times achieving the sort of inspired drive that the old trio had so effortlessly attained, especially behind Evans's own playful solo.

Whatever the album's drawbacks, at least the pianist was testing the water again, however tentatively. His life was at the beginning of a large and long-lasting change. Now married and looking as ever for increased financial security, Evans had opened negotiations with Creed Taylor, new A&R boss at Verve Records, to join his label. Taylor had known Evans casually for a number of years and had been reminded of the pianist's abilities while using him as a sideman during Taylor's short stay at Impulse! Records. Taylor was attempting to re-cast Verve in a new image different to that set by its founder, Norman Granz, who had recently sold the label to MGM. Taylor was convinced that Evans would be an artist capable of considerable musical and commercial development – and with similar aims in mind he would sign Wes Montgomery, also from Riverside, Cal Tjader, from Fantasy, and Jimmy Smith, brought over from Blue Note.

Like Miles Davis moving from Prestige to Columbia in 1955, Evans would not be free of his recording commitments to his existing label, Riverside, for some time (in fact it would not be until early 1963, although the first Verve session took place in August 1962). But the new deal was arranged in late 1961, as reported by *Down Beat* dated December 7th that year. In the following issue the Readers Poll results declared Evans in third place on piano, behind Oscar Peterson and Thelonious Monk and ahead of Dave Brubeck and Horace Silver. Evans's reputation was growing at a time when his own life was in disarray. Apart from being unable to pull together a regular working trio, he also suffered from another attack of hepatitis. According to Brian Hennessey, who met him for the first time in New York in early 1962 while the pianist was in the midst of this illness, the result was "permanent and serious liver damage".[2]

Desperate for money to keep his addiction going – his wife was now also a user – as well as to pay the rent, Evans began working in early 1962 with his new trio, retaining Paul Motian on drums and permanently hiring Chuck Israels on bass. Despite the pianist's poor health and low spirits, the group found work sporadically around the New York area at clubs such as Birdland and the Village Vanguard. Evans also appeared on a Tadd Dameron big-band album, *The Magic Touch*, for Riverside in February.

The new group began to gel, but work remained occasional as Evans attempted to pick himself up. His prevailing mood can be heard in the four selections recorded in April 1962 as the first part of a projected solo album. It was never completed and the performances set aside, not to be heard until issued in the 1970s. On a 'Danny Boy' which lasts for over ten minutes, Evans is by turns ruminative, disconnected, intense, faux-jovial and content to swing things along at mid-tempo. The music is intensely personal and private, sounding less like a shaped performance than time spent privately at the keyboard which happened to be overheard.

Other pieces from the date are treated in a more formal manner, but there are still strange moments, such as the unnerving pause at the end of the first full statement of 'Like Someone In Love' where Evans seems simply unsure whether to continue playing. 'In Your Own Sweet Way', a tender and sweetly affectionate medium-tempo Dave Brubeck portrait, finds Evans curiously unable to bring to bear his vaunted gradations of touch and dynamics, and his left-hand accompaniment to his own improvisations is unusually lumpen. He hardly bothers to give the performance a coherent ending. 'Easy To Love' comes off best in terms of shape. He supplies one of his trademark out-of-tempo introductions before falling into an easy mid-tempo improvisation where the melodic line often achieves a cantilena (a long, flowing instrumental passage) not apparent elsewhere that day. Even then, there are passages which sound like filler, where the hand rather than the brain is making the note choices. It is understandable that Evans stopped the session after this track.

Clearly spring 1962 was a bleak time for him, yet it was also the period when the seeds of his pre-eminence in the later 1960s were planted. The trio he was now rehearsing for a series of booked gigs was to stay together for close on four years and would tour the world together. Evans was also introduced to Helen Keane, the woman who would fashion his subsequent career, by close mutual friend Gene Lees, who was only too aware of the calamitous state of Evans's private and professional life in that period. According to Lees, Evans had even allowed himself to be signed to two booking and management agencies at the same time – neither of which were doing much for him. Keane was then striking out on her own in management after a highly successful career as a talent agent for TV and live shows. By the summer of 1962 she had offered to become Evans's manager after Lees had extricated him from his two previous agreements by involving the American Federation of Musicians.

Evans took his new trio into the Riverside studios in May and June and recorded enough material for two albums, *Moonbeams* and *How My Heart Sings*. This was unusual: until now, Evans would never have entered the studio as a leader without clear artistic reasons. He had also been winding down his sessions as a sideman in order to concentrate on his own band. Suddenly he went into a period of frantic studio activity. There were a number of reasons for this, but two of the most pressing were his curtailed earnings from live work in the wake of LaFaro's death and his remorselessly voracious heroin addiction, a habit that could be fuelled by money alone. His desire to fulfil his contractual commitments to Riverside quickly so that he could move on to his new career at Verve coincided with this need for extra income. Apart from the session money he could make as a sideman on dates for others, Evans could ask for advances against future sales from his record company for sessions he led, irrespective of their anticipated release dates.

Keane remembered clearly this transitional time. "Bill was struggling, and I was able to struggle with him," his new manager said later. Her income was considerable from two of her key clients, actor-choreographer Geoffrey Holder and dancer Carmen DeLavallade. "I was very active in dance, and I was able to give the dedication and commitment to Bill and build him without starving to death,"[3] said Keane.

Much of the material recorded that summer would remain unissued for decades, but the trio date *Moonbeams* was issued within months of its studio completion. It starts with the anagrammatically titled 'Re: Person I Knew' (= Orrin Keepnews), an unaccompanied piano statement of an original theme – yet again on an out-of-tune studio piano. (Evans used a blues-based chord sequence for this tune which he would re-fashion as 'Story Line' for his 1966 Town Hall Concert.) After the theme, the bass and drums enter for a mid-tempo but ruminative minor-key statement, dominated by the piano's melodic eloquence. Israel's bass style and sound is completely different from that of LaFaro's, more traditional in every respect. The melodic, rhythmic and harmonic choices he makes for solos and accompaniment are similar to those heard from many other top bassists at the time, from Oscar Pettiford to Paul Chambers. As might be expected, Israels had a difficult time in the spring and summer of 1962 settling into the trio's structure. Evans himself noted, "He was in a very sensitive position … [It] was all happening when we played earlier this year at the Hickory House … I had a slight apprehension about whether his self-consciousness would prevail for a long period, obstructing or misdirecting the natural way the group could develop. About the time we left the Hickory House, Chuck had a big overhauling job done on his bass … During the month-long lay-off, many of the problems, musical and otherwise, must have settled or resolved themselves for Chuck."[4]

Those resolutions gave Israels the confidence to concentrate on simple melodic patterns, to leave space where appropriate, and to explore extensively the deeper registers on the instrument, often driving Evans along on faster repertoire in a way not heard since the pianist had left Miles Davis. Evans happily admitted that the trio with Israels was "different", while Israels pointed out that "only with Bill have I begun to realise my conception of music. It's a melancholy thing to say, but … if Scotty hadn't died, I'd be struggling still to find a situation in which I could play what I want to play. I like to make the bass sound good. If playing time in a deep and firm and flowing way sounds good, then that's the way I like to play. If playing more delicate counterlines and filling [patterns] sounds right … then I want the bass to sound light and clear."[5]

The working practice established on *Moonbeams* would remain in place while Israels was in the group, giving it a very tight, disciplined character and style. The inessentials were all but eliminated, the spotlight trained firmly on the pianist. Unfortunately, on *Moonbeams* this tends to lead to too much of a good thing, for although the repertoire is of high quality – all but the first track and 'Very Early' are well-known standards – and the playing largely flawless, the group has not yet developed its musical interaction to sustain such a programme of essentially similar material. The album remains one best approached in samples, where specific highlights become easier to appreciate and the similarities do not overwhelm the listener. Worthy of note is the interplay between Israels and Evans on the theme statement of 'Polka Dots And Moonbeams', and the wonderfully concise and precisely played but wholly romantic conception of Tadd Dameron's 'If You Could See Me Now' which had been reintroduced into Evans's working repertoire by the recording session with Dameron a month or so prior to this date. It was also surely somewhat self-defeating to record a whole programme of ballads where the pianist is often reliant on sustain and overtones when the upper registers of the supplied piano are so evidently in need of proper tuning.

Of course the tuning problem is also present on *How My Heart Sings*, but the issue of pacing is less pronounced because a swinging groove can be interpreted in a variety of ways. The presence of two waltzes also helps create different moods and expectations – and this is tangible when a clearly delighted Evans tackles the melody statement of the title track, using pauses, sudden emphases and elisions to create aesthetic tension and release in much the same way that Miles Davis was currently doing – for example on the waltz 'Someday My Prince Will Come', which Davis had recorded the year before. Evans's trio version of 'In Your Own Sweet Way' is utterly different in mood and conception to the hesitant solo performance made just one month ago. The trio swing lightly, much in the manner of Brubeck's original rhythm team, Joe Dodge and Bob Bates, while Evans retains the light and affectionate atmosphere indicated by the song's bright harmonies and spare, skipping melody. Only a poorly recorded and rather dull, unvaried bass solo from Israels spoils the continuity of an otherwise superior performance.

The other notable event on this album was the appearance of three Evans originals. 'Walking Up' is an exercise in fourths across a descending progression of related keys in the verse, while the bridge uses two scales and the chords rise in major sevenths across them, much in the manner of Evans's version of 'Milestones' or his playing on 'So What'. Not a classic composition, it is at least harmonically stimulating and suits Evans's approach. '34 Skidoo', another waltz, points up his fondness for verbal humour, the title being a variation on an old pre-war saying. The tune is Shearing-like, the construction artful, hiding shifting metre through skilful rhythmic displacement of the same melodic kernels. The theme is not memorable, however, and Evans seems to be trying a little too hard to make things work during an unusually busy and decorative solo. 'Show-Type Tune' finishes up the record but has the misfortune to follow the beautiful Cole Porter song 'Everything I Love', which is given a relaxed and assured performance by the three men. Evans's tune, by contrast, sounds happy but superficial, his improvisation full of what by now could be identified as personal clichés, both rhythmic and melodic. Still, the overall level of inspiration and cohesion of this album, though recorded at the same time as *Moonbeams*, is a good way ahead of that all-ballad programme.

While Riverside was pressing ahead with a busy recording schedule for Evans, during that summer his new company, Verve, began to show its hand. An announcement in *Down Beat* in June 1962 claimed that "Gil Evans has signed a contract with Verve. His first record will be with pianist Bill Evans".[6] The great arranger and composer did in fact sign to Creed Taylor's Verve that summer, but he and his pianist namesake never made a record together. It is entirely possible that the Verve project for piano and orchestra was kept alive by drafting in for the arranging and composing duties another recent Taylor signing to the label, Gary McFarland; an Evans/McFarland album was indeed made the following January. On a less ambitious scale, Bill Evans was lined up with drummer Shelly Manne and bassist Monty Budwig to cut an all-star trio session for Verve in August 1962. Meanwhile, the pianist did not allow Riverside's Orrin Keepnews to relax: he had already proposed a quintet date to the surprised producer, who readily agreed. On July 16th Evans went into the studio with Freddie Hubbard (trumpet), Jim Hall (guitar), Percy Heath (bass) and Philly Joe Jones (drums).

Riverside was clearly pleased that one of its more prominent artists wanted to abandon his parsimonious strategy to recording, but had few illusions as to his motives. In his liner notes to an early-1980s vinyl release that reissued the Hubbard sides (alongside an unissued Zoot Sims/Jim Hall session from the same summer) Keepnews refers to Evans's "severe dependency on narcotics" at this stage of his life. He goes on: "This dependency uses up a lot of cash; the most feasible way for a musician who had not been working much in the past year to get money was from his record company."[7] The junkie in Evans had realised that as he was in the process of winding up his recording contract with Riverside – and beginning another with Verve – he could make extra money to feed his habit by proposing Riverside sessions one after another during the summer and fall of '62 – while simultaneously asking for advances from Creed Taylor at Verve.

The quintet sessions that became the *Interplay* album were released within a year, suggesting that all concerned were relatively happy with the results. All but the title tune – an Evans blues – were standards that needed little in the way of preparation. 'When You Wish Upon A Star', 'Wrap Your Troubles In Dreams', 'I'll Never Smile Again' and 'You Go To My Head' all have strong melodies with a calculated impact and nothing particularly hazardous in their chord changes. The presence of Philly Joe Jones alone guaranteed a harder drive than normal for Evans, while the other band members made only rudimentary contributions to what are clearly head arrangements. The open, swinging approach brings out the best in Freddie Hubbard, with whom Evans had profitably appeared on Oliver Nelson's *The Blues And The Abstract Truth* a year or so before. Hubbard's playing, both on open horn and mute, are unusually melodic, unfailingly swinging and unerringly tasteful. Brimming with ideas but avoiding the flash and inelegant, he displays a full and beautiful tone and an eagerness to shape his solos, alongside a varied rhythmic conception that gives his playing drama and freshness, even on ballads. Of the others, Jim Hall comes off less well, his understatement an insufficient contrast to Evans's own when used as a foil for the incisive solos of Jones and Hubbard. At times Hall simply lays out in an effort to keep clear of Evans's accompaniments (their justly praised duet albums avoid the problem of passages where both men are simply being accompanists). Evans plays with such restraint and sensitivity that it is hard to believe on aural evidence alone that he is the date's leader. His solos are no longer than any others, he rarely solos first, and at no time does he wrench the listener's attention away from what else is happening by demanding to be heard. The overall impression is of a swinging, happy date with a gifted young trumpeter in particularly good form on a bunch of well-worn standards.

August 1962 saw Evans placed first in the *Down Beat* International Critics Poll piano section (Monk was second, Peterson third – although Peterson would, with just one exception, maintain an iron grip on the Readers' Poll results for some years to come). Evans's success in the poll confirmed the worldwide impact of his first trio now that its final recordings were emerging. The same month saw Evans in the studio on consecutive days: on the 20th with a trio for his initial Verve recording date, and on the 21st and 22nd for Riverside for another quintet session, this time with Zoot Sims and Ron Carter subbing for Freddie Hubbard and Percy Heath. Both sessions were more ambitious than *Interplay*, with markedly different results.

For the trio session, Creed Taylor at Verve had drummer Shelly Manne specially flown in from Los Angeles. Manne brought along his own group's bassist, Monty Budwig, guaranteeing a working approach markedly different from Evans's own band. The record bears similar signs of organisation and close collaboration between peers that Manne had brought to *2,3,4* – a small-group session for Impulse! earlier in the same year featuring Eddie Costa and Coleman Hawkins, among others. Manne's record with Evans, *Empathy*, covers a variety of moods within a session of standards. There is a tongue-in-cheek, off-centre arrangement of Irving Berlin's little-heard 'The Washington Twist' – a musical trinket from a failed 1962 Broadway show *Mr President*, and little more than a blatant re-working of the traditional song 'Frankie & Johnny' – and here Evans exhibits his funk credentials. This contrasts with an affecting, intense, concise exploration of 'Danny Boy', a number that Evans had already recorded at length that year. Throughout the studio date, Manne's patented and stimulating conversational style adds dimensions and angles to the music which continually pull Evans away from his normal melodic and rhythmic patterns, providing a welcome freshness of approach and inspiration. The music is concentrated and thought-through. Simple touches bring more distinction to the performances, for example on another Berlin piece, 'Let's Go Back To The Waltz', where the move from waltz to quicker common time and back again serves to highlight Evans's own solo.

The longest tune on the session, 'With A Song In My Heart', lasts for over nine minutes and contains an unexpected coda between Evans and Manne which may well have occurred spontaneously after the usual trio performance had ended. Reflecting the give-and-take of a piano-drums duet from that February session featuring Coleman Hawkins and Manne, this tempo-less section finds Evans light-heartedly imitating a number of pianists, from Powell to Tatum and Ellington, while Manne paces his ideas superbly. Their rapid and sure responses to each other make for a satisfying unity in each tune, whatever the overall shape may eventually be, as the depth and simplicity of Gordon Jenkins's ballad 'Goodbye' makes equally clear. Just how strongly Evans and Manne felt about the rare quality of their intercommunication can be gauged by the fact that, not long after, they appeared opposite one another with their own groups at New York's Village Vanguard.

This initial Verve date may well have been partially driven by marketing, pairing Evans with a jazz heavyweight who was at the top of his profession and highly visible in a series of performances for hit TV shows, as well as being well-known for his new club, Shelly's Manne-Hole, in Los Angeles. Certainly the advertising campaign that Verve launched suggests a carefully considered effort to bring Evans to wider attention and to project him as distinctive and artistically important. In September 1962 the Evans/Manne session was released and promoted extensively in specialist magazines. "This is *Empathy*," ran one of the ads. "The subtle interplay and projection of the emotions of three major jazz personalities on each other. A one-time-only meeting that resulted in such sensitive improvisation the album could be titled only *Empathy*."[8] A further set of ads in November placed the LP alongside new records from Ella Fitzgerald, Stan Getz, Jimmy Smith, Oscar Peterson and Johnny Hodges, proclaiming: "The giants of jazz in new and provocative settings."[9] Verve was determined to raise Evans's public profile, placing him in the company of these proven jazz icons and best-sellers, and surrounding him with such portentous copy. Yet, as Gene Lees recalled[10] many years later, Evans's life was in such personal disarray at the time that the electricity had been cut off in his apartment and he was constantly having to deal with loan-sharks following desperate attempts to finance his and his wife's drug habits. Not that his addiction was allowed to impair his professionalism. He always conscientiously fulfilled his responsibilities – even if his need to make a drug connection occasionally determined that he would miss a gig or arrive uncomfortably late.

Riverside too was in the business of promotion, and in the same month as Verve's *Empathy* they released *Moonbeams*, the Evans/Israels/Motian trio session from June, advertised in *Down Beat* along with new albums from Bobby Timmons and Milt Jackson. Riverside's copywriter claimed the album to be "a rare and hauntingly beautiful experience".[11] Meanwhile, in the same November 1962 issue of *Down Beat*, an entirely different and previously unheralded Evans project surfaced for review. *Undercurrent* was a duet album with guitarist Jim Hall recorded for United Artists in the autumn of 1962 as a sort of afterglow from a summer that had seen them working together in the studios on Evans's quintet dates for Riverside. This pairing, to recycle Riverside's marketing words, was indeed rare and haunting, for the two men combined in a way that the more crowded environment of the quintet sessions had made largely impossible.

Evidently UA were well aware of the quality these two men brought to the project, for the album was packaged in a high-quality gatefold sleeve with special art-paper finish to offset a stunning black-and-white photograph of a woman drifting underwater. Unfortunately the company overcooked the recipe with the fatuously arty liner notes by Barry J. Titus, whose stream-of-consciousness attempt to portray the musical alchemy of Evans and Hall through stretched syntax and hyperbolic imagery makes for painful reading. To quote the concluding sentences: "'Naked day?' puffed sound slices blush. Tongue stuck inside teeth. Torso immobile inflame face cheeks ticket counter leaned hat veined hat pulled hat swivel, 'I don't know what to say.' Jagged leaning brown limbed face. His eyes crumbled smiles smoke dust wound warm bricks."[12]

The music itself is much more successful. The similarity of texture and the typically reduced dynamic range favoured by both men melds their ideas and interplay in an intimate fashion. *Undercurrent*'s rather short programme – just six numbers that barely make a half-hour's worth of music – covers a wide canvas, from originals (Hall's 'Romain') to standards ('My Funny Valentine', 'I Hear A Rhapsody', 'Darn That Dream') and the recent John Lewis composition 'Skating In Central Park' that Evans had first come across during the *Odds Against Tomorrow* film-soundtrack session with Lewis's studio band.

Each musician's special skills at improvisatory counterpoint and sensitive accompaniment are prominent throughout this mostly ruminative date. Their equal but differing abilities in caressing a melodic line through gradations of touch and tiny rhythmic displacements keep the listener fascinated at each new unfolding of a song's deeper levels of meaning. It is no great surprise to find a number of pieces in 3/4 time, 'Dream Gypsy' being one of the most poignant and evocative of the set. Both musicians sound remarkably at ease in the presence of the other, and the musical conversations that arise are seemingly organic in their natural evolution. One wonders whether this date nudged Evans further along the path to his three-piano excursions on *Conversations With Myself*, now just six or so months away. The one overall drawback to *Undercurrent* is its poor recording quality that renders the upper ranges of both instruments curiously subdued and dull.

In an otherwise slow-tempo programme, 'My Funny Valentine', normally performed by jazz musicians as a moody ballad, is the single up-tempo romp on the album (it was the last-recorded piece on the date, though the record company programmed it to open side one on the original LP release). Both men employ a harder and more incisive touch and attack, bringing added drama to their conversations as they shape a perfectly conceived and unified joint improvisation, Evans in particular enjoying his spinning-out of long single-note walking bass lines to support Hall's efforts. The relationship between Evans and Hall that had blossomed for this autumn 1962 duet recording had only been fleetingly heard when they had appeared on the Riverside quintet album recorded on August 21st and 22nd. The quintet session was important to Evans, regardless of any financial spur that may have come from his chemical requirements. For a start, he brought to the date no less than seven previously unrecorded originals; secondly, with the exception of the late replacement of bassist Percy Heath by a young Ron Carter (whose playing on the date is exemplary), Evans had long admired all the musicians involved – in addition to Hall and Carter, there was tenorist Zoot Sims and drummer Philly Joe Jones. He trusted them under studio conditions to deliver on a set of tricky tunes that were not the sort to be knocked off routinely in a couple of hours. However, the ambitions of Evans and his Riverside producer Orrin Keepnews were largely unrealised, thanks in part to the typical shortcomings of an early-1960s recording session: limited studio time, a minuscule budget and no prior rehearsals.

This led to what Keepnews later remembered as an uncomfortable date. He admitted to feeling "pretty edgy going into the studio, which surely didn't help".[13] Problems with sound balances and other technical matters added to the difficulties, including some poor tuning which dogged Hall in particular on day two. On the first day the group recorded 'Loose Blues', 'Fudgesickle Built For Four', 'Time Remembered' and a tune dating from the mid 1950s, 'Funkarello'. Of these, only 'Time Remembered', an intense and lyrical ballad, posed major interpretative problems. Even the detailed part-writing of 'Fudgesickle Built For Four' resolved into a chord sequence which sits comfortably for the soloist (the title's puns refer not merely to 'Bicycle Built For Two' and an American popsicle or ice-lolly, but also to the John Lewis-like Baroque-style four-part canon which forms the theme). 'Time Remembered', however, moves unexpectedly in its harmony and has an unusually long verse structure, forcing the soloist to concentrate hard on his shifting position within the maze. Coming cold to this in the studio seems to have fazed Zoot Sims, who plays very tentatively, though with occasional flashes of lyric beauty. The edit between the solos from Sims and Evans – presumably jumping between takes – is particularly evident. Yet the piano solo is very fine, being concise, emotional and full of colour. Jim Hall carries the recapitulation of the melody with more assurance than Sims could muster at the theme's onset. The other two pieces have Evans tinkering with established forms. 'Loose Blues' is a relaxed investigation into using certain harmonic intervals in a descending pattern through a I-V-VI-I cyclic structure, while 'Funkarello' inverts the harmonic basis used by Bud Powell, among others, for 'Un Poco Loco'.

The second day proved more troublesome. Three songs were completed: 'My Bells', 'There Came You' and 'Fun Ride', with 'My Bells' needing no fewer than 25 takes, many of them breaking down or incomplete, before all concerned were convinced that there was sufficient of quality to edit together into a passable performance. 'There Came You' is a pretty ballad, taken here at medium tempo with Jones on brushes, and featuring an interesting set of modulations in the B section of the song, while the recapitulation of the A section is given added twists to lengthen it and make its harmonic movement that bit more intriguing to soloist and listener. Hall in particular shines in his solo here, bringing poise and eloquence as well as abrupt shifts of pace to his chorus. Evans relishes the challenges he has set himself, taking one of his longest solos of the date and avoiding many of his personal clichés until his final verse, where he introduces Ron Carter for some exchanges and falls back on over-familiar block-chord patterns. Sims does not solo.

'Fun Ride' is a straightforward blowing vehicle of the type Evans played many times with Miles Davis; his own sparkling, inventive solo shows a playfulness not often evident in his improvising. 'My Bells', though, is by far the most ambitious of the pieces here, asking for a quasi-orchestral interpretation which the small-group setting simply cannot provide. Moving between a number of tempo shifts and rhythm patterns, including a semi-mambo opening figure on the drums, the song's different parts refuse to combine properly. Evans's piano counterpoint to Sims's melody statement sounds leaden and clumsy – his parts would have been better handled by other reed instruments – while Hall doesn't even play until the recapitulation of the theme, where he is painfully flat. The second time through this heavily-edited recording Evans takes the theme himself and makes more sense of it, finding continuity and proper weight to each voice, but the song still refuses to settle properly. Its contradictions and inadequacies would be resolved three years later when Evans and Claus Ogerman recorded it for Verve accompanied by a fully-scored string orchestra. Given the many difficulties and the manifest unevenness of the two days' playing, it is no surprise to find that Riverside and Evans only managed to edit one track, 'Loose Blues', to the pianist's satisfaction before his final move to Verve, the project then being shelved. Riverside entered a period of financial instability soon afterward which led eventually to its temporary demise within a year. It would be 1982 before this music was given its first release, as part of an LP, *The Interplay Sessions* – two years after Evans's death. Considering the ingenuity of the compositions that Evans brought to the session, and the fact that only three were subsequently prepared for another attempt in a recording studio, these events must have been especially frustrating for him. It may well have been the case that he had over-estimated Riverside's enthusiasm for ambitious projects at this late stage in their relationship. At the very least, material of this type demanded a significant amount of rehearsal time, especially if the group was not a regular working unit. Perhaps the difficulties he encountered made Evans realise that he had to severely curb his expectations about what Riverside would – or could – do for him in order to fulfil his outstanding contractual commitments.

Whatever the case, it is evident by the time of the pianist's next session for Riverside that he wanted out. His mind was on the future, and for him that evidently lay elsewhere. Orrin Keepnews wrote later: "Bill had left Riverside. The terms of his departure included provision for two final projects, to be recorded rather promptly. It seemed to me that a solo session … and an in-person performance trio set would present fewest problems."[14] It may have seemed that way, but the second attempt by Keepnews inside a year to get Evans to make a solo album was in many ways even less convincing than the first. During the January 1963 solo session Evans simply sounds like he's alone in his apartment, playing for his own gratification. Often he doesn't even bother to pause between songs – something Keepnews had specifically requested that he do. "He managed to ignore this caution a number of times," wrote the producer, "most spectacularly when the last note of the 'Spartacus Love Theme' was identical with the first note of 'Nardis' … [As I was] trying to obtain an album that met normal requirements, I found it highly aggravating."[15]

No fewer than 14 performances were recorded. One was discarded as being sub-standard, and three proved to be medleys of sorts. While there are beautiful and unusual things to be found, including the abstractions of 'All The Things You Are' or the sombre tone of 'My Favorite Things', this is deeply private music that does not seek to communicate or to reach an audience. Even the early treatment of 'Spartacus Love Theme' reveals an almost naïve opening sequence where Evans's inspiration, Satie's 'Gymnopédie No.3', is noodled over before he wanders into the theme. At other points he capriciously abandons a stream of musical thought for a few bars before returning to it, oblivious to how this may affect the overall performance.

Evans is not looking for shape or form here, and consequently this set of recordings is fascinating to fellow pianists or students anxious to penetrate the Evans process of creation. On his version of 'How High The Moon'/'Ornithology' he is deliberately and consciously evoking the improvisational methods of both Tristano and Powell in what amounts to a brilliant, good-humoured pastiche that says much for Evans's own pianistic roots as well as his affection for these pianists. A similar spirit is evident on 'Love Is Here To Stay'. It is as if Evans is unaware of the recording studio and unconcerned for posterity in any form: he is revealing much of his working methods in a way he would not normally allow. He is also taking many more technical and creative chances than usual, especially evident in right-hand flourishes, severely disruptive rhythmic displacements, and jagged patterns. His abandon is clear from the unusually high level of mistakes and technical imperfections he allows. The recital, eventually released in 1984, is much prized by Evans completists as an insight into his creative muse at unguarded moments, but has little to offer the uncommitted listener. The reasons for it not being issued at the time are obvious at every turn. Perhaps Evans had meant it to be that way. But he still had the live album to make to fulfil his Riverside commitments. It would be agreed and cut on the last two days of May 1963, some time after Keepnews had left the label, and would not appear until Riverside had changed ownership and was briefly revived in late 1964. But Evans's musical ambitions now lay elsewhere, as the next two sessions for his new company, Verve, would amply demonstrate.

CHAPTER 8

Conversations With Myself (1963)

"BILL'S HANDS WERE THRUST IN THE SLASH POCKETS OF HIS WINDBREAKER, AND HE WAS ALL HUNCHED UP WITH THE BITTER COLD. I THOUGHT: SO THAT'S WHAT GENIUS LOOKS LIKE."

WRITER GENE LEES, IN AWE OF HIS GOOD FRIEND

For Evans personally, 1962 had been a harrowing year, but he'd also had ample evidence that his professional star was on the rise. He had won his first poll as an established artist when in August the *Down Beat* critics named him above all others as their pianist of the year; four months later in the same category the magazine's readers placed him second only to the perennially popular Oscar Peterson. He was also working more regularly with his own trio, although in the autumn bassist Chuck Israels was often absent from the group for long periods. At one point Israels got as far away as Italy, where he purchased an antique bass that gave him an impressively rich, enhanced sound upon his return. The trio

In Europe – thinking, smoking, playing – in the early 1960s

was still not working every week, but Evans was busy with plans for his new record label, Verve. He was talking through ideas with a group of associates including his manager Helen Keane, writer Gene Lees and Verve boss Creed Taylor. Meanwhile, his popularity was buoyed by the release of recordings he'd made over the previous few years. *Down Beat*, for example, reviewed *Moonbeams* and *Know What I Mean?* together in their January 31st 1963 issue, and a few pages further on evaluated Dave Pike's Epic-label album, *Pike's Peak*, with Evans. Also in that issue, Verve repeated their ad for *Empathy*, Evans's trio LP made with Shelly Manne.

The same week as that *Down Beat* hit the streets, Evans was in the studio contributing his part to the next large-scale Creed Taylor venture for Verve. This one featured recent signing Gary McFarland, who had met Evans through John Lewis, an early admirer of McFarland's arranging and compositional abilities (Lewis had organised McFarland's attendance at a Lenox Music Inn summer school and recorded his music for Atlantic in various settings). The hard-working McFarland's first outing as a leader for Verve had been the well received and commercially successful jazz version of the tunes from *How To Succeed In Show Business (Without Really Trying...)*, a current Broadway hit. He had also collaborated with Stan Getz on *Big Band Bossa Nova* in August 1962 – though Getz was its undisputed star – and that album became both critically acclaimed and commercially successful. As we've seen, there had been talk at Verve of getting Gil Evans and Bill Evans together on a project, but as with so many ideas involving Gil this never materialised. McFarland's success, as well as his undoubted freshness and imagination, made him a natural alternative.

Like the Getz album, the Evans record was certainly conceived as McFarland's project, but this time McFarland's picture was on the cover and his name was out front instead of the star soloist's. This makes its own statement about McFarland's growing success as well as the differing artistic egos of Getz and Evans. The music itself reflects the most absorbing and deeply-felt aspects of McFarland's composing and arranging at that time, his instrumentation alone suggesting something very different from the more conventional jazz practices of the day. The pieces are scored for clarinet, flute (or alto flute), two violas, two cellos, guitar, bass and drums, with McFarland's vibraphone used as an alternative solo instrument or, occasionally, in duet with Evans's piano. In his engaging liner commentary, McFarland claims: "I built this album around Bill – around everything he is, his melodic gift and harmonic conception, his magic … On one track you will hear examples of the blues feeling that Bill is capable of. Many pianists have limited resources, but not Bill, he has such broad resources … He does not sit back with cotton wool in his ears. He listens. For my taste, he is the perfect pianist: he does everything perfectly."[1]

The music ranges from quasi-classical ('Night Images', 'Tree Patterns', 'Reflections In The Park') to open-ended constructions of the sort often employed by Duke Ellington, where intriguing ensemble passages are contrasted against and defined by the consequent solos. 'Misplaced Cowpoke' in particular exemplifies that combination of easy swing and conversational improvisation with tart, evocative group figures and counterpoint. The loping bassline under the theme explains the title, while the improvisational sections recall the more adventurous MJQ dates. 'A Moment Alone' prominently features McFarland's vibes with a sustained sound very close to Milt Jackson's, beginning as a romantic ballad before moving into swinging common-time solos. These two pieces made up side two of the original LP release. On side one the music ranges further and Evans's own role is more fully integrated with the ensemble. Indeed, on 'Peachtree' Evans states the ballad theme unaccompanied at the beginning, leaving McFarland to re-state the theme in waltz time against strings and rhythm before returning for a solo: again, a procedure strongly reminiscent of the MJQ.

Side one starts with the skittish, involving rhythmic piece, 'Reflections In The Park', in which Richard Davis's astounding facility and musical imagination is brought to bear on the bassline assigned him by McFarland, to the benefit of the unfolding piece of music. The second piece is 'Night Images', a reflective item of near-chinoiserie, where McFarland starts by stating the simple unaccompanied theme in thirds, accompanied by spare piano from Evans. They use harmonies more associated with the French group of composers 'Les Six' and Darius Milhaud than with jazz, along with the occasional John Lewis touch. Evans's echoing of McFarland's delicate, touching tracery reveals completely different musical, imaginative and emotional contexts as the statement unfolds. At one point McFarland uses a semitone interval struck between two mallets in a percussive way, almost as if he were chuckling at what was evolving between the two men: Evans responds with awe-inspiring spirals of echo-like arpeggios taken from ever more remote inversions of the original harmonic underpinning. It is a defining moment and one of the most imaginative pieces of intuitive piano accompaniment in jazz – and all in free time.

With the introduction of a metre and the rest of the ensemble, the form crystallises and reveals an ABA structure built around variations on a two-chord harmonic core. Evans then solos on a jazz-based slow-medium tempo, re-using many of the ideas he employed during the opening dialogue as well as some of his more typical patterns, including a three-against-four triplet displacement all the more welcome for its use in a completely novel context. A woodwind re-statement of the A section punctuates his solo and gives it two clear halves, the second consisting of a closer reading of the melody as the piece fades to a finish with Evans accompanied by hushed strings. The whole piece is an extraordinary demonstration of McFarland's talent with voicings, timbres and composition as well as Evans's full-blooded intellectual and emotional response to a challenging musical environment.

If the album as a whole can be taken as a triumph for both the composer/arranger and the featured soloist, then it is also a pointer to what is missing from much of what was to come in Evans's music: only rarely would he return to such a stimulating and unusual musical environment. Nonetheless, the project that he started recording almost immediately after this involvement with McFarland was one of the most imaginative and groundbreaking he would ever devise for himself. It remains, next to the 1961 live-at-the-Vanguard recordings, his most revered. These were the three sessions from February 1963 that resulted in the Grammy-winning album *Conversations With Myself*.

To understand the full impact of this record, one has to reconstruct the then-normal recording methods used not only by the jazz industry but by studios in general. In the early 1960s most jazz fans – and I would include the average critic in this description – believed that the best jazz recordings were those that more or less "just happened". A group of musicians were playing and a microphone happened to record what they did. Even though the editing of performances had been common practice since the widespread adoption of magnetic-tape recording in the early 1950s, virtually no one noticed such things. Solo piano recitals using this "documentary" approach had been part of recorded jazz since Jelly Roll Morton and beyond. It was rare that such sessions would be treated as raw material from which to make an edited "construction".

"Bouncing" between two recording machines to build up a number of individual performances into one recording had been undertaken by Sidney Bechet with RCA as early as 1941 and had been extensively explored by guitarist Les Paul in the late 1940s and early 1950s, but was still widely regarded as at best a gimmick, at worst a way of bolstering the performance of a below-par musician or singer. With most studios of the early 1960s operating on two or three-track tape recorders, often with a direct mixdown to a mono master, engineers could do little in terms of bouncing before a build-up of tape hiss and a loss of recording quality became all too evident.

Everyone involved in Evans's *Conversations With Myself* album – and most of the initial reviews from critics – obsessively discussed the gimmickry of the technology before any consideration of the music. They finally decided that Evans's artistry somehow made the use of multi-track recording "all right", as if there were something sinful in such a technical process, or some sort of cheating was involved. Evans himself was sufficiently worried (as well as excited) that he wrote a justification in the liner notes of the gatefold LP release, explaining his reasoning. To be so defensive is entirely understandable in a world of such musical orthodoxy as jazz. After all, this writer can remember a well known jazz critic using the fact that the singer's voice was overdubbed at another session as a valid reason for describing *Blue Rose* as an artistic failure. This mid-1950s collaboration between Rosemary Clooney, Billy Strayhorn and Duke Ellington is now rated by many as one of the most successful of all Ellington's meetings with a vocalist, Sinatra included. The date of this Luddite criticism? 1995.

Yet by 1963 a slim but artistically convincing catalogue of multi-track recordings had built up in jazz. The aforementioned Sidney Bechet's 'Sheik Of Araby' for RCA Victor in 1941, Lennie Tristano's solo piano experiments of 1955, later released on Atlantic, Erroll Garner's 1956 and '57 piano-and-orchestra outing, *Other Voices*, for Columbia, and *Sing A Song Of Basie* by Lambert, Hendricks & Ross for ABC in 1957 (with Creed Taylor as a producer) were all seen by jazz fans as worthwhile projects. Even musical hipster-comedian Slim Gaillard had experimented in 1951 with the technique when he recorded 'Genius' for Norman Granz. Like Bechet, Gaillard played every instrument, including organ, bass and drums, but the recording was left unissued until the mid 1990s. Given the genuine interest in the idea – and Creed Taylor's success with Stan Getz's 1961 LP *Focus*, where Getz played at least some of the programme on a different date to the Beaux Arts group – it is understandable that Evans found the concept intriguing and that his record company would be willing to try it out. The author of the album's liner notes, Gene Lees, was careful to acknowledge the willing co-operation of artist, manager and record company personnel. "One thing I remember vividly is the atmosphere of permissiveness that Creed Taylor established," wrote Lees. "He didn't make this LP happen, he let it happen."[2]

The most fascinating aspect of *Conversations* is the series of challenges and dilemmas that Evans poses for himself in the allocation of piano roles. Three individual piano parts were recorded on to the two-track stereo master tape: the basic part (always heard in the right-hand speaker) we shall call "piano one", and then two further parts, "piano two" (left speaker) and "piano three" (heard in the middle). Evans's most obvious musical demarcation was to accord each recorded piano part a rhythmic, harmonic and melodic role in direct parallel to his own trio's work, emphasising the interaction that would take place between piano, bass and drums during a normal Evans trio performance. At times this is readily identifiable, as in 'How About You?', but for the most part he is forced into supplying subtly different commentaries against the underlying musical fabric of piano one. This is especially notable on the three Thelonious Monk pieces and the Evans original, 'NYC's No Lark'.

During these performances, Evans is sufficiently stimulated by his material to continually break free of a preconceived role on any given piano part, leading to some of his freshest and most daring playing. Such inspired bending of his normal rules of practise reaches its apotheosis on '*Spartacus* Love Theme', a piece that we will consider in more detail below. Paradoxically, but perhaps also predictably, this shifting of roles and abandoning of strict demarcation is liberating for Evans. As he no longer has to provide all the elements of a piano performance in one take, he can allow himself the luxury of single-note arabesques, staccato chord patterns in unusual rhythmic shapes, and a host of other imaginative interjections which stretch and redefine his pianistic and musical vocabulary. This sense of creative excitement which we share with Evans is a key element in the album's artistic impact.

Conversations is also remarkable for Evans's choice of repertoire, often far removed from what he had been happy to record before. Apart from the three Monk compositions – 'Round Midnight', 'Blue Monk' and 'Bemsha Swing', the latter not issued until some years later – there is also 'Just You, Just Me', the structure of which Monk had re-cast as 'Evidence'. More typical of Evans are the standards 'How About You?', 'Stella By Starlight' (from the suspense film *The Uninvited* and a tune that he'd already re-cast once for Miles Davis), 'A Sleepin' Bee' (again held over at the time and first issued decades later) and 'Hey There'. Both 'Bee' and 'Stella' would remain part of his working repertoire for many years. The other film soundtrack tune, '*Spartacus* Love Theme', is unusual in that it was current at the time of Evans's recording and, in its original context, is not an obvious choice for jazz treatment. One wonders if the choice was influenced by the astonishingly successful transformation of Richard Rogers's 'My Favorite Things' by John Coltrane two years previously, though it seems to have been Evans's choice and was not suggested by his manager or record company.

The album was completed in just three sessions. 'NYC's No Lark', the first and only piece to be recorded on February 6th, is a brooding, quasi-funereal piece in A minor (hints of Chopin), its theme arising from an ostinato pattern of fourths over a tonic and dominant bass. It is a tribute to the recently deceased pianist Sonny Clark, Evans's friend and a fellow heroin addict. Evans was very clearly aware of the original contexts of his sources, for one of the musical models for this composition, especially its B section, is Stravinsky's ballet *The Firebird*, which tells a story of death and transfiguration. In a typical play on words, Evans had constructed a telling title from the letters of Clark's name. He had also put much thought into the structure of this piece, which runs for close to six minutes and at first listening sounds almost completely spontaneous. Piano one, which carries the repeating chordal and rhythmic patterns as well as the frequent modulations, registers the form. There is an initial ABA pattern, and then roughly halfway through, when the piece has arrived back at the tonic, piano one signals a cessation of metre and a remarkable unaccompanied right-hand chordal passage that recalls nothing so much as the keening, passionate trumpet playing of Miles Davis on 'Solea' from *Sketches Of Spain*. Then Evans picks up the initial rhythmic and scalar pattern, albeit in truncated form and with a gradually disintegrating rhythmic base, before a short finale in suspended time, saturated in upward-swirling right-hand passages from two of the parallel piano parts. It is like cold, driving snow in wintertime New York City.

Evans's playing on 'NYC's No Lark' is very forceful. The rather dull recorded sound may rob his piano of some of its impact, but his left-hand passages in the finale are tripleforte stabs at the keys – reminding us that, like Garner, he was a natural left-hander – while a blues-drenched, bitterly angry right-hand octave figure from piano three (central) during the B section of the recapitulation carries such force as to be comparable with Bud Powell's attack, or even Cecil Taylor's during this period. It is Evans's misfortune – and the listener's – that this tune was the first recorded, for some technical problems allied to the nature of the recording mean that piano three is a quarter-tone flat compared to the other two. This certainly increases the bleakness of the performance, but the sourness wasn't something Evans was actively looking for, and it is significant that no other songs were attempted that day.

The other problem with 'NYC's No Lark' is the tentative nature of Evans's own pianistic commentary on the musical base of piano one. Although the music he makes is fascinating, the second and third piano parts are often very untidily played in relation to what is going on around them, with late or early entries, occasional racing in front of the (implied) beat, and other distractions. In the liner notes Gene Lees wrote about Evans's mood during this session: "At the first date, Bill began to feel that what he was trying to accomplish was, perhaps, ultimately impossible."[3] There are also notable imbalances in sound levels, especially between piano one and piano three, as well as a degree of tape hiss due to the mechanical process of recording three pianos on to a two-track master. All this must have led to a general agreement to suspend operations after just one number in order to consider these problems.

Three days later, February 9th 1963, Evans, his manager Helen Keane and Creed Taylor were back in the Webster Hall studio in New York City that Verve preferred for their recording projects. The six selections completed that day for *Conversations* show that the technical and musical challenges had been met and overcome, although one or two keys on the piano were now out of tune. In all of these recordings, the unusual power and élan in Evans's attack, in the absence of bass and drums, is especially evident. On the first tune of the day, 'How About You?', Evans keeps up a bright tempo on his original piano-one "guide" part, moving from syncopated chordal accompaniment, where he uses his carefully worked substitutions, to a full-on single-note solo, before returning to his opening chordal treatment. The performance concludes with a brief unaccompanied resolution. Both additional parts share the theme-stating responsibilities at the front and end of the song and add arpeggio swirls at the finish, while also increasing the rhythmic heat during piano one's brief solo, when piano two lays down a chorus of romping walking-bass notes. All exits and entrances are neat and unfussy and the playing is confident and full of fresh ideas (including a host of paraphrases and quotations from other songs with relevant titles).

'Just You Just Me' was recorded next. It follows a similar procedure to the first piece, except that Evans uses piano one to state the melody more clearly through his voicings. He also solos confidently on this piano track, offering involved, rhythmically virile ideas with good continuity and a remarkably boppish tinge recalling Bud Powell's long, fluent lines. The other two pianos – two and three – restrict themselves on this brisk number to commentary and embellishment, the most notable addition occurring at the end where piano three delivers a delectable octave-unison middle-register flourish over quiet held notes from the other two pianos. By the time he tackled the third piece of the session, 'A Sleepin' Bee', Evans was more ambitious in his arrangement, beginning with a swirling eddy of tremolos and arpeggios from all three pianos that comes directly from the Erroll Garner book of dramatic entries. After this his simple statement of the theme on piano one echoes the arrangements of Art Tatum, who would pick out a medium-tempo melody between elaborations to telling effect. The commentary from piano two alternates between ascending and descending fourths, echoing the melody's contours, and occasional octave runs. Once the theme is out of the way, a moderate tempo is set and pushed along by left-hand proddings and off-beat chordal jabs from two pianos. The recording is very busy, with all three pianos playing for most of the time, and though Evans succeeds in keeping the lines relatively disentangled and the pianos hitting the beats together, the lack of contrast and development over four minutes makes for a meretricious rather than musically impressive result. The closing sequence with its modulations and repeated tremolos is uncomfortably close to what Evans would choose for 'Stella By Starlight' and 'Hey There', which he recorded next. Considering the general superiority of form, pacing and inspiration on 'Stella' and the greater variety and winning humour of 'Hey There', one can understand why Evans and Taylor kept back 'A Sleepin' Bee' from appearing on the original album.

'Stella By Starlight' is a superior performance, partly because Evans allows himself space at this slower tempo to evolve a moving and dignified theme statement that is embellished beautifully by the other two pianos, and partly because his collective improvisation after this – against the same perky, prodding left-hand rhythm he uses throughout this day's work – is unusual, constantly varied, and rich in melodic and harmonic nuance. The following piece, 'Hey There', is less well developed, with Evans blocking out the tune's chords on piano one while piano two provides the melody, mostly in octaves and with rhythmic displacement. Piano three is tentative in its variations until a brief solo well into the piece. Originally used to open side two of the LP, 'Hey There' has a jaunty humour and optimism appropriate to the words of the original song, but apart from some concise and electrifying double-time right-hand runs during the collectively improvised solo slot, there is a lack of variation in texture. There is also some over-busy playing at this point from the two accompanying pianos, presumably because they were recorded prior to the double-time piano track. For all these reasons, 'Hey There' is the least successful of the originally released pieces.

The final recording of the day, 'Round Midnight', was eventually slated to open side one of the original LP. It is the first of three Monk covers recorded at these sessions and is a magnificent statement of a theme that Evans, a self-professed Monk fan, knew well and played often. By this late stage in the session Evans had worked out how to keep a slow ballad buoyant, avoiding the more obvious tricks to maintain the listener's interest such as playing in double-time. He uses the Miles Davis arrangement of Monk's great ballad which, by 1963, had been in circulation for over eight years and had become the standard. This undoubtedly helps Evans to shape the overall performance, allowing him to build the atmosphere lovingly through the three layers of piano before launching into his improvisations in the "release" section. (Piano three employs some touches of Ravel at the opening, most notably from 'Ondine', the first movement of *Gaspard*.) Piano one takes the lead in the solos, with pianos two and three content to add colour and arabesque, and the title of the record comes vividly to mind as the three pianos enter into a close and beautifully balanced dialogue. This level of performance is maintained throughout the recapitulation of the theme, achieving a near-perfect recording. At 6:33, 'Round Midnight' is by far the longest recording of the day.

Ten days passed before Evans returned to the studio to complete *Conversations With Myself*. The February 20th session began with his fully developed treatment of the 'Love Theme From *Spartacus*'. He had made a brief foray into the piece for Riverside just over a month earlier, but had only dallied with it then before launching into the harmonically related 'Nardis'. Now he was ready for a completely rounded creation. He had come across the theme while watching the movie at a Florida drive-in with pianist Warren Bernhardt. Evans's reaction on hearing the movie theme was not remarkable; Bernhardt only remembers him saying, "Oh, wow, listen to that theme, that's a beautiful theme."[4] But it is instructive to consider for a moment its context. In the film the theme is first heard at the moment Kirk Douglas's Spartacus, locked in his prison cell, is given Jean Simmons's (very) British slave-girl Marian to sleep with for the night, so long as the guards and the slave-owner are allowed to watch the proceedings. Put in this degrading position, Douglas, in the process of falling for Simmons, recoils from the intended debauchery and shouts to his tormentors, "I am not an animal!" Simultaneously Simmons looks at him with love in her eyes, and the theme commences as Douglas responds in a similar fashion. Perhaps it is not beyond credibility to suggest that Evans saw a parallel of a kind: he was slowly emerging from a most distressed and degrading period in his life and recently settled in a long-term relationship with Ellaine, a woman many presumed to be his wife (although they never married). Certainly his treatment of the theme is overflowing with love and tenderness, as if his soul is speaking.

The minor theme is simple and direct, as is the static two-chord harmony which underpins it, and the tune has no B section (presumably the film had no need of one). Evans overcomes this structural oddity by ingeniously dressing up his melody-repeats and with judicious but sparing modulations as a means of bringing proper cadences into the overall form. He also uses different tempos, as he did on other *Conversations* performances, moving into his preferred 3/4 time during the central improvisational section.

But all this is mere depiction of the skeleton. The flesh of the performance is in the utterly inspired combination of all three piano voices. It goes beyond what is done elsewhere on the album, where one piano will often anticipate or complete a phrase played by another, or where constantly shifting backgrounds give sumptuously appropriate musical contexts to melodic invention. Here, the pacing, contrast and drama that occur through the interchanges are a constant marvel. Evans takes enormous risks, such as the miraculous tracery of the fast right-hand lines embroidering the final collective improvisation. For once, he largely ignores the project's allocation of general registers to each recorded piano. It is also worth saying that this piece is perhaps the furthest from conventional jazz piano of the day, and closest to Evans's classical inspirations – especially Debussy, Gershwin, and Russians such as Borodin and Mussorgsky. But his spontaneous interplay and jazz techniques anchor this firmly in the improvised music of its time. Considering the ultra-Romantic setting, some of his playing retains a marked blues identity, precluding any mere quasi-classical pastiche. The sessions for this milestone in Evans's career were concluded with spirited performances of two further Monk compositions. 'Blue Monk' came first, and is the only piece on the LP where Evans lays down just two pianos instead of three. There is no external musical necessity for this, as Monk's famous theme is no busier than others tackled during the date. Evans must simply have wanted to keep this straightforward reworking of the blues as basic and uncluttered as possible, to enhance its funky nature. Again the ghost of Tatum hovers, especially in the two-part harmonies and walking left hand which Evans uses to accompany the majority of the improvised section. His solo, played on piano two, combines earthy blues intervals and phraseology with more angular, challenging double-time runs that stretch the harmonic and melodic basis of the piece.

'Bemsha Swing' was the last tune recorded. This piece was not released until the late 1960s when – oddly considering that it was an out-take – it appeared on a *Best Of Bill Evans* collection. Once again all three pianos are present. The pianist retains his method of playing the supporting chords and rhythm on piano one at the outset, using piano two for the melody and piano three to embellish this. The following improvised solo passage stems from piano one – but the variation here is that Evans makes plenty of space for the anticipated notes of the other two pianos in this section, allowing all three pianos a share of spotlight and accompaniment. The piece is brought off very well, runs under three minutes, and is full of sparkle and wit. One can only assume that it was held back originally to reduce the proportion of Monk pieces on the LP.

Conversations With Myself would be released in the early autumn of 1963, to universal critical acclaim. It has sensitive and lyrical liner notes by Evans's friend, ex-*Down Beat* editor Gene Lees, which were important in their own way. Lees treats Evans and the album's particular creative process with a reverence close to awe. This struck a new note in jazz writing, for although jazz from the 1920s onward has never been short of enthusiasts espousing the cause of one artist or another, few pieces of jazz writing had ever made assumptions like this. There are no apologies for Evans's methods, his stance or his choice of repertoire. There is no uneasy sense of jazz's insignificance next to other, more mature musical forms. There is a basic assumption that Evans, and the music he is making, is and will remain significant, and that the pianist is intellectually equipped to deal with the aesthetic and creative consequences of his position. This is all at distinct variance with, for example, the writers dealing with so-called "third stream" jazz-meets-classical music at this time, where the attitudes to jazz are almost invariably patronising. It is also significantly distanced from the fan-based writing in the 1940s and 1950s about such giants as Parker, Gillespie, Monk and Powell, or even celebrated descriptive pieces such as Dan Morgenstern's famous description in a 1958 *Metronome* magazine of Lester Young playing at a club late in his career. Even there, Morgenstern is assuming Young to be a more or less unconscious and involuntary font of originality and beauty, firmly separating art and life.

The way Lees writes on *Conversations* is similar to the way in which LeRoi Jones would soon be describing the music of John Coltrane. In both cases the assumptions are clear. Lees spells them out in the last, most poetic lines of his essay: "Bill was walking ahead of us, close to the buildings, looking thin and frail. He has a somewhat pigeon-toed walk. Those hands were thrust in the slash pockets of the windbreaker, and he was all hunched up with the bitter cold. I thought: so that's what genius looks like."[5] From now on, the stakes would be raised in terms of critical expectations of Evans, and this would in turn influence perceptions of every other project in which he involved himself. It would remain a double-edged sword for the pianist. Evans's record with Gary McFarland was released in April 1963 and, like *Conversations*, scored highly with reviewers, although Verve's advertising campaign concentrated exclusively on McFarland. Meanwhile Evans had to earn a living, and during the spring he made the most untypical record of his career, *The Theme From The VIPs And Other Great Songs*, and then went back on the road with his trio, reaching Los Angeles in May, where at Shelly's Manne-Hole he was reunited with bassist Chuck Israels.

The *Theme From The VIPs* album, released on the MGM label (then Verve's parent-company), was a piano-with-strings-and-voices affair with Claus Ogerman supplying the charts. It was Creed Taylor's idea, and it smacks of the producer trying to kill a few too many birds with one record. Evans later recalled that Taylor had suggested an LP where he would play with a larger group. "I thought fine," said Evans. "But as it turned out … there was no room for me. So I just read the parts and it was really very pretty. In other words, I didn't know until I got into the studio that it was going to be this kind of album, in the pop field … I wanted to use my Russian name on it, Gregorio Ivan Ivanoff. That's William John Evans in Russian. Then I thought, well, what the hell, I've played lots of lousy jobs, and lousy music; certainly this is nice, and pleasing, a lot better than the things I'm referring to."[6]

Critic John S. Wilson did not mince his words in his *Down Beat* review of *VIPs*, commenting accurately: "The fact that Evans is present is thoroughly incidental, no matter how you look at it."[7] Evans, fulfilling a very limited commission, is unrecognisable. Indeed the record was considered so far outside his legitimate work that it did not even merit a place in the vast 18-CD *Complete Verve Bill Evans* set released in 1997. Evans remained refreshingly practical, saying soon after to Leonard Feather, "If this record could have done something for widening my audience, getting better distribution for my other records, I am all for it, because it's a cold, hard business."[8] Creed Taylor concurred: "[Evans] was totally pragmatic inside the shell of the artist that he was … he had no hesitation whatsoever about doing something that might widen his base. As long as we came back to the music he felt so deeply about."[9]

The recording at Shelly's Manne-Hole club, meanwhile, would fulfil Evans's last recording commitments to his old company, Riverside, and conclude a harrowing but vitally important phase in his career. His trio had been working only fitfully as winter gave way to spring 1963, and Evans arrived in California without a bassist or drummer. The bassist on the date was Evans's regular, Chuck Israels, who told the story of his involvement in the original LP's liner notes. "I had been filling in a slow period with a few weeks of work [elsewhere]," said Israels. "Bill, unsure of my whereabouts or availability, decided to work Shelly's as a pianoless duo with some suitable Los Angeles bassist. However, a happy coincidence left me in Denver at the end of [my] tour just at the time when Bill could fly me to Los Angeles to join him for the two weeks at the Manne-Hole."[10] The two men began the engagement as a duo, later adding drummer and vibes player Larry Bunker, an ever-present audience member for their sets: he came recommended by composer and arranger Clare Fischer. As Israels recalled, the three men blended from the outset: "Larry was hired on the spot to finish out the job with us. The following week, Wally Heider came in to record the group for Riverside."[11] Engineer Heider was supervised by Richard Bock, an LA-based producer and owner of the

Pacific Jazz label, who had a keen ear for maintaining technical and performing standards. Portions of the last two nights of the engagement were taped, with the first evening contributing 11 of the 17 selections that have survived. Israels noted that "this recording … is one of those rare, candid accounts of how a jazz group actually sounds in a club. The performances here are ones in which the feelings of the musicians, the attention of the audience, and the atmosphere of the club inspired a creative range and joy of expression that surpasses the usual perfunctory nature of nightclub jazz".[12]

This is true enough in that there is a palpable sense of relaxation and enjoyment in the music, especially from the first night. But during that first night there are few instances of Evans and his companions digging much more than superficially for their inspiration. Bunker, discreet to a fault, keeps well out of the spotlight. Israels, however accurate in pitch, strong in rhythm and telling in his choice of notes, rarely opens up any really imaginative musical dialogues with Evans, who is for the most part content to skate along on his own musical power. In the beautiful Gershwin song 'Our Love Is Here To Stay', for example, Evans picks a tempo for the trio's entry which is nothing less than jaunty, reflecting little of the tune's inner depths. Nothing is badly played, but there is little to grab the attention. This contrasts strikingly with the previous trio: in Paul Motian, Evans had a drummer who could make any tempo come alive through deft and unusual emphases of the beat or interesting combinations of percussive texture. Even on the rare occasions when Evans and his bassist would coast briefly, Motian more than held the attention. Nothing like that happens here.

On this evening, Evans is continually falling back on familiar improvisational devices in his solos, indicating a lack of sustained concentration. There are rather too many bass and drum features – the downside of having a group sound just like they really do in a jazz club. No fewer than three selections from the recently completed *Conversations With Myself* were played on the first night: 'How About You?', 'Stella By Starlight' and 'Round Midnight'. Of these only 'Midnight' aspires to better than average nightclub music and preserves a portion of the pianist's solo conception, again at a bright medium tempo. In fact, Evans gives over the melody statement and initial solo on 'Stella' to Israels, who acquits himself well but cannot compete with the bass greats, let alone Evans, in sustaining the listener's interest. The second night brings an immediately appreciable difference, with Evans no longer eager to push tunes and tempos. The music remains unambitious and small-scale, but Evans is several layers deeper into the meaning of his chosen material. His partners respond accordingly, though there is no radical redefinition of styles and roles. 'Everything Happens To Me' is a perfectly judged statement of bittersweet memory, while 'My Heart Stood Still' carries some of the elation of discovery which the tune and its lyrics indicate. Evans, for once supported by Bunker on sticks instead of brushes, takes off during his improvisation, finding new twists to his familiar patterns and reinvestigating his debt to Bud Powell in particular. 'In A Sentimental Mood' is blessed with a poised opening, but does not really work, the treatment too knowing and elaborate to sustain the simple eloquence of Ellington's line. This could be any number of clever piano trios rather than that of Bill Evans.

A different story emerges on Evans's own 'Time Remembered', inexplicably omitted from the original LP release in 1964. (There was no competing released version: Evans's summer 1962 quintet recording of the piece for Riverside would remain unissued for decades.) This is one of Evans's deeply-felt ballads, its strong melody arising from a very busy harmonic pattern, recalling music by Rachmaninov and Chopin. The work was later recorded in a number of settings by Evans, including a 1965 session where Claus Ogerman supplied a string and woodwind arrangement. Here it inspires Evans's most intense playing of the recorded portion of the Manne-Hole engagement, his solo after the theme both reflective and dramatic. The form is spoiled by a bass solo that provides very little in the way of an alternative viewpoint on the song – indeed, Evans's discreet accompaniment continually teases the ear – but the power of the piece is still strongly communicated, and Evans concludes with appropriate feeling. As a snapshot of a working group the recording has its value – even if they did not survive beyond this May 1963 engagement. Their lack of ambition and the relative conservatism of their interplay coupled to Evans's own evident lack of inspiration on the first evening makes this a predictably patchy farewell from an artist to his old record company. Evans would go on to much better work with Israels and Bunker, but with other record companies and in the pursuit of different goals.

CHAPTER 9

Everything Happens To Me (1963-1965)

"BILL IS JUST ABOUT MY FAVOURITE PIANO PLAYER, SO FRESH AND IMPECCABLE. HE CAN DO ANYTHING HE WANTS, AND HE HAS ALL THE FACILITY HE NEEDS."

GEORGE SHEARING ON BILL EVANS

During the spring and summer of 1963 Evans continued to experience the worst of heroin addiction. He was always short of money and was unable to keep his group together for lack of work. Evans and his partner Ellaine were constantly scuffling to pay for their addiction and suffered from chronic ill-health. Gene Lees related that Evans would play nightclubs at this time even when unable to use his right hand after he'd damaged a nerve shooting-up.[1] During his tenure at Shelly's Manne-Hole club in May 1963 Evans was thin and wan, but in relatively good spirits. That summer the Newport Jazz Festival once more passed him by, and he had no regular group right through to the autumn. At least his new

Evans in 1964 (opposite), ignoring jazz fashion and looking deep into the music

record company stayed faithful, advertising all three of his Verve albums regularly in the wake of the August release of *Conversations With Myself.*

Chronically fatigued, he took a break with his parents in Florida again, catching up with his brother, and this allowed him to stabilise his heroin habit. His return to New York in the autumn coincided with the signing of an agreement brokered by Helen Keane. This long-term contract to provide the house trio at the Village Vanguard in New York City afforded him, as *Down Beat* put it, "the kind of security a jazzman rarely receives".[2] Another *Down Beat* report[3] confirmed Evans's long-term associate Paul Motian as drummer in the trio, but by this time Chuck Israels had joined Stan Getz's group. Evans turned to Gary Peacock, a young Californian bassist newly resident in New York who had impressed him.

The trio settled in at the Vanguard during autumn 1963. When Evans felt they were ready he had Verve producer Creed Taylor drop in to see the group. Taylor quickly agreed to a studio recording, which took place in December. On the resulting album, *Trio '64*, the group sounds ill-balanced, with Peacock's remarkable bass playing often suggesting musical ideas that simply aren't echoed elsewhere. Motian is particularly subdued. The choice of material doesn't help, with Evans attempting to demonstrate that he can miraculously transform the most banal material such as 'Santa Claus Is Coming To Town' and 'Little Lulu'. The listener's reaction is more often "why bother?" when there are so many good tunes that Evans never recorded.

Added to these handicaps are entirely avoidable ones, such as poor track sequencing on the original LP. Side one consists of four tunes, all in major keys, all mid-tempo. Track one, in G, is the trite 'Little Lulu', a joke that worked with 'Washington Twist' on *Empathy* but falls flat here. The second and third tracks, 'A Sleepin' Bee' and 'Always', are both in A, while 'Santa Claus', which closes the side, is in C. The relentless rhythm, major tonality and a succession of related if not identical keys makes it very difficult to maintain interest, especially when coupled with so many problems between the players.

The listener is involved more completely on side two, where medium-tempo songs are mixed with ballads and major keys alternated with minor. The beauty of Evans's more connected melodic ideas surfaces occasionally on superior material such as 'Dancing In The Dark' and 'Everything Happens To Me', a particular Evans favourite at the time. Bassist Peacock recalled many years later that the session was an unhappy one. "The circumstances of the date were unbelievable," he said. "Creed Taylor had come down to the Vanguard, and he'd heard us playing, so he knew exactly what we were about, what we were doing. We got in the studio, and we played a little bit to get a sound level. We were listening to it back in the booth, and I said, 'Wow, that sounds great, man, let's go.' Creed Taylor said, 'Ah, hmmm,' and I said, 'What's wrong?' And he said, 'Well, you know, I don't really hear you playing the time.' I thought he was joking, I couldn't believe he was serious." But Taylor was serious. Things got worse when he and the engineer removed Motian's tom-tom, ostensibly because its resonance created microphone and balance problems. Peacock was enraged and an argument began. The date was soured. Many years later, Motian could still remember the atmosphere as "awful"; Peacock recalled in the same conversation that "it was the worst vibe I ever heard". Evans, ever the professional, kept the trio on course until the end of the session, producing some coherent, occasionally inspired music, especially on the ballads. But Peacock summed it up: "It was so far below what we had been doing up to that point, in the clubs, just in terms of us playing together."[4]

The trio did not get another chance to record, for Peacock went off in another direction soon after. The *Down Beat* review of the album by Don DeMichael unknowingly echoed Taylor's concerns about time-keeping. "Since Evans on this record is very much in his stop-and-start bag," wrote DeMichael, "when Peacock begins starting and stopping at the same time – with Motian seemingly out of touch with them both – the result is like exaggerated Swiss cheese – too many holes … The best non-ballad [music from] Evans on the record is to be heard on 'Santa Claus' and 'Dancing In The Dark' when Peacock unclutters his section playing and lays down the time in back of the pianist."[5]

Evans always regretted the shortlived nature of this trio. Talking of Peacock many years later, he said, "I thought he was a rare talent with tremendous potential. Unfortunately he took a detour into diasthetic spiritualism and his bass playing was left by the wayside. [*Trio '64*] was prepared hurriedly and it did not really represent what we could have done together."[6] Peacock turned also to areas of jazz occupied by the avant-garde, and later in 1964 toured Scandinavia and recorded with saxophonist Albert Ayler's group.

The day after the trio cut their session, *Down Beat* published its Annual Readers' Poll results for 1963. Evans charted for the first time in its Hall Of Fame list, at number 25, sharing that position with Sonny Rollins, and came second in the Piano category with 1,444 votes, outdistancing the third-placed Thelonious Monk by some 300 votes, and a similar number again short of Oscar Peterson, who that year won for the eleventh time. Evans's popularity and reputation were on a steady upward curve. As 1964 arrived he was poised to capitalise for the first time on this popularity. With his record company and manager carefully building his career, step by step, he had brought his personal problems under control and was busy planning the year's activities. Included was his now regular break in the early spring to visit his family in Florida. While he was there, *Down Beat* reported that he had "gained 25 pounds"[7] and had re-formed his working trio. There was much work in the offing, the report added, including a potential appearance at the Newport Jazz Festival that summer and his first European tour in the autumn. Evans did not, however, continue the residency at the Village Vanguard, which by now had decided (briefly) to host only folk and, a little later, ragtime gigs.

During Evans's absence in Florida, *Conversations With Myself* continued to gain attention and admiration, peaking in May 1964 when the album was awarded a Grammy for best instrumental jazz performance by small group or soloist. It was Evans's first. That same May, he attempted for the second time to make a successful record with Verve stablemate Stan Getz (an April '64 date using Gary Burton, Chuck Israels and Joe Hunt from the two leaders' rhythm teams had been abandoned after three songs, and has since disappeared from the tape archives). Evans and the notoriously mercurial Getz were joined on this occasion by bassist Richard Davis and drummer Elvin Jones, two inspirational musicians capable of lifting any soloist.

Getz was in high spirits at the time, amply demonstrated by the first song tackled on May 5th, the Evans favourite 'My Heart Stood Still'. Getz and Elvin Jones here enjoy a mutually uplifting relationship, with each man stoking the creative fires through a succession of takes. Yet Evans is tentative and seems uncomfortable on this piece and most of the rest of the date. He recalled many years later, "Both Stan and I had a mutual desire to do a record together, but when it was over we both felt that we had not got to the level we wanted."[8] Certainly at times Evans's mind seems to be elsewhere, as in 'My Heart Stood Still' where his disconnected and rather aimless snatches of line and idea are uncharacteristically listless and unformed. Davis and Jones both pull back, waiting for something to happen, but nothing much does. Evans stumbles messily through the solo introduction to a Getz staple of the time, 'Grandfather's Waltz', on which Getz again shines as his limpid tone caresses the melody. Even in his favoured 3/4 metre Evans manages only strings of personal clichés in his solo spot. Getz and Evans's men play sensitively on the Lerner-Lane ballad 'Melinda', with Jones (on brushes) and Davis accompanying the soloists with a wonderfully inventive musical dialogue. The slapstick fun of the 'Dark Eyes' fragment underlines the generally upbeat atmosphere that day, Evans playing Teddy Wilson-style stride and Getz imitating the sound of a smoochy swing-era tenor saxophone. But it was a day when Evans failed to shine.

The following afternoon the quartet re-convened with bassist Ron Carter replacing Davis, and opened with a reworking of Evans's own 'Funkarello'. Evans solos first (tellingly, Getz had soloed first throughout the previous day) and produces in a relatively short space his most coherent and flowing playing of the sessions so far. Getz continues at a level of inspiration close to that of the day before but with less continuity of phrasing, while Carter and Jones provide a light, smooth but intense rhythmic pulse. Getz gives Jimmy Van Heusen's 'But Beautiful' a relaxed yet involved reading with attentive support from Evans, but the pianist's solo is uninspired, providing few insights into the song. 'The Theme From *The Carpetbaggers*', a superior Elmer Bernstein melody previously recorded by Evans on his *VIPs* session of 1963, is brushed aside in less than two minutes. It was in all probability recorded as a sop to MGM, Verve's parent company, who were often pushing their movie themes on Verve boss Creed Taylor. As Taylor later admitted, "Occasionally I gave in."[9]

Still lacking enough material for a full LP, the group tried two more tunes: the Cole Porter standard 'Night And Day' using Elvin Jones's patented "caravanserai" rhythm during the intro, and Larry Green's 'WNEW', named after a New York radio station. On the Porter piece Evans again solos first. He uses stop-time breaks confidently but without real fire, although he does manage to construct a worthwhile improvisation. Getz uses those breaks more effectively and builds a driving solo, with Jones matching him throughout. The short final piece, 'WNEW', finds no one in outstanding form, and generally the players seem keen to finish the session. This frustrating event for all concerned was left in the can until 1974, long after both artists and Taylor had left Verve. Most of the frustrations seem to have stemmed from a clearly below-par Evans.

That the pianist was capable of quickly turning things around is demonstrated by his appearance at Shelly's Manne-Hole club later in May 1964 with Chuck Israels and Paul Motian. Evans was usually a magnet for all self-respecting jazz pianists currently in town. George Shearing, a confirmed Evans fan, spoke with huge enthusiasm to journalist Jack Hutton as they enjoyed an Evans set at the club. During 'I Should Care', Hutton relates, "George whispered to me: 'If Art Tatum were alive, this is where he would be coming: to hear Bill. His legato playing is incredible. The way he sustains notes and chords to the nth degree. The changes! Gee! I reckon Bill is just about my favourite piano player. Peterson and Hank Jones are great for different styles, but Bill is so fresh and impeccable. His thoughts flow so easily … He can do anything he wants and he has all the facility he needs for his approach."[10] Shearing was unusually well qualified in the jazz circles of the time to judge Evans, with a knowledge of classical music to match Evans's own. But this appreciation from an important peer came as a prelude to the first series of public rebuffs aimed at Evans from a variety of sources, most notably the jazz avant-garders, currently building their efforts to take jazz and improvising to new areas of expression and theory.

Whether through the desire to compensate for the aborted session with Getz or for more mundane reasons, Evans was recording again for Verve within two months, this time near San Francisco in Sausalito, California, at a club called The Trident. A friend of Evans, the pianist and composer Denny Zeitlin, had recently recorded there for Columbia to considerable acclaim, and this new West Coast venue was being looked upon kindly by record producers at the time. The Evans trio had Chuck Israels and Larry Bunker, who officially took over from Paul Motian with this engagement. Bunker told *Down Beat* that he was celebrating his release from the Hollywood studios that had provided his musical life for the previous two or more years. Evans, he felt, "kind of fulfilled all the ideal requirements for me. He says the most musically for me. Working with him makes the most sense to me. Now I can play some music for a change".[11]

But the results of the Trident recordings with Israels and Bunker are no more inspired than the session almost exactly a year earlier at Shelly's Manne-Hole. This time, however, Evans and Verve agreed to shelve the recordings. Israels remembers this as yet another period when Evans was in poor physical shape and battling against drug abuse. "There were a couple of nights where he was absolutely unable to play," said Israels. "He may have [been] distracted by those problems and then didn't want to hear whatever [it was] in the recordings that reminded him of that."[12] Eventually in 1973 Verve released an album from these two July 1964 dates, years after Evans had left the label. More recently, over two hours' worth of previously unissued music was made available on the *Complete Verve Recordings* package. The extra recordings add detail to the picture of Evans and his trio at the time but provide no revelations.

July saw Verve placing ads that declared: "This Is The Year of Bill Evans – 1964 is the year of fulfilment for Bill Evans." In some ways this became a self-fulfilling prophecy. Not only was Evans winning Grammys but he was also beginning to enjoy a firmly established reputation worldwide, demonstrated by the successful European tour that he would start in August and by his position as top pianist in the *Down Beat* Critics' Poll that same month. Evans may still have been suffering from a deeply chaotic personal life that centred on his continuing drug dependency, but his professional life as a leader was at last in full swing.

The working trio of Evans, Israels and Bunker left for Europe in summer 1964, beginning their tour with appearances at a festival in Comblain-la-Tour, Belgium, on August 8th and 9th, moving on to Copenhagen, where he appeared on a television show on the 10th, and ending in Stockholm with a club date and radio broadcast. The tour was short and unambitious, with no dates in France, Britain or Germany, for example, but it brought Evans in front of enthusiastic crowds and proved to him and his management that there was in Europe a most willing audience for his music. Evans's stay was capped by a recording for the Swedish arm of the Dutch Philips label with the trio accompanying the talented Swedish singer/actress Monica Zetterlund. The resulting album was titled *Waltz For Debby* – the second to be so named. By August 28th Evans, Israels and Bunker were back in New York, where they followed tenorist Zoot Sims's group into the fashionable Café Au Go Go.

In the autumn of 1964 Evans's contract with Verve came up for renegotiation. Considering the relative failures of the December 1963 and May 1964 sessions and the undistinguished results at The Trident, both parties must have been unsure about continuing. By late September *Down Beat* was reporting a "flurry of jazz activity" at Capitol, which had signed Cannonball Adderley and Shelly Manne, while "at press time [Capitol] was negotiating a contract with pianist Bill Evans, most recently with Verve".[13] It is not clear whether this was merely a clever manoeuvre on the part of Evans's manager, Helen Keane, or if the pianist really was on the verge of leaving Verve. In an October *Down Beat* Creed Taylor talked of his continuing efforts to balance commercialism with artistic integrity at Verve. Explaining that albums rarely sell unless "there is a number on [them] which takes off", Taylor said: "I always try to get one single from each album and ... give that one the full DJ exploitation." But he also claimed "I'm trying to be less deliberately commercial and more musically logical. Some deliberately commercial efforts do attract attention to jazz artists, but if we can capture what an artist really wants to do – and this catches on – we find it does better than anything we can work up."[14] There was an all-out blitz of publicity in *Down Beat* in October and November, with Evans the front-cover interview in the October 22nd number, along with the first part of his two-issue appearance in a Blindfold Test. The following issue carried part two, as well as a review by Nat Hentoff of the Evans trio's appearance at the Café Au Go Go. Neither magazine carried Evans ads from Verve.

Whatever the precise details of the stand-off, the final result was a renewal of the Verve contract. Evans was slated to return to the Van Gelder studios in early February 1965 to make a new trio album with his working group. In the October '64 *Down Beat* interview with Dan Morgenstern, Evans had already hinted at how he might feel about such a deal and a new studio booking for his trio. He pronounced himself "extremely happy" with the group. "Larry [Bunker] is a marvellous musician," said Evans. "He plays excellent vibes as well as being an all-round percussionist, and being so musical he just does the right thing because he's listening." Evans expressed his own good spirits when he noted "we probably make a stronger emotional projection than at almost any time in the past".[15]

Elsewhere in that interview Evans allowed himself to be drawn into a contemporary public debate about the so-called "new freedoms" being introduced into jazz by musicians such as John Coltrane, Eric Dolphy, Ornette Coleman and Cecil Taylor. For the most part he was careful to emphasise that his own preferences were just that – a personal choice. But Evans did make some wider comments in the interview: "The only way I can work is to have some kind of restraint involved – the challenge of a certain craft or form – and then find the freedom in that, which is one hell of a job. I think a lot of guys either want to circumvent that kind of labour, or else they don't realise the rewards that exist in one single area if you use enough restraint and do enough searching."[16]

This was perfectly justifiable as a personal method of working, but in the highly charged atmosphere of the mid 1960s it would have been generally interpreted as a previously innovative musician deliberately aligning himself with the old guard of jazz rather than the new wave. Later in the interview he again attempted to define his own position with regard to freedom, this time giving it a qualified embrace. Speaking about his group's music-making, he said: "By giving ourselves a solid base on which to work ... If we have the skill, we can just about do anything. Then we are really free. But if we were not to have any framework at all, we would be much more limited, because we would be accommodating ourselves so much to the nothingness of each other's references that we would not have the room to breathe and to make music and to feel. So that's the problem."[17]

In these musings Evans had revealed not only his deep immersion in a particular style of and approach to jazz music making, which was mostly based upon pre-existing forms such as the popular song, but also his own imaginative failure to grasp the emerging forms in the new music. This is no great surprise: few practicing musicians care about or need to look deeply into new and evolving musical forms in an attempt to reinvent themselves. They prefer to build up an image and identity through a long initial process of trial and error and then, by and large, to stick with that identity, expanding or contracting it depending on each musical situation that they find themselves in. The few exceptions – in jazz, people like John Coltrane and Miles Davis come to mind – seem only to prove the rule. Evans had no real need to embrace the ideas of the newer generation: in fact they may have done more harm than good to his conceptions. But his reactions to these evolving ideas would inevitably lead him to an increasingly narrow stylistic field which would slowly detach him from the mainstream of jazz development for a number of years during his later career. It was a course he felt he could do nothing to alter: he had to stay true to his own musical instincts.

"What many people mean when they say 'atonal', I think, is more a weird kind of dissonance or strange intervals and things like that," he continued in his *Down Beat* interview. "I don't feel it. That isn't me. I can listen to master musicians like Bartok and Berg when they do things that people would consider atonal – although often they're not – and love and enjoy it. But here's someone just making an approximation of this music. It really shows how little they appreciate the craft involved, because there's just so much to it. You can't just go and play by what I call 'the inch system'. You know, I could go up eight inches on the keyboard and then play a sound down six inches, and then go up a foot-and-a-half and play a cluster and go down nine-and-a-half and play something else. And that's atonality, the way some guys think of it. I don't know why people need it. If I could find something that satisfied me more there, I'd certainly be there, and I guess that's why there are people there. They must find something in it."[18]

Topicality and fashion have no real bearing on the evaluation of Evans's musical output. Quality can never be identified with style alone, but it explains his curious position and subsequent neglect in an age when some of his peers – Miles Davis, John Coltrane, Charles Mingus, Cecil Taylor and Roland Kirk, for example – continued to invent and reinvent the boundaries of jazz and improvised music. Evans admitted to *Down Beat*, "I don't really feel that I have to be avant-garde or anything like that. It has no appeal for me, other than the fact that I always want to do something that is better than what I've been doing … If it stays right where it is, and that's the best I can find, that's where it's going to have to be."[19]

Evans was played tracks by Coltrane, Davis and Taylor in the Blindfold Test in that same *Down Beat*. He gave approval to Cecil Taylor's 'Trance', noting initially: "I really got with that – it was interesting … I like it a lot. I think that what they were going for they realised very well, and I would give it five stars, except that I feel that with that wonderful beginning they could have realised a lot more with change of texture and dynamic exploration. But I was moved by it in a particular way which was unique." On further reflection about the form of the piece, he added: "For what it is, it's realised almost perfectly, but it just didn't explore enough area of expression … All dramatic effect is achieved by change: by setting up one thing and then bringing in some sort of contrast. And that's the very thing that's lacking in this."[20]

By expressing this opinion of a relatively early live recording by Taylor, Evans clearly identified his own reference points and criteria in music, but it's interesting that he had no yardsticks beyond classical music and jazz with which to measure what Taylor was attempting with his "tuned-percussion" approach to the piano. Around the same time in New York, composer Steve Reich was watching marathon John Coltrane sessions at Birdland and similar clubs, matching it to his interests in Far Eastern music, and coming up with new ideas about form, pattern and contrast in modern music. Within a couple of years Taylor would write in the liner notes to his *Unit Structures* album, "Form is possibility."[21] Taylor would also soon have his trenchant opinions about Bill Evans published in the pages of *Down Beat*.

In the meantime, while Evans practiced privately for long hours on a newly acquired harpsichord, he and his group prepared for what was to become *Trio '65*, the follow-up to *Trio '64* and the first Evans recording project in a year to make it to general release. The preparation was underscored by the knowledge that in December 1964 Evans had, for the first time, won the *Down Beat* Reader's Poll for pianist, at last out-polling Oscar Peterson. Considering it was a working group that made *Trio '65*, there were a worrying number of re-treads from previous recording ventures, mostly done before with Riverside (which at this time was officially in the hands of the receivers). Included among them was a 'Round Midnight' that Evans takes no further than his previous arrangements of its formal splendour. The trio works very closely together and shows all the attention to dynamics and overall coherence that one would expect from a group led by a man who said all those things quoted above, but nothing remarkable happens. It is simply the now-familiar Evans treatment of a bunch of well known tunes, plus one new "standard" – a convincingly-rendered 'Who Can I Turn To?' (from the Broadway show *Roar Of The Greasepaint, Smell Of The Crowd*). A possible exception to this well-worn air is Tadd Dameron's 'If You Could See Me Now', which receives a slow and rapturous treatment packed full of feeling. Away from the keyboard, Bill and Ellaine were still battling to pull their lives from the powerful grip of heroin. On this record, Evans generally sounds happy enough and reasonably relaxed, but he does not linger where in the past he would have allowed dramatic pause, and the interplay with Israels and Bunker is severely limited. Evans leads from the front and produces a well conceived and finely executed set of performances, but this is a set with no particular depth. His friend and fellow pianist, Denny Zeitlin, had some insightful comments about the album when played 'Israel' in a *Down Beat* Blindfold Test later in 1965. "I just wonder whether Bill has had a chance to sit down and listen to what Verve has done to his sound," said Zeitlin. "This is really a travesty, compared to the beauty that Riverside was able to give what his trio produced in the past. Especially in listening to a tune like 'Israel', which I heard him do so many times in person and on the Riverside version, I find this leaves *everything* to be desired."

Zeitlin went on to mourn the death of Scott LaFaro, claiming: "I don't think any bass player in the immediate future is going to replace the role that Scotty filled. I don't think Bill's approach to music has changed so much that one doesn't feel the lack of someone similar to Scotty." He was also critical of the drumming. "I have never been happy with any of Bill's drummers. Paul Motian's approach seemed a little stiff. Larry Bunker's is, for me, far too cluttered: a busy, almost sophomoric kind of approach." Zeitlin ultimately summed up his feelings: "Bill is one of the true greats of our age. I wish I could hear him in a context that would really do him justice, force him to get outside of himself and explore the new parts of himself that I know from talking to him he wants to get into. This album should never have been released."[22]

Critic John S. Wilson caused waves when given *Trio '65* to review for *Down Beat* on its release in July 1965. Wilson's digs at Verve's marketing of Evans were intertwined with his low opinion of the pianist on this occasion. "The more I hear of Evans," he wrote, "the more I become convinced that the propagation of the Evans mystique must be one of the major con jobs of recent years. Evans' performances … are clean and polished, but they neither seize nor hold the attention; not mine, anyhow … This is great jazz? It's more like superior background music."[23]

Back in February of the same year, Cecil Taylor had let fly at Evans in response to Evans's opinions on jazz form and musical freedom. "Obviously, Evans has the right to go his own way," Taylor said, "but I do not think his playing is a particularly powerful argument for his thesis. I've heard him in clubs, and I know at least ten pianists – without even thinking about it – who better deserve the amount of page space he gets. I can't take what he says too seriously because what I hear when he plays is so uninteresting, so predictable and so lacking in vitality. He's a competent cat. That's all."[24]

This was a peculiar combination of artistic insight and professional bitterness, but it articulated many previously unexpressed reservations about the extent of Evans's creativity, reservations that were being more widely aired during the course of 1965 and led, eventually, to his being roundly dismissed by the majority of so-called "progressive" critics and fans for the next 20 and more years. As such, Taylor's outburst set the tone for what was to come. Evans had for some time been aware that he was no longer in the vanguard of the music, and had also been at a low ebb personally for much too long. He had allowed his professionalism to pull him through too many crucial musical situations, when he really should have been outpacing his previous achievements. But now it was clear that the tide of jazz fashion, in America at least, was about to drift away from around him. As one of the many who wrote letters to *Down Beat* in reaction to Wilson's review put it: "Alas, everybody does not dig Bill Evans."[25]

CHAPTER 10

Both Sides of the Atlantic (1965-1966)

"WHEN THINGS ARE GOING WELL – SAY ONE NIGHT IN TEN – BILL AND I HAVE A DIALOGUE GOING. BUT WHEN THINGS ARE GOING REALLY WELL – SAY ONE NIGHT IN 30 – IT'S JUST PERFECT."

BASSIST CHUCK ISRAELS ON THE MATHEMATICS OF PLAYING LIVE

S oon after making the *Trio '65* album for Verve in February 1965 Evans took off once again for Europe, *Down Beat*'s announcement of the tour noting that "Larry Bunker rejoined the pianist's group for the tour, replacing Arnold Wise".[1] This was a strange statement, considering the ten days or so which fell between the recording session (which included Bunker) and the trio's departure for Europe. Perhaps Bunker was already showing signs of the restlessness that would lead to his departure from the regular group by mid-year, with Wise regularly depping for him at gigs.

This second tour of Europe was more extensive, taking in France and Britain as well as the previous year's destinations, Sweden and Denmark. Evans

Behind you! Evans in a Danish TV studio, 1966

met up once again with Swedish singer Monica Zetterlund, giving a concert with her at Uppsala University, and was video-recorded for posterity in England by the BBC. The European audiences for Evans were far less blasé than the average nightclub crowd in America. They were not used to seeing the stars of modern jazz from Evans's generation, let alone those of the emerging US avant-garde: the arrival of Evans's trio in any European capital was a major jazz event that spread ripples to the wider musical and cultural communities. The trio stuck to a relatively limited repertoire which they had been exploring since the previous summer's Trident sessions, some tunes of which had turned up on *Trio '65*. Evans, Israels and Bunker had an enormous impact on these new listeners, some of which can be gauged by the two television programmes made for the BBC in London in March 1965, two weeks into the tour. They were part of BBC TV's *Jazz 625* series, hosted by British jazz personality Humphrey Lyttelton, and have recently been made available by the BBC on two videos. They feature Evans with Israels and Bunker on the trio's standard repertoire of the time, with Lyttelton making all the announcements. Following contemporary jazz etiquette, Evans remains only dimly aware of his audience and almost entirely absorbed in his playing, turning and nodding his thanks to the audience like a mole surfacing to check the daylight from time to time.

The television recording gives us an opportunity to study Evans as he plays. His is not a classical posture at the piano: he allows himself to bend forward, sometimes as if urgently seeking the first hearing of the sounds he is making, at others as if propelling the rhythm he is laying down. His hands are held with the palms mostly parallel to the keys rather than well above them, his fingers bent but not to the extent of most classically-trained players: his years as a professional jazz musician had led him to evolve his own particular finger "shape". But his fingers in no way approximate the remarkable straightness of, say, Thelonious Monk in action. Evans occasionally pulls himself closer to the piano in order to hear more clearly the overtones, but this is a rare and expansive gesture in what is mostly an introverted presentation of his music.

One is quickly reminded that Evans is left-handed, as his lower-register work is strong and often locked in motion with his right. Surprisingly for one so endowed with technique and the ability for melodic invention across imaginative harmony, Evans on these performances often spends entire solos playing out finger patterns in the right hand which scarcely require him to move his hand from one piano register. Much of what record listeners get to hear as the Evans "style" can be observed in the video as a form of fingering shorthand where he follows patterns that his hands know very well across a restricted intervallic range. This is in contrast to much of his playing of the 1950s, where long lines often alternated with chordal passages and more broken, rhythmically jagged phrases. Back then, his hand was moving across considerable stretches of the keyboard, his left hand often suspended for whole bars or more. But by 1965 the two hands more often play in tandem, the lines rarely reaching the length and melodic elaboration of those earlier years.

This economy may begin to explain why much of Evans's recorded work from this time holds little surprise, and why so much of it lacks the freshness of his work up to 1962 and early '63. He is not doing anything wrong, and his playing never slips below supreme competence, but there is something automatic about it all. One might well use a word more often associated with Erroll Garner: formulaic. This may be as unfair applied to a man of Evans's obvious talents as it is when directed at Garner – after all, Garner when inspired was an overwhelmingly exciting and original musician. But when inspirational energy is not dominant in any creative effort, the bare bones of that effort are always painfully visible. Evans is no exception.

The reference to Garner is not arbitrary: around this time Evans publicly stated his admiration for the self-formed genius. Additionally, his appreciation of Thelonious Monk during his 1964 *Down Beat* Blindfold Test had been noted by someone at Monk's record company, and as a result Evans supplied the (brief) notes for Monk's next Columbia album, simply titled *Monk*. Evans recapitulated his *Down Beat* comments, asserting that "Monk approaches the piano and, I should add right now, music as well, from an 'angle' that, although unprecedented, is just the right 'angle' for him. Perhaps this is the major reason for my feeling the same respect and admiration for his work that I do for Erroll Garner's … Each seems to me as great as any man can be great if he works true to his talents, neither over or underestimating them and, most important, [if he] functions within his limitations." This could be an encapsulation of Evans's views on his own playing – though he would never be so bold as to claim parity with Monk or Garner. It is possible that Evans felt he was playing in a different manner in the current trio to how he had played in the past. He did say repeatedly that he did not expect to meet another bassist who would offer the same level and style of interplay as Scott LaFaro. Chuck Israels offered an interplay of sorts, but his counterpoint was couched in a musical language that articulated a supportive role more firmly anchored in rhythm. Israels preferred the lower registers of his instrument, and was as much at home "walking" through arrangements as he was when suspending his beat and engaging directly in musical dialogue with Evans's right or left-hand figures.

Broadcast tapes from that European tour in the winter and spring of 1965 catch the trio on more inspired evenings than the BBC programme, playing dates where they excite themselves and their audiences. A concert on February 13th at radio station ORTF's studio in Paris found Evans with quickened reactions to his partners and a bevy of fresh melodic and harmonic ideas, with a sparkling performance of 'I Should Care' closely presaging that of his New York Town Hall concert a year later. Evans was now happy to assume the role of musical leader in the trio. He would supply most of the musical material that the group fed off and used to propel itself, but he had not yet worked out a way of consistently freeing himself to explore new areas through the application of his own imagination upon familiar formats and material. On the same evening, his approach to his ballad 'Time Remembered' is routine and rooted in Shearing-isms, despite inspired playing from Israels. By early 1966 he would discover the required consistency, but before he got there a number of important events, personal and professional, would intervene and leave their mark.

The first of these was depressingly familiar. Home from Europe and booked into a number of clubs, Evans and his trio were back at The Trident in Sausalito, California, by late April 1965. The booking was originally scheduled to last the entire month, but Evans suffered a physical collapse that stopped him appearing professionally in public, and the group did not complete the engagement. He had been unhappy and isolated while on tour in Europe, and his heroin addiction had deepened, as had Ellaine's back in the US. Pianist Abe Battat and his group took over the vacant weeks at The Trident. Evans, announced *Down Beat*, "has decided to rest in [California] rather than return to New York after his recent collapse, attributed to malnutrition. [He] was booked by the Jazz Workshop for a two-week stay in July".[2]

Bunker, unsettled by the events of the past few months and back in his home state, took the opportunity to pull out of the trio, and by the time Evans returned to New York he was looking for a permanent replacement drummer. During his recuperation and subsequent search the group had no work, so Chuck Israels filled in with other sessions, appearing, by odd chance, at the Monday-night jams at the Village Vanguard organised by Evans's old boss, Tony Scott, recently returned from a six-year sojourn in the Far East.

Ironically, during this period of instability and confusion a long profile of the Bill Evans Trio, titled Natural Flow, appeared in *Down Beat*. In this highly sympathetic article by John Tynan, the trio – Evans, bassist Israels and drummer Bunker – had been interviewed backstage at Shelly's Manne-Hole and given a good deal of space to elaborate their playing philosophies and how these affected their music. "In this trio," Evans felt, "the fundamental musical principles are happening. There is a bass function, a melody function, and a rhythm function. So, fundamentally, the trio can develop in this direction ... Three things are happening with each other all the time, yet there's no imbalance." Israels expanded on the idea. "My voice is left open," he said, "because Bill doesn't play the bass in his left hand. So I mold the contour of my bass line to fit the character of the piece ... There are only a few other groups functioning like this: Gary Burton's, Gerry Mulligan's and Stan Getz's."[3]

Israels was honest about the hit-and-miss nature of this approach. "When things are going really well – say, one night in ten – Bill and I have a dialog going. When things are going *really* well – say one night in 30 – it's just perfect." He went on to expand this point: "In relation to this group, there are moments when my role is secondary to Bill's ... It doesn't detract from my feelings of artistic expression in a secondary role. Bill does what seems complementary to what I do and I to him. We try to complement each other. This, of course, is on an ideal plane. This is aside from the burden of personal problems, feelings, considerations, and so on." The interviewer said Israels had told him that particular evening that "he felt his morale had been sandbagged". Larry Bunker had no such problems with morale, enthusing to Tynan: "When [Bill] is really on, he's staggering. He probably makes fewer mistakes than any person I've heard on the instrument. I hear just about everything I want to hear in his playing. He's got everything – time, emotion, chops."[4]

Within weeks, the trio had disintegrated. That August, the furore over John S. Wilson's review of *Trio '65* in *Down Beat* broke out in the magazine's letters pages. This temporarily knocked Evans off-balance just as he was beginning a set of projects that would revitalise his artistic life and public profile. The first of these was an ambitious new recording for Verve that put his piano and trio with a large woodwind and string ensemble, released in February 1966 as *Bill Evans Trio With Symphony Orchestra*. This time there were no slick arrangements of film themes but imaginative jazz-tinged treatments of classical music and a handful of Evans originals. Two points about the sessions are immediately noticeable. First is the presence of session man Grady Tate on drums, indicating that Evans had still not replaced Bunker permanently, although Arnie Wise was a regular dep. Second is the lack of any new material from Evans's own pen. Both his compositions on this record are from some three or four years earlier.

The idea for this album seems initially to have involved discussion between Bill Evans and Gil Evans: the second Verve attempt at a joint project for the two men. According to Bill, Gil was responsible for the presence of a Chopin piece on *With Symphony Orchestra*. "We were supposed to do a record together," Bill said. "In fact they had already made the album cover. One of the ideas was to do the Chopin C-minor prelude. It lends itself well to a blues kind of feeling."[5] But Gil moved out of the picture, and Verve eventually replaced him with Claus Ogerman, with whom Bill had already worked on the forgettable film-themes record. Ogerman is a thoroughly schooled composer, arranger and conductor who had come to the US from Germany in 1959 and was then in his mid-thirties. He moved easily between film and commercial commissions, freelance arranging, and the writing of his own music. He came to the Evans project fresh from orchestrating and conducting a bossa nova album for RCA Victor with Joao Donato, having already proved his excellence in that field not long before with a bossa nova masterpiece that had Antonio Carlos Jobim at the piano.

According to Evans's liner notes to the original *Symphony Orchestra* LP, "With the assistance of Creed Taylor and Claus Ogerman, first meetings resulted in the selection of material and agreement of conception on how it should be approached. From then on the load fell on Claus Ogerman's shoulders and my first glimpses of his scores shortly before the dates quickly excited my anticipation."[6] Evans saw his role as that of an improvising soloist, whether unaccompanied or with his trio, playing against the backdrop of the ensemble. Despite the album's title this was by no means a symphony orchestra, there being no brass, no percussion nor even a complete woodwind section. Evans wrote, "The trio's function, and mine in particular, during these performances is largely improvisational. With deep thanks to the sensitive, wide and accomplished talents of Claus Ogerman, the pieces proved to be most satisfying vehicles for trio or solo improvisation."[7]

Evans's notes were in strong contrast to those of writer Lewis Freedman that accompanied his in the original gatefold LP sleeve. Some of Freedman's claims made on Evans's behalf take the breath away. One example: "If Ginsberg can write poetry with references to Baudelaire, then it is time for the jazz musician to be allowed and encouraged to come out of the cultural ghetto. If these resources are to be allowed, then he must experiment with its forms and its sound and its riches. On this record, there are five such experiments. On the one hand are the inventions of such masters as Bach, Scriabin, Fauré, Granados and Chopin. On the other is the inventiveness of a totally contemporary master, Bill Evans. The results are as beautiful and as provocative and as stimulating as Robert Lowell's *Imitations* or Picasso's *Les femmes d'Alger*."[8] The music that resulted from this union of two cultures is stylish, accomplished and highly palatable. It is in no way revolutionary, other than in the area of taste: few non-classical musicians had re-styled selections from the classical repertoire while retaining the poise and dignity of the originals.

With Symphony Orchestra was made in two sessions with the "orchestra", two weeks apart in September and October 1965, and a third session some two months later in December was reserved for drop-ins and other trio overdubs. The first of the "orchestra" sessions was notably more conservative in nature than the second. The first piece attempted, the Scriabin *Prelude*, is an early work of this most visionary of Romantic

Russian composers, coming from his Op.11 book of 24 Preludes, published in 1896 but written during the previous decade. The most striking part of this interpretation is the opening woodwind fanfare, giving textural brilliance to Scriabin's original piano score. The device by which Evans and his men are introduced – a rhythmic pattern which would not have been out of place in a film or TV score – is much less inspired, though the modulation is pleasant. The whole-note string background to Evans's simple octaves underlines the feeling that no one knew quite what to do to shape this piece of music into a satisfying structure. Perhaps it was conceived as a single? It certainly had the inconsequential rumination and lack of development necessary for AM radio play. A further modulation in the theme recapitulation at the end is workmanlike at best. Intriguingly, there is evidence of second thoughts from Evans himself, for his piano obbligato suggests the presence of a further piano track, perhaps added at the December session in an effort to reinforce the rather lightweight interpretation.

The next track recorded at that first session in September 1965 would end up as the opening track on the LP. It is an arrangement of the main (the maiden's) theme from 'Complaint, or the Maiden and the Nightingale', No.4 of *Goyescas*, a piano suite by Enrique Granados published between 1912 and 1914. The second theme (the nightingale's) is abandoned by Ogerman and a brisk jazz piano-trio section inserted instead. Evans opens with an unaccompanied treatment of the recapitulation of the maiden's theme, bringing his own discreet re-voicings to a pared-down setting, especially during the move from minor to major, softening the aching heart of the original in the melody's second section. The orchestrated exposition which follows introduces a mood closer to Granados's original, while the repetitive note patterns behind the melody suggest the hovering nightingale whose theme has vanished. This builds to a satisfactory climax before the jazz trio is ushered in, with Grady Tate's drumming a particular pleasure. Bassist Chuck Israels later recalled the value of Tate's presence. "I thought Tate did a superb job with the trio," said Israels. "It locked in great."[9] The trio swings effortlessly and Evans comes up with fresh and complex melodic and rhythmic ideas. The strings enter under the second chorus, leading Evans into a quick recapitulation of his own accompanied by trio and orchestra. Here is a satisfactory marriage of the two musical styles, even though the grafting of a jazz trio section into the piece makes no particular sense in terms of the music's form.

The musicians next turned to Ogerman's own piece, 'Elegia' from his *Concerto For Orchestra And Jazz Piano*. This is one of the most successful items on the record, developed along classical lines with the solo piano part entirely scored, and a short improvised trio section allowing it a natural and fully integrated environment in which to play. Judging from other concert works by Ogerman which have been recorded more recently, such as his Violin Concerto, this is couched in his mature compositional language. It opens with a melody statement from the strings alone, followed by an unaccompanied Evans covering the same thematic material. Ogerman is in this way following a long tradition in piano concertos, reaching back at least to Mozart, though more recent precedents included the Bartok 3rd Concerto, the chord sequence of which is distinctly echoed as the piano enters. Evans plays with great feeling and the piece marks a highlight of his recording career, the simple eloquence of his playing equal to his best with Davis some eight years earlier. Unfortunately there is a poor tape edit leading into the following treatment of the theme where trio and strings play together, and a momentary mismatch of pitches mars the mood. There is also some painfully inadequate string-section playing in the concluding orchestral passages before Evans's final chords. Presumably this unfamiliar piece posed some problems for the string players.

The final track recorded in that first session was Fauré's *Pavane*, originally scored by the composer for orchestra and chorus. The Pavane form was a dance, a point which Fauré certainly understood in his essentially light treatment, and Ogerman allows plenty of space for the Evans trio to set a gentle medium tempo ideal for elegant dancing. Israels sounds particularly happy and inventive, breaking the rhythm into attractive new patterns behind Evans. The strings follow Evans's opening theme statement, but there is not a great deal of orchestral writing here: Evans has the spotlight. This track is perhaps the closest in approach to that which the MJQ's John Lewis adopted with his similar piano-plus-ensemble projects. Even Evans's solo, while using rhythmic asymmetry and displacement in cunning and inventive ways, is largely in a single-note style in the Lewis tradition, and the bass and drums follow the MJQ's precedent of discreet counterpoint. This was a successful translation, then, of a piece that Fauré intended as a light diversion or entertainment.

The second session, held in mid October 1965, produced four more tracks (the piano and trio additions that would be made at the later December sessions are now impossible to separate from this earlier work). First up was the Chopin piece that had prompted the whole project: the 'Prelude No.20 In C minor', here retitled 'Blue Interlude'. The approach is disappointingly lightweight. The recording starts well enough with a thoughtfully coloured woodwind scoring of the theme – sounding remarkably like Gil Evans's voicings – followed by a mix of flutes and strings. But the orchestra exits entirely to give way to the Evans trio for one chorus before entering, re-stating the melody as a slow fugue behind the trio's jazzy embellishments but – considering it is Chopin – in a rather ponderous manner. This is the closest that Evans and Ogerman come to the style of Jacques Loussier and Michel Legrand – a style that was taken up by distinctly lesser European talents in search of a few more marks and francs. It was a mid-1960s fad, where pseudo-jazzy workings of classics were often used in breezy European films and released as singles or soundtrack themes. Here, only the opening scoring and the unaccompanied Evans ending are worthy of Chopin's original.

A good deal more weighty is the first Evans composition to be tackled by the assembled company, 'My Bells'. This and the other Evans piece of the day, 'Time Remembered', were not new: both had been recorded during his Riverside days, although 'My Bells' with Zoot Sims and Jim Hall remained unreleased at this time. Evans had clearly been attempting to solve the tune's problems, including its abrupt metre changes. The score opens brightly with sensitive but quite literal orchestrations of his original piano passage in an orchestral introduction that lasts just under a minute. The trio then enters, unassisted by the larger ensemble, for a relaxed mid-tempo common-time exploration of the chord changes before Evans is left to complete an unaccompanied recapitulation of the entire theme. The orchestra plays the final tonic chord with Evans adding a delicate arpeggio. This is a sensible arrangement of the piece, allowing it to tell a story from three different angles, although there is virtually no interaction between pianist and orchestra. It is more a series of contrasts. The group moved next to a piece listed simply as 'Yesterday'. It remains unissued and was possibly never completed. Its identity is unknown, although the title suggests it may have been a first attempt at the next number, 'Time Remembered', which was certainly finished to everyone's satisfaction. It had been part of the trio's working repertoire for at least two years and often began with the pianist, unaccompanied, stating the full theme. Here the orchestra takes over that role before giving way to the trio once more, which plays elegantly on Evans's minor progression. Interaction between trio and orchestra is again minimal, with strings and flutes supplying a single whole-note chord for Evans to vamp over on a fade-out. It all works, largely through Ogerman's arranging skill and the taste with which Evans solos, without flash or filigree and with a lightness of texture that remains delightful, even if these are not Evans's most deeply-felt improvisations.

The final piece is an arrangement of an arrangement: an excerpt from a Bach flute trio based on a theme by Vivaldi – Bach greatly admired Vivaldi and used his work on a number of notable occasions to provide raw material for his own inventions. Here, the piano trio and orchestra interact for closer to the full length of the piece, and Evans himself excels as usual in the 3/4 metre, teasing out the grace and elegance of the original melody. The performance is a somewhat literal interpretation, hardly profound, using only the colour of the orchestration and the trio's innate good taste to steer clear of glibness, but Evans and bassist Israels manage to conjure up some substantial contributions, with Israels again inspired to a complete dialogue with Evans throughout the jazz-trio improvisation section. Happy enough with the results to end with a flourish, Evans finishes with an octave arabesque over the orchestral coda that echoes similar passages on *Conversations With Myself*.

The *With Symphony Orchestra* album is unquestionably of its time. It has often been written off as something of a commercial aberration in the pianist's career, but this writer finds no reason to do so. It is a sincere if somewhat conservative attempt to marry together jazz and classical using material susceptible to that kind of arrangement. It is also often rather beautiful, always tasteful, and enjoyably relaxing. As Franz Liszt would perhaps have said, it is a "Consolation" in a busy and fraught world. Certainly Evans and producer

Creed Taylor remained proud of it. Reminiscing about his involvement with the pianist, Taylor later commented on his favourite Evans albums: "I still go back to the Oliver Nelson [*Blues And The Abstract Truth*] LP and … the Evans with symphony orchestra. I really like that."[10] Evans himself was equally enthusiastic, telling Mike Hennessy, "As I travel around, I find people have worn out copies of [*With Symphony Orchestra*]. I have worked hard over the years in developing the language of jazz, and sometimes I think that if I have made any contribution at all it is in terms of motivic development. I really enjoyed making this album with Claus and record my deepest respect and admiration for him."[11]

Within a week of the October 1965 session for the album Evans was off to Europe for a month or so as a solo act, picking up rhythm sections and other players as he went. This led to impromptu appearances in Berlin and Stockholm with saxophonist Lee Konitz's trio, with Niels-Henning Ørsted Pederson on bass and Alan Dawson on drums, and as the leader of a trio at the Golden Circle in Copenhagen. His playing on these dates varies wildly, according to the evidence of various pirate recordings, though they consistently reveal him playing more freely and with less concern for overall form and concision than he did with his own groups of the time. He sounds more like the aspiring New York sessionman of the late 1950s. Reports of the tour suggest he was once again using heroin heavily and suffering physically as a result.

Back in New York by December, Evans finished off his remaining work on the Ogerman album, picked up some jobs around the city with Israels and his newly permanent drummer, Arnie Wise, and noted the relative fall in his US popularity when the annual *Down Beat* Readers' Poll results placed him third on piano (he'd been number one the previous year). His combo dropped out of the top 10 and his sole new record for the year, *Trio '65*, scraped in at number 17.

Still, he had a major album completed and ready for release and his manager Helen Keane was busy finalising the arrangements for his concert debut in New York, scheduled for Town Hall on February 21st. This was his second large project of recent times and an ambitious showcase, displaying Evans in trio, solo and large-group settings. A January 1966 issue of *Down Beat* announced that "he will introduce several new compositions at the event"[12] but this turned out not to be the case. The change of plan may have been directly related to the sudden death of Evans's father, Harry, from a stroke just days before the concert. Bill returned to Florida to be with his family, and it is quite possible that the suite played at the concert in tribute to his father took the place of a section meant to showcase newer material.

At the same time, the *With Symphony Orchestra* album was released by Verve. The company's advertising trumpeted, "With This Album Jazz Moves Ahead A Giant Step,"[13] and this immodest statement would in itself have been enough to feed the flames of controversy. But contrasted with the kind of chaos, confusion and intemperate debate at large in the jazz community amid the rapid emergence of the second wave of avant-garde players – epitomised at the time by Albert Ayler, Archie Shepp and Pharoah Sanders – this claim by Verve for the new Evans album seemed distinctly out of touch and faintly ridiculous.

This was not the reaction, however, of audience or critics to the February 1966 concert at Town Hall. *Down Beat* reviewer Dan Morgenstern gave a long and detailed account of the music played that evening, noting that the trio section of the evening came first and absorbed the entire first half of the concert. Eight pieces were played, only seven of which have been issued by Verve, who taped the entire evening's proceedings. The missing track, a version of 'Very Early', remains unheard by all but the concertgoers. One other Evans original was played, a tune Morgenstern identified as 'My Lover's Kiss' in his review and described as "a beautiful ballad".[14] This performance was finally issued in the mid 1980s on Verve's CD version of the event. Its title was then disclosed as 'One For Helen'; the tempo was bright, though the melody was rhapsodic in typical Evans style, and the pianist plays with drive and urgency, his ideas tumbling out. A clue to the track's original non-appearance comes with the hesitation between ideas midway through his solo. Bassist Israels and drummer Wise swap fours with Evans at the close.

Other medium-tempo numbers receive similarly sparky attention from the trio. The opener, 'I Should Care', benefits from 12 months of club appearances, making for an integrated and cohesive arrangement. Evans is again in debt to Shearing for his reading of the melody, with octaves in both hands and a boppish, long-lined, intensely melodic first chorus. 'Who Can I Turn To', its out-of-tempo exposition aside, is driven along with a poise only occasionally glimpsed on record since the Riverside days, the tone and touch of Evans's playing amplified by the unusually rich sound of the concert-grand piano and by the engineer on this location recording. After the often compressed and jangly sound of the piano on the Van Gelder studio recordings – a pitfall for many jazz pianists throughout the 1960s across different record labels – it is a pleasure to hear a proper balance and extended range of overtones from a more sympathetically recorded instrument. In his review, Morgenstern felt that "Evans wrought a near-miracle" on 'Who Can I Turn To', "avoiding all bombast and sentimentality".[15] This is in part achieved by his extensive use of fourths to perk up the otherwise mawkish conventional harmony of the show tune, as well as his decision to pick up the tempo for the solo.

A similar transformation takes place on another old show tune 'Make Someone Happy'. Following his usual practice, Evans takes the theme-statement solo then moves into a bright allegro which has Wise moving to sticks from brushes. The piano improvisation on this tune is perhaps the most closely shaped and well paced of all the medium-tempo pieces that night, with the single-note opening building considerable tension and excitement, released by some typical Evans block-chords in the second chorus. The piece ends once more with an unaccompanied Evans pushing the theme hard. An unexpected flourishing arabesque, evoking both Tatum and Powell in its speed and nakedness, brings the tune to a dramatic close. Toward the end Evans misses a note, but thankfully it is not edited and we get to hear exactly what he played.

The final medium-tempo swinger, Victor Young's 'Beautiful Love', was also the last trio number of the evening. The group sounds confident and relaxed. Evans seems less concentrated, as if he is already looking ahead to the music to come following the interval, but Israels and Wise shine in their features, with the drummer taking his only solo of the night. Morgenstern noted, "Wise is the best drummer Evans has had. Working mostly with brushes, he was a model of good taste and comprehension of Evans's musical aims, unintrusive but always there."[16] This track and a ballad, 'My Foolish Heart', were left off the original LP of the concert, appearing for the first time in the late 1960s on *The Best Of Bill Evans*, a Verve compilation. Presumably they were put aside originally because they featured extended workouts by bassist and drummer.

If the medium-tempo performances were the best Evans had managed for Verve since the Shelly Manne/Monty Budwig outing more than three years earlier, his ballads rank alongside his best on record. 'My Foolish Heart' does not have the clear recording quality of the 1961 Village Vanguard sessions, but finds Evans pacing his phrasing impeccably, bringing an astonishingly acute level of feeling and stretching his lines to a tautness that only the masters can sustain without breaking – an ability that Evans's erstwhile employer Miles Davis also had at his mercy. The pianist's conception of the piece had not changed in five years, but the emotions were expressed with equal force and presence.

The other slow ballad was 'Spring Is Here', described by Morgenstern as "a shimmering impressionistic canvas".[17] This is accurate, for the pianist starts with a progression of open sevenths whose dense dissonance directly echoes such Debussy pieces of the 1890s as the two books of *Images*. The pace is very slow, the group marvellously poised and interlocked. Evans puts aside long and elaborate improvisation, relying on simple paraphrase and alternative voicings and allowing the mood to build through each echo of the original line. His recapitulation adds to the gentle resolution of the intensity, the dissonant harmonies of the opening section returning to give logic and balance to the overall picture. It is a masterful performance.

After the interval, Evans returned alone to the stage to open the second half of the concert and play what the programme announced as 'In Memory Of His Father, Harry T. Evans, 1891-1966'. It was presented as a new composition but was in fact a collation of some of his earlier pieces, one just months old, the others from years ago. They were prefaced by an introduction that uses whole-tone harmonic devices similar to those in 'Peace Piece' and 'NYC's No Lark' and with roots in Satie's Gymnopedies, the melody being almost literally an inversion of No.3. The form of Evans's suite is simple but effective, and this introduction gives way to probing improvisation on two themes. The first theme was noted at the concert as 'Story Line' but was in fact originally released in slightly different form during his Riverside days as 'Re: Person I Knew'. The other theme was from a ballad composed in the fall of 1965, 'Turn Out The Stars', the original lyrics by Gene Lees not required on this occasion. The symmetry of the work was sustained by the use of Evans's brief and cryptic 'Epilogue', originally used to conclude both LP sides of *Everybody Digs Bill Evans* and here enabling a return to the mood and style of the suite's opening.

Such a bare description of the music's basic shape does little to suggest its impact and its beauty. Evans plays with great intensity and almost infinite gradations of feeling, touch, tone, rhythmic adjustments and emphases. The overall mood of the music is elegiac, the melancholy at its heart becoming progressively darker and more intense until, touching despair, it is resolved by the enigmatic 'Epilogue', newly poignant in its latest role. Evans moves from a carefully controlled and accurate exposition of the simple contours of the scored introduction into the slight, fragile but very beautiful theme of 'Story Line' and its attendant improvisations, with little effort to conceal the joins but with a strong artistic continuity. 'Story Line' starts as if it were the second part of a conversation already begun by the first section. It does indeed seem to be telling a story, in the most intimate and confessional passages of music that Evans had recorded since *Conversations*. There are conspicuously few personal clichés, with Evans's rhythmic variety and creativity pulling the listener into the unfolding drama without resource to bombast or sentimentality.

Returning to the theme, first in chords only, then in octave depictions of quiet, spine-chilling beauty, Evans slowly turns the mood of the music down through a series of minor chords until a pause introduces the theme of 'Turn Out The Stars'. Once more the melody is of extreme simplicity, embedded within a harmony that reveals a bleak, agonised beauty. As he extemporises on the chords, Evans uses Art Tatum's device of extreme rubato, sometimes within a single phrase, to emphasise the dreamlike quality of his own emotional isolation. He also falls into 3/4 metre for half a chorus, as if he is acting out a half-recalled scene, and delivers some fiercely articulated, lightning-fast right-hand passages. He returns constantly to the theme, as if emphasising the role of fate in a universal story that leads to inevitable death and dissolution. He ends this section on a restatement of the theme in extreme diminuendo, leading to a pianissimo chord virtually inaudible on the original vinyl release but brought out cleanly by the CD. The brief 'Epilogue' communicates loss and simple human dignity in the face of pain – a set of emotions that Evans knew only too well.

Reviewer Dan Morgenstern noted that the audience had been asked to refrain from applause at the conclusion of the suite, but long and rather muted applause follows on the original vinyl release, where it was the last track on the record, and on all the CD reissues. The applause, superfluous from the beginning, no longer signals the end of one side of an LP and should perhaps now be removed by a sympathetic producer. CD releases have also failed to reflect the concert's running order, placing some later-released trio performances after the solo recital so as to preserve the original LP's sequencing. One would have thought it possible for Verve to have researched Evans's original concert order by now, especially for their *Complete Verve* collection of 1997.

The big-band section of the concert which followed has never been made available on record, even though in the liner notes to *At Town Hall, Volume I*, Helen Keane writes: "Verve Records taped the concert live and is releasing the proceedings on two separate LPs - *Bill Evans At Town Hall – Volume I and II*."[18] The non-issue of the big-band tracks may well have something to do with the way they were presented. Four pieces were played: two standards – 'What Kind Of Fool Am I?' and 'Willow, Weep For Me' – and two from Evans's pen – 'Waltz For Debby' and 'Funkarello'. Morgenstern's review says these four "were performed without interruption, with brief transitions between tunes by either woodwinds or piano".[19] Perhaps the challenges of editing this uninterrupted cycle were insurmountable; alternatively, there may simply not have been enough of a spotlight on Evans himself. Morgenstern's review noted that although Evans was well featured, "the arrangements were not piano showcases".

Morgenstern found arranger Al Cohn's writing for the big-band segments of the Town Hall concert outstanding and the section playing excellent, with lead trumpeter Ernie Royal earning special praise, and admired solos from Clark Terry (trumpet), Eddie Daniels (tenor), Jerry Dodgion (alto) and Bob Brookmeyer (valve trombone). Only on 'Funkarello' did the reviewer pick out Evans's contribution. Whatever the reasons, the music has not been heard publicly since February 21st 1966 and remains part of Evans's legacy only by reputation. In an oddly dislocated passage in the *Complete Verve* boxed set of 1997 someone is quoted talking about the second, unreleased volume. It is uncredited, but seems to be Creed Taylor: "MGM, the producer, and myself decided that the big-band segment wasn't what we had hoped for so we didn't put that part of it out. They may some day. They have the right to do it." Elsewhere in the same booklet, critic Phil Bailey claims: "An unissued big-band segment with arrangements by Al Cohn has never been in Verve's holdings."[20] Curiouser and curiouser.

After this concert triumph it would have been logical to consolidate with live appearances using Evans's newly cohesive and inventive trio. In fact, faced with going out on the road, bassist Israels decided it was time to make a break. Drummer Arnie Wise stayed on, allowing Evans to hire an old colleague, bassist Teddy Kotick, in order to make a sold-out March booking at Boston's Jazz Workshop. The group's first work together, however, came earlier that month at the Village Vanguard, part of which is preserved on *The Secret Sessions*, a boxed set of eight CDs of material recorded between 1966 and 1975 by amateur enthusiast Mike Harris and his wife Evelyn. Harris had become an Evans devotee during the early 1960s, rarely missing his appearances at the Village Vanguard. By 1966 he was determined to do something about the fate of Evans's live performances, aggrieved that they were gone forever as soon as they were played – a common feeling among devotees of many performers. Harris acquired portable recording equipment and taped at least part of every Evans set at the club that he could attend over those nine years. These recordings were private though not especially furtive, as Harris cleared his activity with the Vanguard's owner, Max Gordon. The recording quality of his tapes overall is decent, although the crowd noise is higher than a professional date, given that the microphone was in the crowd rather than onstage. The first recordings date from the time of this transitional trio and provide a clear indication of Evans's thinking at the time. Bassist Teddy Kotick plays in a similar vein to Israels: muscular in his rhythm playing and inventive melodically, he spins a series of involving conversations with Evans's piano.

By mid April 1966 when the group reached Chicago's famous London House, Kotick had departed to be replaced by the young New York bassist Eddie Gomez. Gomez had first come to notice as a member of Marshall Brown's Newport Youth Band, for whom he auditioned at the age of 13. "He was the youngest kid ever to join the [musicians'] union," said Brown, "and when we went out on the road playing those ballrooms, it was really illegal for him to be onstage, but I'd sneak him on to play one number … When I broke up the band in 1960, he was then technically one of the better bass players in town, and he was only 16. The only thing was, nobody knew it except me, but I knew it was just a question of time before Bill Evans found him. He's like another Jimmy Blanton."[21] While Gomez is inevitably compared regularly to Scott LaFaro, Blanton does make a more suitable comparison. Gomez certainly learned from LaFaro, but his more forceful playing and powerful rhythmic drive leads back more clearly by way of Ray Brown to Blanton's example, especially his famous 1940s bass-and-piano duets with Duke Ellington.

By the time he joined Evans, Gomez was a widely experienced player, having worked with Marian McPartland and Paul Bley, to name just two widely diverse leaders. McPartland often said afterward how she regretted seeing Gomez leave. She told interviewer Steve Voce, "I think he enjoyed playing with me, but he never made a secret of the fact that he always wanted to go with Bill Evans. I always felt that, for him, being with me was just like a little trip along the way. And it was. But naturally I loved his playing and hated to see him go."[22] In the months before joining Evans, Gomez was working alternately with Jim Hall and Gerry Mulligan. Mulligan's group was for a time resident at the Village Vanguard, which is where Evans heard him. Gomez had always idolised Evans, and when Helen Keane rang him on the pianist's instructions and offered the job, Gomez was stunned. He said to Marian McPartland shortly afterward, "I'm ecstatic! I can hardly believe it."[23] Evans expressed similar feelings to McPartland around the same time.

This line-up, with Gomez on bass and Arnie Wise on drums, remained solid until the end of 1966, when Wise moved on. Evans chose not to take them into the studio, despite their obvious cohesion and Evans's fast-growing harmony with Gomez. In fact, at the start of April 1966, the same month that the group came together at the London House, Evans had paired up in the studio with guitarist Jim Hall to make their second duet record. This and an early-May session would see the completion of what was released by Verve as *Intermodulation*, an apt title considering the harmonic approach of the two musicians and their abilities as accompanists and duettists. Once again, the recording was made at the Van Gelder studio in New Jersey, and while marginally better recorded than their initial foray for United Artists in 1962, the sound still lacks presence and seems somehow blunted: perhaps this was the effect the players themselves wanted.

The two men respond to one other instinctively, interweaving ideas of great beauty. Their work on 'My Man's Gone Now' is on a par with their earlier LP in unity of vision, while 'Turn Out The Stars' has not yet evolved very far past its solo piano conception of a month or so earlier. 'Angel Face', from the May session, suffers from a lifeless and blurred recording, and despite Hall proving a wonderful rhythmic accompanist to Evans at a slow-medium tempo, there is not a great deal more to ponder. Claus Ogerman's 'Jazz Samba' suffers from the lack of a drummer and a relatively undistinguished rhythmic and harmonic basis. Hall's one original – brought along, Hall says, at Evans's insistence – is 'All Across The City', an elegant ballad and one still in the guitarist's repertoire at the time of writing. Hall remembered the session as fun, in common with all his professional associations with Evans. "He was so easy to work with," said Hall. "It was just like he read your mind all the time."[24] The feeling was mutual, for Evans later confessed: "I loved working with Jim Hall. The wonderful thing about him is that he is like a whole rhythm section … He just propels it along, and you do not have to make any great effort with his support."[25]

Intermodulation was released later in 1966 to great acclaim. Once again Verve tried something new in its presentation, asking the classical conductor Skitch Henderson to provide liner notes. These naturally emphasise the connections between the endeavours of the two jazzmen and concert-hall music. "Pianists are a strange group," Henderson wrote. "They live in a world of instruments which never satisfy them – they're either out of tune or the action isn't comfortable … There is very little difference between the classical artist and the popular artist in this field. They both develop a style and become complete individuals … I have listened to Bill play for many years, mostly on records, and have always been struck by the skill with which he produces the sound or tone. In many ways he is reminiscent of the great classical composer, Rachmaninoff."[26] Evans would have been gratified by the comparison.

While the Hall record was still being recorded, Evans's music was the subject of a harsher evaluation in a rapidly changing jazz world. 'Time Remembered' from the Ogerman *With Symphony Orchestra* collaboration was played to Archie Shepp in a particularly trenchant Blindfold Test for *Down Beat*. After admitting that he'd had to look at the cover to find out who it was, Shepp ignored the specific track and instead launched into a set of pronouncements on Evans. He claimed, as did many of his generation at the time, that he thought Evans's best work had been done with the Miles Davis Sextet.

Shepp then brought up the subject of Cecil Taylor's criticisms of Evans, clearly siding with his erstwhile boss. "Bill is in many ways one of the most overrated pianists in the country," said Shepp. "I like him on ballad material. He can do that type very well – Satie, Debussy, everyone knows that Bill can do those things. But … there's nothing particularly original about that, as far as I'm concerned."[27] This somewhat patronising put-down was in line with the accepted contemporary musical/political view, and in fact would fast become a cliché itself. But Evans suffered increasingly from this attitude as rock took over American popular music; and jazz, still reeling from the second wave of avant-garde musicians like Shepp and the Ayler brothers, would become polarised afresh as critics and musicians alike had to decide where they stood in relation to jazz-rock fusion.

Just two weeks before Shepp's Blindfold Test, Evans's *With Symphony Orchestra* album had been reviewed by Mike Zwerin in *Down Beat*. Zwerin was something of a critical maverick at the time, unpredictable in his reactions. He had distinct reservations about what the LP set out to do and how Verve had packaged it, but ended with a perceptive comment on Evans's current direction. "I think," wrote Zwerin, "that Evans's growth has been more qualitative than quantitative. He is playing what he has always played, only better than ever, rather than playing much that is new. But that same old thing is *so* beautiful."[28]

CHAPTER 11

Further Conversations (1966-1970)

"USUALLY HE WAS SOLEMN AND RETICENT, AS ALOOF IN HIS DREAMS AND THOUGHTS AS HE WAS IN HIS MUSIC."

WRITER RANDI HULTIN ON EVANS IN 1966

The Evans trio's "same old beautiful thing" was heard again at the Village Vanguard in early July 1966 with Eddie Gomez on bass and Arnold Wise on drums – at a time when the cream of the performing jazz world was concentrated in Newport, Rhode Island, at the annual Festival. Evans had been absent from Newport since 1958 and had never appeared there as a leader.

When it came to recording this new working trio, Evans hesitated. He decided instead to revisit the formula of *Empathy*, the record he'd made with drummer Shelly Manne and easily his most successful trio LP for Verve to date. This time, however, Evans retained his new bassist, Eddie Gomez, tilting

Eddie Gomez, Bill Evans and Jack DeJohnette at the Montreux Festival, Switzerland, 1968

the stylistic balance in his favour. The recording session took place at the Van Gelder studios in New Jersey in October 1966. It would be the last of Evans's Verve albums to be produced by Creed Taylor, who very shortly afterward left the company to set up his own label, CTI Records, through A&M.

The new record with Manne, *A Simple Matter Of Conviction*, was curiously conservative, consciously evoking past attitudes and impressions. The opening (title) track is a medium-fast minor key Evans original using blues changes. It is characterised by a nervous dotted-note 3/4 metre that perhaps picks up on the intensity of McCoy Tyner's piano playing (especially the prodding left hand) in the same metre with the John Coltrane Quartet. The irony is that Tyner learned a great deal from Evans, but Evans does little with what he has re-imported from the younger player. The trio hangs together well and Manne is a study in tasteful invention, but the fact that the track was faded suggests that the conviction was perhaps not quite 100 per cent. On 'Stella By Starlight' Evans is at his most clichéd, finding nothing new to add to the many approaches he had made to this tune. Even his theme displacement seems clumsy rather than exciting. He gives the opening solo to Gomez. Manne holds the listener's attention more successfully with the variety and surprise he brings to his subsidiary role, and his beautifully natural rhythmic pulse is a joy in itself. Another Evans original, 'Orbit', brings out the Shearing style again, and features Gomez playing high and with no great coherence compared to his later work with the pianist. Evans's single-line solo after Gomez is clear and concise, specialising in some fantastically long melodic arcs, but it continues his tour of Shearing-like styles.

During 'Laura', the old film song, Gomez and Manne engage in a musical dialogue that is a high point on the record, their wit and interaction suggesting an entirely different set of musical aims than those of Evans here. Strangely for someone who understands the value of contrast, space and dynamics, Evans is quite relentless in his playing on many of these tracks, especially the standards, as if he were attempting to play right through all his personal licks to the other side and then break free into new ground. It is a problem faced by every improvising artist, and was articulated most acutely around this time by John Coltrane who admitted that it often took him more than 30 minutes in a given solo to work through all the ideas he had rehearsed many times before in order to arrive at new configurations. Bandleader Stan Kenton understood this when in a *Down Beat* Blindfold Test he listened to an Evans solo from Oliver Nelson's early-1960s *Blues & The Abstract Truth* album. "I wasn't too impressed by the piano," Kenton said. "He's tasty, but suffers from the same fault of a lot of modern pianists – they get into one idiom, and they keep it going, and there are so many possibilities … He could have gotten a little more colour from the piano by broadening it out a bit, getting away from just the stabbing left hand and the single-finger right hand – in spite of the fact that he did play some thirds."[1]

Evans must have been aware of the problems too. After all, his own appreciation of music was unusually broad and well-informed. But perhaps the task of continuing to develop his own style from within was for the moment proving a little too daunting. Although the new partnership with Eddie Gomez suggested fresh ways to escape such paralysis, only time would allow for the development. A new composition on this disc, 'These Things Called Changes', shows Evans toying with a range of permutations of 'All The Things You Are', but the harmonic relationships are so stretched and the rhythmic interest so low that the result is listlessness, not unlike some of the more unfocused latter-day performances by Bud Powell.

Meanwhile, tunes like 'Star Eyes' with an obvious lineage stretching back to Parker and the bop era suggest that the pianist was on artistic hold at the session. Evans was of course aware that he had to evolve, as he demonstrated in his written tribute on Bud Powell's death that autumn. "His was the most comprehensive composition talent of any jazz player I have ever heard presented on the jazz scene," Evans wrote. "He had the potential of a true jazz player. He expanded much in a legitimate, organic way. Because of his history, he never got to use that potential that much, though he did plenty. His insight and talent were unmatched in hard-core, true jazz."[2] Evans later reinforced that opinion in a 1970 interview with Norwegian journalist Randi Hultin, a friend to many musicians and especially close to Powell in the 1960s. "There are some feelings which don't make you emotional," Evans told her. "They don't make you cry, they don't make you laugh, they don't make you feel anything but profound, and that's the feeling I got from Bud. It's like the feeling you get from Beethoven, maybe … When I think about Charlie Parker, Dizzy Gillespie and Bud,

I think that Bud is very underrated … Bud comes in there among those names, too, it's just that he has never got the attention he deserves."[3] Evans shared the early weeks of October 1966 at the Village Vanguard with Ray Nance (backed by Walter Bishop Jr), Horace Silver's quintet and Sonny Rollins's quartet, and then took Gomez to Denmark for a quick visit later that month, making radio and television appearances again with Monica Zetterlund and playing in a trio using local drummer Alex Riel. They then moved on to Oslo in Norway for a concert that was witnessed by Randi Hultin: "The concert had been taped for television, and the audience, which consisted mainly of musicians and jazz aficionados, had been asked not to applaud after each solo. But when Gomez had played, the house came down. We couldn't resist applauding him."[4] At Oslo's Fornebu airport the next day Hultin saw Evans meet up with musicians from Charles Lloyd's quartet. "Seldom was he so glib and full of laughter," she reported. "Usually he was solemn and reticent, as aloof in his dreams and thoughts as he was in his music."[5] After this successful interlude Evans and Gomez headed back to New York, in November resuming the regular stint at the Village Vanguard with Arnie Wise back behind the drum set. At this stage of the group's development Wise had become a great deal more assertive and varied in his playing, evidenced by a stirring November 10th Vanguard performance of 'Come Rain Or Come Shine' (subsequently released on *Secret Sessions*) where his stick work is smooth, colourful and driving.

Yet Wise was not a happy traveller, remaining reluctant to stick with the group on out-of-town engagements. This uncertainty troubled Evans, who in January 1967 invited drummer Joe Hunt to come into the trio. Hunt, who'd had connections with Stan Getz, stayed just four months and never recorded officially with the band, but does appear on three evenings from the Village Vanguard preserved in *The Secret Sessions*. Sensitive and swinging, Hunt fitted in well without stamping a wholly new personality on the music. Evans very rarely recorded Duke Ellington compositions, but *The Secret Sessions* preserves an 'In A Sentimental Mood' showing the group's arrangement of the theme to be light and swinging, avoiding the sentimentality promised by the song's title. Evans's solo, however, is heavy-handed and careless of the ballad's wistful character, an oversight uncharacteristic of the pianist. His playing now was harder, more brittle and less meditative than at any other time in the 1960s. Perhaps it was the stimulating influence of the energetic and brilliant Gomez – or maybe Evans just felt differently about his music.

The trio now played and toured regularly, including a successful stint at Shelly's Manne-Hole in LA in mid April 1967 that confirmed his audience as loyal and numerous. During the spring months Hellas Music Corp published "a must for the sophisticated musician", a set of transcriptions of the arrangements for the *Bill Evans With Symphony Orchestra* LP. It confirmed the wide interest among professionals, piano students and amateur players about the mechanics of the Evans method. Verve, meanwhile, on the release of *A Simple Matter Of Conviction*, seemed to have run out of marketing ideas for their star pianist, preferring to trade on past achievements by picturing *Conversations With Myself* and *Intermodulation* alongside the new album under the heading "Solo - Duo - Trio!" The copy is equally at a loss: "Bill Evans … alone or in a crowd, this quiet man comes through soft and clear."[6]

In the late spring of '67 Evans took part in a panel discussion on the future of jazz at the University of California in Berkeley, along with John Handy, Leonard Feather and Ralph Gleason. As with most discussions of this sort it produced a lot of hot air and few conclusions, but Evans made some succinct points, as reported in *Down Beat*. When faced with the old chestnut "What is jazz?" he said, "Jazz is a mental attitude rather than a style. It uses a certain process of the mind expressed spontaneously through some musical instrument. I'm concerned with retaining that process." No one else even went this far over the formal aspects of the music. Feather pointed out that other cultures used improvisation in their music, but this didn't qualify that music as jazz. There had to be a cultural and stylistic dimension too, he said. Following this point at a later stage of the discussion, Evans commented: "[Jazz] has to do with everybody. It can be traced to a variety of ethnic backgrounds. The Negro was trying to make music – not Negro music. He drew from his culture, just as I did." Handy added that "racial pride is one of the things that has kept our heads above water", while Feather thought that "jazz resulted from a segregated culture". Gleason, arguing as a newly-converted rock enthusiast, had little patience with the views of Evans or Feather, clearly feeling they were too conservative. His parting shot was: "A lot of things that go on now in rock are more interesting than in second-rate jazz. Some rock bands and some rock musicians can knock you right out of your mind – like Miles."[7]

Evans, Feather and Handy were content during the discussion to be identified as reactionaries when it came to new rock music. On the same subject, Evans would later comment to Randi Hultin: "There is more music in jazz. I don't mean to be snobbish, but I know for instance what it cost me to learn a little bit about music. I also know how much shorter the trip is for a pop artist to reach the top, or to learn how to play his instrument."[8] This reluctance to embrace new popular-music forms gradually forced Evans into an ever more constricted musical and stylistic corner, especially as the 1970s began and contemporary music moved even further away from the areas he valued. It would leave him out of the limelight in the US until the final years of his life late in the 1970s, when fusion and soul-jazz were no longer at the music's popular cutting edge.

Meanwhile, Evans continued to try to improve matters for his working trio. In May 1967 he invited his old friend and drumming favourite Philly Joe Jones to join the group. Jones accepted, and the difference he made to the group – as well as to Evans's playing – can be heard from a May 19th tape from the Village Vanguard. The sole up-tempo number from that date, 'On Green Dolphin Street', positively steams along, Jones laying down a beat as grooved as Shelly Manne's but with his own special brand of dynamism. The trio was swinging in a way that no other Evans working group had done before. Jones was always sensitive to the leader's intentions in any given song, but his primary concern and responsibility was always with the rhythm, the pulse. These are inescapable when a group is being propelled by Jones, and it helped lighten the load on Evans, who could dig in and swing without attempting to dominate the rhythm with an over-heavy left hand.

In July '67 this trio played the Los Angeles Festival, in concert with Gary McFarland's big band, and at the Newport Jazz Festival – his first appearance there as a leader. Little notice was taken of them at Newport among all the festivities and musical fireworks. Dan Morgenstern, in a long report, noted that the Evans trio "played a strong set, egged on by Philly Joe Jones's drive and power",[9] while Burt Goldblatt merely reported that "Bill Evans, with drummer … Jones behind him, emphasised the contrapuntal".[10] As the song goes, when you're hot you're hot, when you're not you're not. Back to the Village Vanguard, then.

But this was not to be the only pattern of activity for Evans over the summer and autumn of 1967. In August, a month after the Newport set, Evans went into the Webster Hall recording studio in New York to make his next album for Verve and his first under the guiding hand of Helen Keane. The result, *Further Conversations With Myself,* seemed to be another exercise in retrospection, or even retrenchment – although as far as Evans was concerned it was partly to correct what he saw as the deficiencies of *Conversations With Myself,* the 1963 LP with three independently recorded piano parts from Evans. As he commented to Morgan Ames, who wrote the new record's liner notes, "My main criticism, and the main problem in making the original *Conversations,* was that of heavy texture. Since the third voice functioned only as commentary and wasn't basically significant, I preferred to try a two-voice conversation this time. Even so, I found that in many cases one track would have sufficed … I wouldn't be surprised if my next album were to turn out to be a solo effort."[11] A solo album would be recorded in due course in the fall of 1968.

Listening to the music on *Further Conversations* one can sympathise with its creator. Although there are some exquisite high points, such as the opening cut, 'Emily', with its swirling obligato and beautiful voicings, there is the nearly unlistenable 'Yesterdays' where Evans's rhythm piano track is so insistent and aggressive in its feeding of ideas, and his later overdubbing so close in concept to the first track, that the performance sounds more like a garrulous windbag shouting down a more softly-spoken, thoughtful conversationalist. The harsh sound of Evans's piano – including microphone distortion on loud notes – only adds to the ugliness of the recording. Technical problems mar the whole album, though some of the less dense tracks are only intermittently affected. From 'Yesterdays' Evans moves on to 'Santa Claus Is Coming To Town', a song that caused puzzled expressions the first time he'd recorded it (on *Trio '64*. Why he should want to record it a second time will remain a mystery: its essential flimsiness does not improve on further exposure. Evans finishes side one with a brusque treatment of his own new ballad, 'Funny Man'. Here he breaks into a walking bass line, then plays at swapping eights with himself. As with the previous two tracks there is scarcely room to breathe, the pianist apparently forgetting one of his own basic rules, that the use of space and contrast is fundamental to creating a fully satisfactory improvised excursion.

The potential impact of such an approach is immediately felt on the long opening track on side two, 'The Shadow Of Your Smile', where Evans allows his phrases to breathe naturally, to expand and fall away again, rather than crowding out each phrase with a consequent one. This is such a controlled and shaped performance that when Evans double-times midway through it seems a logical investigation of the tune's possibilities and a successful part of the performance's form rather than a random desire to do something different. This is the one track from this session that would have sat proudly on the first *Conversations* album. The following tune is another re-make, 'Little Lulu', and a revival even more questionable than 'Santa Claus'. Evans tries hard to inject humour with countless silent-movie-style madcap endings, but it is too forced and does not work. There is also the problem on records of repeatability. The tune gives him little musical sustenance: as a joke, it could have stood maybe 30 seconds of album time as an end-piece. The disc ends with Evans's first attempt at Denny Zeitlin's 'Quiet Now', which quickly became a staple of his live sets. This first attempt at it is a fine and controlled performance, sombre and full of feeling. Perhaps unexpectedly, Evans's playing here recalls the richly-coloured harmony and measured dignity of Dave Brubeck, a San Franciscan like Zeitlin.

The year 1967 would turn out to be a terrible and tumultuous one for jazz: Billy Strayhorn, Rex Stewart, Stuff Smith and John Coltrane died, while the music itself came under increased commercial and artistic pressure from a newly mature rock industry. A younger jazz generation, mixing elements of avant-garde and more traditional methods, was meanwhile finding new audiences. By the end of 1967 Charles Lloyd and his group would be the most popular in jazz, while the previous holders of that title, the Dave Brubeck Quartet, would break up after more than 15 years together. Like Evans, Brubeck would continue to serve up appetising musical feasts for his audiences, but he would never regain a popular ascendancy. That had moved on to another generation. Only John Coltrane had pushed on remorselessly, keeping his ideas at the cutting edge, but now suddenly he was gone, leaving a huge chasm at the centre of the avant-garde movement that proved impossible to fill. Of that generation, it would be Davis who later rose to the challenge and reinvented himself for the new rock generation. In the meantime, Evans's public profile continued to shrink, partly perhaps due to his inability to arrive at a settled line-up for his trio, and also perhaps because Evans, now in his late thirties, was perceived as part of a relatively older generation of jazz musicians. For the average jazz fan, and in particular for younger music lovers, Evans had become "predictable". No matter that his output was not inferior to before – indeed, his next session, a welcome return to recording at the Village Vanguard, was an outstanding addition to his discography – but it seemed like old news. The music that Evans played with Gomez and Jones at the Village Vanguard that August indicated that he was not even attempting to maintain his former position at the forefront of the music.

Their repertoire at the Vanguard in August '67 is a little wider than had been the leader's habit for a while, with the aforementioned Ellington composition included alongside a 1940s hit, 'Happiness Is A Thing Called Joe', while the old show tune 'California Here I Come', as well as 'I'm Getting Sentimental Over You' and 'Gone With The Wind', all regularly sneak into the sets. Yet these songs were so old – almost veteran – that it seemed as if Evans was consciously evoking musical scenes and styles from his youth. Only Burt Bacharach's saccharine 'Alfie' was taken into his performing book from a wealth of contemporary popular material. Other established jazz artists, including former Evans collaborators like Oliver Nelson and Gary McFarland, were investigating the new pop repertoire, so it is curious that Evans never attempted a Lennon-McCartney song, for example, at this time. Perhaps he saw no need. Perhaps he had no interest, or saw little relevance to what he was attempting. The music that the Evans trio created during the nights of recording at the Vanguard is consistently inspired. The trio worked for the most part as a cohesive team, though the pianist is still figuring out how best to integrate bassist Gomez's obvious talent into his music. Gomez occasionally sounds ill-directed in his forays across the octaves on his instrument, especially in his frequent solos. Although he has immense speed and dexterity and a style not dissimilar to that of Scott LaFaro, the young bassist is not at this stage of his time with Evans as melodically interesting and rhythmically surprising as LaFaro had been some six years earlier. This is especially noticeable in his solo spots, no doubt a legacy of the live circumstances of the recording, where he is often all over his instrument but less often sustains a clearly shaped musical argument. An example to the contrary is his very LaFaro-like solo on 'Gone With The Wind' from August 18th, the solo falling in a set which is markedly relaxed and swinging, with close communication between all three players. It would be wrong, however, to suggest that Gomez is somehow inadequate in his playing on these August evenings: his consistent flow of ideas, his spirit of adventure and his constant search for variety, as well as his ability to revert to swinging walking basslines when required, mark him out already as the most impressive bassist Evans had used since LaFaro's death.

Evans plays throughout the recordings with considerable intensity as well as a noticeably more buoyant emotional state: he swings impetuously, rarely allows reflection and introspection to dominate, and generally gives the listener the impression that he is in control and enjoying himself. But it is noticeable that he is not especially well integrated with Gomez's playing, preferring at this point to follow the logic of his own ideas and let the others follow. This does not preclude successful music-making: here is a working group that conspicuously exudes contentment, with Jones's imperturbable pulse the creative wellspring of the entire project. Had this trio survived for as long as the group with Israels and Bunker or Wise then it may well have developed in newly revealing ways. As it was, for reasons unconnected with the music the group was making, Jones had left the band by the close of the year and Arnie Wise was depping once more. A double LP released in the early 1980s, *California Here I Come*, marked the first release of any of the music from the Vanguard sessions; in 1998 around four hours of the material appeared on the *Complete Bill Evans On Verve* CD boxed set. A poorly tuned piano may have been one of the reasons for its being held back at the time.

It was Wise who crossed the Atlantic with Evans and Gomez for a brief European visit just before the end of 1967, with concerts in Italy and Switzerland as well as an appearance at Ronnie Scott's club in London. The sets at Ronnie's were witnessed by packed houses of fans as well as many local musicians in awe of Evans's harmonic abilities and musical command. The trio also appeared at the London Jazz Expo '67 on the same bill as groups led by Charles Lloyd, Max Roach, Roland Kirk, Gary Burton, The Newport All-Stars, Son House, Bukka White, Miles Davis and Archie Shepp. The Evans trio were there as substitutes for a Teddy Wilson/Albert Nicholas band which failed to materialise, and with the audience primed for music of an altogether different era of jazz their performance was not well received.

That same autumn Evans appeared on film, still a rare medium for jazz. He and his manager had an idea that stemmed from an appearance on American television where Evans combined playing piano with talking about his music. The interviewer was, according to *Down Beat*, his brother "Dr. Harry Evans, supervisor of music education in Baton Rouge, LA".[12] Harry Evans was not the only interpreter: veteran TV star and amateur jazz pianist Steve Allen contributed "the introduction, and also [appeared as] transitional narrator later in the film". *Bill Evans, Jazz Pianist – On The Creative Process And Self-Teaching* was a 45-minute attempt to look seriously at the complexities of its subject, and as such was a first in jazz education.

Evans said, "We tried to go into the psychological things you have to go through to master this nebulous craft, not put it in terms that were so theoretical."[13] During the course of the frank and engaging film, Evans asserted some of his principles, including his strong feeling that "in an absolute sense, jazz is more a certain process – a spontaneity – than a style". This, he said, meant it was vital that people teaching jazz started from musical principles rather than stylistic traits. Evans made his opinions clear: that he would uphold his own areas of interest and concern in contemporary improvised music, and continue the methods and processes that he had used throughout the 1960s. While all this made sense to Evans and his management, his record company was becoming increasingly perplexed. How could they promote him in the face of the rising tide of rock and its application to jazz by younger musicians, some of whom were now proving popular and fashionable with rock listeners? Given rock's close identification at this time with social ferment, how could Evans be fitted into this newly emerging consciousness? Verve's January 1968 advertisement for the *Further Conversations* LP underlined the company's confusion. Under the title "Conversations continued: additional dialogue by Bill Evans" Verve made some embarrassingly inept comments and inappropriate allusions, apparently pining for the days when Evans was ahead of the game. "It was a private conversation," ran the ad. "And highly personal. Bill Evans alone in a room with three pianos; *Conversations With Myself.* Six years have passed. The dangling conversation is resumed. And the pianist speaks with even more authority now. The dialogue has been perfected as the artist within has grown. With fewer questions, more swinging statements. Other voices, other tunes. The original *Conversations* has remained Bill Evans's best-selling album. And perhaps his best. Now overhear this."[14]

With a company this confused about one of its major artists (how did a Paul Simon song about a declining relationship get into a Bill Evans ad?), perhaps the non-appearance of the Vanguard music is easier to understand. But Verve were not the only ones unsure about the pianist's future. Leonard Feather, in his intro to a Blindfold Test in *Down Beat*, wrote: "Bill Evans, in the context of the 1968 musical scene, is something of an anachronism. His music … relies on introversion and innate beauty, at a time when the trend is to detonation, reverberation and exaggeration." Of the music played to him during this Test, Evans was most enthusiastic about a Herbie Hancock piece, 'Cantaloupe Island', which he guessed as by Horace Silver, but his most pertinent comments came during a Don Ellis track from his award-winning LP, *Electric Bath*. Ellis, an early-1960s radical, was now fronting a revved-up big-band playing highly-charged original music full of eccentric time-signatures and using a rock rhythm section. Questioning the record's staying power past the novelty of its unusual sounds, Evans said: "I would give it about four stars for imaginative sound adventure in music, and perhaps one-and-a-half stars for the actual musical content. To me, of course, the musical content is always primary, and although this is something that can attract one's attention immediately, in 20 years' time it's not going to mean a thing as far as novelty is concerned, and the musical content will be the only thing that matters."[15]

Whatever was going on at Verve and elsewhere, Evans continued to work his trio steadily, mostly in New York clubs but occasionally beyond. He did more on film and TV, appearing in spring 1968 on CBS Television's *Dial M For Music* series along with the Teddy Wilson Trio. By this time drummer Jack DeJohnette had taken time out from Charles Lloyd's quartet and was freelancing assiduously in New York City. Persuaded to come into the trio courtesy of Eddie Gomez, he appeared with Evans on this broadcast. DeJohnette stayed with Evans through the summer and into the autumn, briefly rejoining Lloyd in November for that quartet's final album, recorded live at New York's Town Hall. That same November 1968 DeJohnette would move on to Miles Davis's groundbreaking electric group before going out as a leader in the early 1970s.

During the six or so months that DeJohnette was with the trio their work was fortunately preserved on one of Evans's most famous late-1960s LPs, recorded at the second annual Montreux Festival in Switzerland, in June 1968. Just six days before that auspicious occasion, however, Evans made his second televised appearance of the year, but in very different circumstances to the spring's *Dial M For Music* session. He was one of the featured jazz artists in a hastily assembled but immensely dignified WCBS-TV jazz tribute on June 9th to the assassinated US Senator Robert Kennedy. Kennedy's funeral had been televised nationally the day before. Other artists appearing in *A Contemporary Memorial* included the MJQ, Joe Williams, the Thad Jones/Mel Lewis Orchestra, Woody Herman, Horace Silver and Duke Ellington (in a trio with Johnny Hodges). Father Norman O'Connor, a priest with lifelong connections to jazz, introduced the artists and gave readings from a wide variety of writers, ancient and modern, between the musical tributes.

Evans's portion carried strong echoes of his February 1966 Town Hall concert. Ira Gitler reported in his review that Evans appeared with the CBS Orchestra on Claus Ogerman's 'Elegia', with the trio on 'Time Remembered', and unaccompanied for "the very affecting threnody 'In Memory Of His Father'". Evans's music for the occasion was entirely appropriate, Gitler noted. "The program was already underway when I tuned in but I was almost immediately locked in by the feeling emanating from all the participants. It was neither saccharine nor maudlin but a heartfelt tribute. The occasion inspired the musicians to a uniformly high level of performance." Gitler also made the telling point that "it is a shame that a tragedy of this magnitude had to provide the reason for one of the best and longest programs of jazz ever presented on TV".[16]

Within days Evans was in Switzerland, appearing thanks to the involvement of his friend Gene Lees in the Montreux festival's organisation. Evans, according to Lees, arrived a few days early and became an enthusiastic sightseer, along with his trio and Lees. The festival that year was held, related Lees, "in the nightclub (as big as a concert hall) of the Montreux Casino, an old-time pleasure-palace".[17] In his *Down Beat* report on the entire festival, Lees wrote: "Everyone agreed that the peak of the festival was the Evans performance. Relaxed, tanned, and in a better frame of mind than at any time in the many years I've known him, Evans played at the absolute peak of his form before an audience breathless with attention. The crowd exploded with applause and wouldn't let him get off the stand. Some of it may have had to do with drummer Jack DeJohnette … he played very free time, but without ever losing the pulse, and his taste was impeccable. The audience went mad over him."[18]

The trio played for just a little less than an hour, and the result would later appear as *At The Montreux Festival*. The repertoire was largely familiar to Evans fans, with only Earl Zindars's bluesy ballad 'Mother Of Earl' diverging from his regular performing set. Evans displays the same zest and intensity evident in the previous summer's live recordings with Philly Joe Jones. His rhythmic thrust is heightened by the power and drive of a drummer whose own concepts of time came to maturity in the wake of Elvin Jones and Tony Williams, and whose understanding of Evans's art was strengthened by the fact that he was a fine pianist in his own right. Although DeJohnette is a busy drummer, full of ideas, nuances and complex patterns, he is an immensely sensitive musician fully capable of conceiving ideas and patterns that easily carry the length of a bar or further. Few of Evans's previous regular drummers were capable of such far-sightedness; consequently, the rhythm was often choppy and stop-start as the drummer tried to fit his fills and emphases in between Evans's habitually jagged and insistent phrasings and asymmetries. With DeJohnette's sophisticated but flowing style the music could breathe more naturally, giving Evans the freedom to develop his improvisations unimpeded by a fear of clashes with the underlying patterns supplied by the drummer.

Bassist Eddie Gomez also benefited from this new arrangement and opened up his phrasing accordingly. This happy combination within the trio, with Gomez correspondingly alert and resourceful, was reflected both in the mood in which Evans arrived onstage at Montreux and the unfeigned adulation of an unusually attentive festival crowd. Each tune's arrangement was well conceived and absorbing in execution, with only the rather overlong bass and drum solos on 'Nardis' – one at the front, one at the end – pushing a performance out of shape. Yet this was, first and foremost, a live performance, and such attempts at re-ordering a staple part of the set helped inspire the performers, to the increased delight of their audience.

As a way of pacing the hour onstage at Montreux in June '68 Evans played two unaccompanied ballads, a new favourite, Denny Zeitlin's 'Quiet Now', making its European debut under his fingers, and 'I Loves You Porgy', normally given a trio treatment by Evans (it had appeared thus on the 1961 Village Vanguard recordings with Motian and LaFaro). 'Quiet Now' was the only selection omitted from the original album release of the concert, due to the time restrictions on vinyl LPs. Twenty minutes per side was a technical optimum in those analogue days to achieve the best possible mastering results and the fullest frequency response from a stylus in a groove – the original Montreux LP was closer to 25 minutes per side.

Evans keeps his reading of 'Quiet Now' dark and intense, spare and reflective, using modulations of key to inject drama and shape into his evolution of the piece, while on 'Porgy' he delivers one of his most perfectly conceived improvisations of the late 1960s, a beautifully judged and deeply felt series of variations and extemporisations on theme and harmony. These two performances occurred at the mid-point of the concert, the resulting applause indicating that all present were aware of his achievement. From there on the trio were flying, finishing with a 'Someday My Prince Will Come' that moves easily and sinuously between 3/4 and 4/4 during Evans's involved extended-phrase solo. This concluded the set, but the audience's demand for an encore led to a version of Evans's own 'Walkin' Up', taken at a bright clip and featuring sparklingly integrated playing from all three men. It was a perfect thank-you to the festival crowd.

Detouring through Holland and London, where they once again appeared at Ronnie Scott's, Evans and his trio returned from their Montreux success to another television date, again for *Dial M For Music*. Evans this time appeared separately with both the trio and The CBS Orchestra which had accompanied him on the Kennedy broadcast of a month or so earlier. On this occasion they stuck to less weighty music, opting for the Claus Ogerman arrangement 'Granadas'. The other featured group on the show was The Modern Jazz Quartet; during the course of the orchestral segment John Lewis joined Evans to perform on two pieces, 'Almost Blues' and 'Chazzer'. Reviewing the broadcast, Leonard Feather felt it was the best show he had seen to date in the series of programmes.[19] All this television exposure and increased touring during 1968 would help Evans to regain some of his lost popularity before the year was out. In the meantime, as summer turned to autumn, he returned to regular trio appearances, including dates at the Top Of The Gate and the Village Vanguard in New York. These were done without DeJohnette.

Simultaneously, Evans took the next logical step in his sequence of unaccompanied piano recordings for Verve by cutting *Alone*, a recital entirely devoid of extra piano tracks. Recorded in September and October 1968, this may be seen as a logical extension of his search for further clarity of line and texture, as he had said in the liner notes to *Further Conversations* – but in his own notes for *Alone* he did not mention this. Instead, he wrote about extending the "great tradition in jazz" of solo piano performances and of his wish that his own performances might have "sufficient merit to carry the listener without distraction to the musical feeling I have strived to accomplish". His other overriding concern, as he put it, was to explore a paradox: "Despite the fact that I am a professional performer, it is true that I have always preferred playing without an audience." Furthermore, he noted, "Perhaps the hours of greatest pleasure in my life have come about as a result of the capacity of the piano to be in itself a complete expressive musical medium. In retrospect, I think that these countless hours of aloneness with music unified the directive energy of my life." In a recording studio, alone with his piano, Evans attempted to reconcile these apparently contradictory artistic and personal impulses. "What I desired to present in a solo piano recording," he wrote, "was especially this unique feeling."[20]

Certainly the music on *Alone* is much more unified and intense than that on *Further Conversations* from the previous year. Here, Evans does not have to consider embellishment, accompaniment or any other aspect of multiple piano tracks. He pares his playing to essentials and concentrates on his involvement with the music. Because of the absence of all other accompaniment, Evans can be as flexible as he needs to be and takes appropriate advantage. He adopts the simplest of approaches: exposition, improvisation, resolution. He also allows himself complete freedom of invention harmonically, rhythmically and melodically. Apart from his natural ability, the resulting power and logic is largely due to his certain vision and thorough preparation.

Talking to Marian McPartland just prior to the recording, Evans was in decisive mood. "You can hear that I know exactly what I am doing," he said. "There's no doubt in my mind when I play. I know the reason for everything I do." As if ruminating on his upcoming solo sessions, he elaborated: "If you play too many things at one time, your whole approach will be vague. You won't know what to leave in and what to take out. I would say to a young musician: know very clearly what you're doing and why – play much less, but be *very clear* about it … Take an idea – any idea – play it upside down, backwards, change the rhythm, and so on. Take any combination of notes that might occur to you and try to find 18 different ways of doing it."[21] With a set of standard songs on *Alone*, he practiced what he preached.

As Evans attempts to penetrate the surface meaning of each tune he reaches different and deeper levels of meaning and inspiration, involving himself not only in any "message" a song might have but also in the beauties to be found in the study and redeployment of its components. Again in his album notes, Evans observes: "As you can readily see from the length of the tracks, I did get involved perhaps most successfully in 'Never Let Me Go'."[22] Running for over 14 minutes, the song provides Evans with sufficient raw material to play himself through most of his own personal licks and clichés into fresh and invigorating musical waters. His inspiration is palpable. Other songs are given less magical transformations, but nothing from these sessions is wholly without its own small successes and surprises, the album being a formidable achievement at a time when Evans's relationship with Verve was winding down. Certainly Doug Ramsey in his *Down Beat* review agreed, making one especially prescient point. "When the dust subsides from the meaningless battles for recognition waged by so many of his contemporaries," wrote Ramsey, "[Evans] will still be there, playing his music as he hears it. And he hears it beautifully."[23] By the end of autumn 1968 the uncertainty over personnel caused by DeJohnette's departure had been resolved. After a short series of deputisations by drummer John Dentz at the Village Vanguard and elsewhere – preserved in part on the *Secret Sessions* – Evans brought in on Eddie Gomez's advice a young drummer making an impact in New York jazz circles, Marty Morell. During this period Evans was again on television screens, this time for NBC as part of a *Camera Three* series. He appeared with his trio and, on two selections, with young flautist Jeremy Steig. Evans had long admired Steig's playing and spirit, and four years earlier had declared: "I think a lot of his talent and ability already. I played flute myself for quite a few years and I know how difficult it is. He plays well and naturally."[24] The two had met in the early 1960s when the flautist was in Paul Winter's band, Evans being particularly struck by the intensity of his playing. Since that time Steig had struck out on his own, at first in a modern jazz context, more recently forming his own group, Jeremy & The Satyrs – a jazz-rock group before the term had been coined. Steig had sat in with Evans a number of times since then at the pianist's invitation, and Evans evidently felt entirely at home with the spirited attack that Steig brought to his instrument.

The success of the TV broadcast – which included new versions of Evans favourites such as 'Love Theme From *Spartacus*' and 'Nardis' plus a workout on 'So What' – and the obvious rapport between the two men led to recording sessions for Verve in February and March 1969. Prior to that, Evans had integrated Marty Morell into the trio so successfully that they won an admiring letter in *Down Beat* after a December performance at The Frog & Nightgown in Raleigh, North Carolina. The writer enthused that the Evans group "seemed to communicate with the audience by a kind of musical osmosis".[25] Meanwhile, the last month of '68 had seen the release of the set from that summer at Montreux. This time Verve resolved the complications of previous ads by simply quoting a string of reviews of the concert from distinguished journals such as *The New York Times*, *Down Beat*, *The Montreal Star*, *Melody Maker* and papers from Italy and Germany.

Also in December 1968 the annual *Down Beat* Readers' Poll confirmed the benefits of Evans's higher public profile during the previous 12 months, elevating him to second place in the piano poll, behind Herbie Hancock (then on the point of leaving Miles Davis) but in front of old rival Oscar Peterson. Confirming the impact of the trio's live work, bassist Eddie Gomez placed eighth in the bass poll, a rise of some six places on the previous year. This resurgence is the more notable for the absence of any Evans recordings in the album-of-the-year section of the poll. In the other main categories, vibes player Gary Burton was voted jazzman of the year, Don Ellis's *Electric Bath* was the top album, and Wes Montgomery, who had died following a heart attack in the summer, was voted into the Hall of Fame – all indicating the public's turn of interest toward a newly confident rock genre. With jazz entering a new phase of eclecticism and diversity in its increasingly fraught attempts to survive the commercial and cultural impact of rock, Evans was being appreciated for his musical consistency and a sustained return to form.

It's ironic, then, that the move to make a record with Steig in the winter and spring of 1969 must be seen at least in part as an attempt by Evans, his management and his record label to re-position the pianist closer to contemporary trends. The young Steig had a stylistic fluency in both jazz and rock, being a technically gifted player with a personalised tone who had the imagination to combine elements of Eric Dolphy's approach to the flute with the style of more mainstream flautists. Still in his twenties, he sported an of-the-moment look, an ideal bonus to help Evans begin to move away from an image that had not progressed since the death of Kennedy and the arrival of The Beatles in the US. The sleeve and title of the Steig record, *What's New?*, was part of this re-positioning. For the first time on a Verve cover, Evans is not dressed in a dark suit and tie, instead choosing a red roll-neck under a sports coat. Beside him an impassioned Steig, his long hair and flute prominent, is caught mid-phrase. The album's title, emblazoned in the latest trendy typeface, directly reflected this new Evans departure. The music, however, is closer to Evans's taste than Steig's: the repertoire is all drawn from songs that Evans had either been familiar with for some time or had written himself. What Steig brings to the record is fire, enthusiasm and constant risk-taking. He makes it into more of a jam session than any record Evans had been involved with since his Riverside and freelancing days.

The presence of two blues numbers aids this impression of looseness. Monk's 'Straight No Chaser' immediately sets the mood, at a brisk tempo, as Evans and Steig move each other to exciting and unusual improvisational paths. The sections on this and other tracks on the album where Evans drops out altogether leave Steig to push ahead in his solos, forcing Gomez and Morell to respond with some hard swinging – something they were not normally called upon to do in this trio. The other blues, the Evans original 'Time Out For Chris', is taken slowly, giving all the participants time to shape their phrases and build the late-night atmosphere. At times here Evans sounds uncannily like Art Tatum on a slow blues, especially during his accompaniment of Steig's heavily vocalised, expressionistic passages. Evans's accompaniment is unusually dense, constantly supplying counterlines to Steig's angular, darting phrases. Steig responds in the way that Benny Carter and other Tatum guest stars did, alternating between heightened and more starkly delineated versions of his normal idiomatic playing, and tending to let Evans fill the cracks.

Other tunes tackled on these dates emphasise similar strengths as well as the basic compatibility of the two men. 'Autumn Leaves' uses the patented Evans intro, but Steig is allowed to state the theme persuasively before a convincingly dynamic improvisation, while Gomez solos not only with great dexterity but also with increased continuity and coherence. Evans himself takes a single-note solo of considerable drive and authority. 'Lover Man' receives a slow, sultry treatment in tune with its character and the performers' own leanings, while 'So What' raises a considerable sweat from all four musicians, with levels of raw excitement seldom reached elsewhere on Evans's recordings as a leader. But there are unresolved problems. The '*Spartacus* Love Theme' finds Steig expressive and tender in the theme statement, but Evans cannibalises his original 1963 recording for the arrangement and even parts of his own solo and accompaniment, crowding Steig uncomfortably and refusing to allow the performance to breathe. For once in his career he could be accused of not listening closely enough to others. On 'What's New?' Steig handles the melody beautifully but seems at sea when he tries to fashion a mid-tempo ballad statement of clear emotional depth – something that comes easily to Evans.

Before *What's New?* was issued by Verve, the label released a compilation, possibly to capitalise on Evans's second Grammy, awarded in the spring of 1969 for the *Montreux* album. *The Best Of Bill Evans* collected some choice cuts from his previous Verve records and added two unreleased trio performances from the 1966 Town Hall concert. The *Montreux* album was given a half-page advertisement in the same *Down Beat* issue that carried the news of its Grammy award, and noted that Evans had been nominated for nearly a dozen more Grammys in as many years.[26] With the release too of *Alone*, which would eventually win its own Grammy nomination and award, the Steig collaboration was largely overlooked. Still, that album could be construed an artistic success and a step forward for both men in different ways; it is perhaps unfortunate that, although the partnership would later be occasionally renewed, nothing more concrete developed from this promising collaboration. Appearing at the Newport festival in July 1969 for the second year running, Evans's trio delivered an energetic closing set on the first evening of the event with Steig guesting on a rapt version of the ballad they had recorded earlier that year, 'Lover Man'.

Evans continued to pursue his career in its familiar pattern for the rest of 1969, playing the best jazz clubs in the US on both coasts and in between, appearing in Europe in the spring, summer and autumn, and providing solid performances at some of the larger theatres that operated a music policy. Evans appeared on the Steve Allen TV show in July, just days after his Newport set. His trio's appearance at the Pescara Festival in Italy in the same month was recorded for Italian radio broadcasts, and later appeared on Italian records – Italian copyright laws until quite recently being notoriously liberal. November performances in Scandinavia and Holland also appeared on record, although many years later Helen Keane would put some of this activity in order by issuing official, professional-quality recordings of one of the Dutch concerts. A special event during that November visit to Europe was a trio performance with the Royal Danish Symphony Orchestra and Danish Radio Big Band. It drew on parts of the repertoire recorded for *Bill Evans And Symphony Orchestra* including 'Blue Interlude', 'Time Remembered' and 'My Bells', plus tunes such as 'Speak Low' and 'Waltz For Debby'. Orchestrations were by Palle Mikkelborg, who also conducted. Evans's performance was taped by Danish radio but at the time of writing has still to appear on CD. The released recordings from Italy and Amsterdam reveal the trio in excellent form and in expansive spirit, while the level of audience appreciation shows conclusively that Evans was treated as something special by European jazz fans at this time (the November 28th concert in Amsterdam has been issued and reissued many times on the Affinity label, boasting superior recording quality and with Evans in particularly fine form). As well as Evans, other major jazz stars such as Miles Davis, Sonny Rollins and Dave Brubeck were finding appreciation for their work in Europe as their options in the US polarised. The US situation was neatly summarised during 1969 by the fate of New York's Village Gate, then one of jazz's most famous clubs. Owner Art D'Lugoff had opened a smaller upstairs room, Top Of The Gate, mainly for piano trios – Evans included – while downstairs he experimented with different musical genres in the main club. He made this switch because across America nightclubs were being deserted by young audiences, who were more likely to light up and go to a "happening" than have a drink while listening to jazz in a glorified bar. D'Lugoff along with many other club owners tried to bring back these high-spending clients by hiring rock-oriented acts, but generally the policy did not work, and by the end of the year he closed his Village Gate "indefinitely".

D'Lugoff said at the time of the closure, "We [cannot] compete with a 3,000-seat auditorium like the Fillmore East … The younger element doesn't drink as much as they used to. We like to keep the prices down, but the artist or their managers won't go along with it."[27] His solution, and one that allowed him to re-open the club, was to give the performers the admission receipts and keep the food and drink money for himself. Other clubs, not so famous or flexible, failed to survive, leaving a much smaller circle of traditional clubs in which jazz musicians could play. Ironically, in the same May '69 *Down Beat* that carried the news of Evans's Grammy was an item headed "Fillmore Jazz Bites Dust; Attendances Low". The article identified a number of causes for the famous rock venue's failure with jazz acts: the Fillmore's neighbourhood was not conducive to visits from older, middle-class people, apparently, and young Fillmore fans spent their dollars on the big rock acts on Fridays and Saturdays rather than waiting until Sunday for jazz.

Aware of these tightened economics at home, Evans welcomed the newly expanding European market, especially the emerging summer festival circuit. In conversation with Brian Hennessy years later he emphasised that he was one of the lucky ones then, rarely going without work involuntarily. "The whole rock scene pushed jazz into a corner in the 1960s," said Evans. "Work and recording opportunities were less frequent … I was fortunate because I had obtained some recognition prior to the rock explosion and I could never complain that I had no work … I play for myself first, not what I think people want to hear. Perhaps I am less flexible as I get older. There will always be those in the avant-garde as I was at one time. They come along and contribute but I do not think there are a great number of genuine avant-garde artists. There are not that many people ahead of their time."[28] This was not a new thought from Evans. In 1970 he told Leonard Feather there was no such thing as the avant-garde. "You can identify it in quotes," said Evans, "but there are some things that are successful musically and are musical; and there are some things that are just a lot of hogwash and a lot of complaining and frustration and affectation. And I think that all you must ask of anything is that it's musical and it's saying something within the musical language, and that's all I want from anything that purports to be music."

Asked by Feather whether he admired any pop music, Evans said: "I do relate to the authentic creations within those idioms; they are, in their own way, little masterpieces. But there aren't many special things, and to think that 100,000 groups can be producing *very special music* is to delude yourself. There just aren't that many talented, creative people around. In the history of classical music there's never more than three or four a generation in the world. And in jazz it's very limited … So you just can't think that this entire rock phenomenon has quality. A lot of it is just a lot of noise, nothing more." In the same unusually expansive Blindfold Test spread over two issues of *Down Beat*, Evans offered more thoughts about worth and the idea of progression in music. "I don't care about the era or anything," he said. "If it's good, it's good … So many of the so-called 'free' things, I think, are trying to be sophisticated in getting out into a weird or strange sound area that was used to death at the turn of the century by classical composers, and certainly is nothing new. The sound area of dissonance or polytonality is nothing that's going to surprise anybody who's sophisticated. The important thing is to make music wherever you're at … the idiom is not important."[2]

Whether Evans was consciously waving goodbye to all that as the decade came to an end or was simply continuing to make his own way in an increasingly diffuse and turbulent music scene is open to conjecture.

But his next projects suggest that it was the latter. Certainly as 1969 ended and 1970 began there were more pressing concerns than whether to hanker after a place within an avant-garde which, in jazz, showed increasing signs of being stuck for a direction in which to be avant.

Evans's next LP project underlined some of those concerns. Recorded during the winter months of 1969 and '70 and completing his relationship with Verve and parent company MGM, *From Left To Right* was a peculiar stab at so-called "easy listening". Evans used an electric piano, the then-fashionable Fender Rhodes. It was the preferred electric instrument of many jazz pianists because, in contrast to cheaper and more primitive models made by other companies, the Rhodes could approximate some of the gradations of tone and touch of an acoustic piano. Its sound too had the volume and flexibility of an electric instrument without being completely divorced from that of its acoustic antecedent. Given these qualities, it was the obvious instrument for Evans when he wanted to try an electric piano. "The only danger," Evans told Leonard Feather, "is that if a pianist plays on [the Fender Rhodes] exclusively, the touch is so light, he would, I think, find it a problem to play piano again. Chick Corea has mentioned this problem to me. Then I mentioned it to Harold Rhodes, the inventor, and he said the action could be regulated, and he's going to have my personal piano regulated to my touch."[30]

From Left To Right set simple popular themes and limited developments against an orchestral backdrop supplied by composer and arranger Michael Leonard, and the record's liner notes consisted of glowing endorsements from Leonard, Harold Rhodes, and Evans's manager Helen Keane. The whole session, though pleasant to the ear, is as close to musical saccharine as Evans came in his entire recording career. Even on the small-group take of 'The Dolphin – Before' the musicians are still never far from easy listening. Evans disingenuously revealed the level of thinking behind the record when discussing a particular track with Leonard Feather. "I had written a little tune called 'Children's Play Song' which I always felt was just a simple little nothing," said Evans. "But Mickey [Leonard] fell in love with it and wrote what was a very austere, slow version of it – because I'd shown him how you'd harmonise it if you wanted to play it in a slow way. The way I conceived of it was the type of tune kids would whistle while out playing hopscotch or something."[31]

By the end of spring 1970 Evans was out of contract and in the middle of a programme of heroin withdrawal and substitution. It involved moving to the synthetic chemical methadone, and eventually proved successful: audiences at concerts that year would notice a subtly different Evans walking out to the piano. All this gave him an opportunity to take stock and to plan fresh moves as the new decade opened. He was certainly aware of an increasing gap in appreciation between audiences in America and in Europe. "I think one of the qualities that the European audiences have a little more," he said in that same Leonard Feather interview, "is that they can enjoy a greater historical spectrum of jazz than the American audiences. We tend to identify with one era – it's got to be the most modern, or else we like Dixieland and we don't like bop, or we like swing … and it seems that European audiences do like the history of jazz, as long as it's got that quality. I find that some of the later-generation jazz players experience a much more welcoming audience in Europe that in the US. People like Ben Webster, the great players, whom American audiences somewhat ignored as they grew older."[32] Whether or not Evans was unconsciously putting himself in that role – or anticipating it – he would find European critics and fans providing something of a safe haven during the first half of the 1970s. Indeed, interviewed in summer 1970 by Randi Hultin in Norway, he took up this theme again. "This is an excellent audience," he said of the local Kongsberg festival, "and it's weird to think that a little place like [this] can hire musicians from all over the world just because they like jazz here. I admire the enthusiasm of the organisers who do all of this without earning a penny for it. Every jazz musician should appreciate this. At least I do … Jazz can't exist without somebody working for it with love. These days here … have really meant something to me. It's a beautiful place, and I've been able to relax."[33]

At the same time, Evans displayed his age-old ambivalence to appearing live. Continuing her line of questions, Hultin felt that what bothered Evans most was constant moving, always under pressure to keep the trio together and take responsibility for them. Evans concurred: "Can you imagine if somebody would give me a scholarship award? I would really be happy to be able to just sit and write music for a year."[34]

CHAPTER 12

Great Expectations (1970-1972)

"BILL ALWAYS SAID THAT HE WAS VERY CAREFUL ABOUT WORKING A TUNE OUT AT HOME AND GETTING IT TO HIS LIKING BEFORE HE WOULD PLAY IT IN PUBLIC."

PIANIST AND INTERVIEWER MARIAN McPARTLAND

Following Evans's success at the 1968 Montreux festival, his appearance there in 1970 was eagerly anticipated by European audiences, musicians and media. It was to be at the same venue, the Casino, with Eddie Gomez along for a second time but with Marty Morell in the drum chair in place of Jack DeJohnette. The trio played two sets on the evening of June 19th, part of which appeared on the subsequent LP, *Montreux II*, on CTI. Creed Taylor's CTI label was his next step on from A&M, for whom Creed Taylor Inc had made a string of highly successful albums by musicians such as Wes Montgomery, George Benson and Paul Desmond. Gaining the rights to the Evans concert was something of a coup for Taylor's fledgling company

Preparing for a concert in 1970

and underlined its ambition and intended scope. It seems that just one of the two Evans Montreux sets was recorded, and only half of that set was released by CTI. The other eight selections – none duplicating repertoire on the CTI release – were taped by Radio Suisse Romande and are apparently still in existence in that corporation's archives.

Taylor was doubly fortunate in that the concert turned out to be an outstanding one. Evans was well aware of the level of inspiration that night: "We had a good reception … in 1968 but this evening surpassed it. Enthusiasm is infectious, even though the artist never really believes that one specific performance to which an audience responds is really that much better than a hundred others … Jazz will never be a mass-appeal music, but there is nothing more that I can give an audience that I give myself … I'm the only one who can tell if I'm reaching the objective. When an audience responds with applause, it can give real impetus, but if I had a choice, I'd prefer no expression of enthusiasm as, to me, it can be a distraction."[1]

Listening to the released recordings of that June 1970 Montreux concert, the audience's overwhelming reception and their complete quiet during the music helped to make it a special occasion. Whatever Evans's qualms about audiences, the heightened responses of Gomez and Morell make for a highly-charged trio performance. The repertoire contains nothing new: Evans had drafted in a couple of his earlier compositions such as '34 Skidoo' and 'Peri's Scope', but they were well known to his fellow musicians and to Evans aficionados. Evans himself seems to be offering nothing beyond his normal levels of thought and creativity. His tendency to push rhythmically and pick tempos that were perhaps a little faster than he would have chosen five years previously provides a hint that he is avoiding the deeper, more resonant emotional states of his earlier career as a leader.

Pianist Warren Bernhardt noticed this in Evans's playing as the 1970s began. "Every time I'd go to hear him when he was with Marty and Eddie, it seemed like he was painting himself into some kind of a corner," said Bernhardt. "I don't know if it was choice of material or chemical or what. He was rushing a lot and going through the motions. And I thought it was odd for a guy who had so much – that's why I suspected it might have been something else. Do you know what I mean, painting yourself into a corner? I mean he almost had no escape from the material."[2] Don Nelson gave *Montreux II* a warm welcome in *Down Beat*, but touched on similar concerns. "If the set sounds a trifle familiar, think of it this way: hearing Evans is like visiting a brilliant friend – you know pretty much what he's going to say, but he says it so well and with such sensibility and clarity that you are charmed every time."[3]

Perhaps Evans felt cornered too by his responsibilities toward the group and its repertoire. Pianist Marian McPartland shed light on the negative aspects of such a task. "Bill Evans used to hone his trio and shape the personalities over a very long period, and he did think along very different lines from me," she said. "Whereas I like to take a new tune and wing it, even if it's a tune I haven't ever played, Bill always said that he was very careful about working a tune out at home and getting it to his liking before he would play it in public. I don't always do that. Bill had some saying … 'I'd rather learn one tune in 24 hours than 24 tunes in an hour.' But that's the kind of musician he was."[4] With such a cautious attitude toward repertoire and taking chances, Evans was likely to hit periods where he would stagnate and lack inspiration. The most direct way out of this was to seek inspiration from the trio, but the chances for Gomez and Morell to catch him unawares, to stretch him unexpectedly, were directly lessened by such careful preparation.

From Switzerland the trio moved on to fulfil engagements in Norway and Germany in summer 1970. In Norway Evans talked once more to Randi Hultin, expanding on his methods of practice. "I play a lot privately, but the trio has never had rehearsals. Not since it started. The cohesion happens on stage or in the studio. The music develops by itself at each concert. There are times when we might need to practice a little more, though," he said. "Including recording [we play] about 40 weeks per year … I want to write more music – something more serious, for example, or music for film. New melodies. But I'll probably play until I go to the grave. I'm never happy if I can't play. After a period without a gig, I get depressed. Everything seems so meaningless. A musician can't just stop playing."[5] Evans's commitment to regular work had the trio returning quickly to America and the clubs, mostly the Top Of The Gate in New York. Even though he'd left Verve, they took a full-page ad in *Down Beat* in April 1970 to publicise the release of *Alone*, keeping Evans's name in front of the public for the summer season. The magazine's review of the LP did not appear until September, but it was unstinting in its praise. Although Newport was not on Evans's festival schedule this year, the trio did appear at Monterey in September and at the Pacific Northwest Jazz Spectacular in Seattle toward the end of 1970. The Monterey appearance was Evans's first there as a leader, but due to pressures on the festival's schedule the trio's time onstage on the Sunday afternoon was limited. Two numbers by the trio alone were followed by 'Elegia', 'Granadas' and 'Time Remembered', accompanied by the Oakland Youth Chamber Orchestra; all three arrangements stemmed from the still-popular Ogerman collaboration album *With Symphony Orchestra*. Critic Harvey Siders commented that the final piece "gave Evans the only real opportunity to hold any conversations with himself".[6]

At the Pacific Northwest event Evans had first appeared as part of an afternoon piano workshop along with Joe Zawinul and Herbie Hancock, appearing for his segment with Eddie Gomez and interspersed by unaccompanied renditions of familiar tunes. The following day he returned with his trio for a more orthodox set, sandwiched between the groups of Miles Davis and Herbie Hancock. The set was described by reviewer Steven F. Brown as something of an anticlimax. "Evans indulged in several rather dead cocktail-lounge tunes," wrote Brown, "made worse by rude color changes in the lighting which would ruffle most musicians. Repetition of the order of solos from one number to the next made things boring after the fourth or fifth number, even (apparently) for Evans himself and Morell. Gomez never ceased to be inspiring or inspired."[7]

The group and Helen Keane did not neglect the television opportunities that came their way during 1970. As part of the *Homewood* series of educational TV programmes, an hour-long special, *Profile In Cool Jazz*, was made in early November: the Evans trio shared the hour with Gary Burton's quartet. The pianist's segment consisted of superior workouts on 'Waltz For Debby', 'Someday My Prince Will Come', 'Like Someone In Love' and 'So What'. Observer Leonard Feather commented: "Evans and his colleagues ... set a gentle mood subtly underlined by the sympathetic camerawork and lighting."[8] The show was syndicated to almost 200 educational TV stations around the US, while the soundtrack appeared briefly on the small label Red Bird (better known as the home of pop girl-group The Shangri-Las).

Also in November 1970 Evans signed a new recording contract, this time with the jazz wing of Columbia, a section run at that time by Bruce Lundvall. Evans went into the studios for his new company and followed the lead of Columbia supremo Clive Davis who was very keen for his jazz artists to play fashionable electric jazz. In an interview the following spring, Davis elaborated on his expectations of the company's jazz signings – which at that time included Ornette Coleman, Weather Report and John McLaughlin. "We're not interested in signing artists still involved with traditional jazz," said Davis, "in the same way [that] I'm not interested in signing people involved with 'rock & roll' ... I am really interested in communicating to new audiences, in people using their skills, using their ideas, to communicate to new audiences in terms that new audiences can understand and accept." Davis used Evans as an example. "A Bill Evans – how do you get him out of what he's been doing for the last few years and say 'use your genius and start communicating, get into exciting areas, use other instrumentation, bring your musical ideas to new people'? If the artist is not interested in doing that, then I'm not interested in having that artist record for us."[9]

The results of Evans's initial duo session for Columbia with Eddie Gomez were unsatisfactory for all involved. As the bassist recalled, the idea was for "an acoustic/electric duo collaboration, containing some new and somewhat experimental material ... We even flirted with the idea of overdubbing the electric instruments. By the way, 'Morning Glory' remains the only example of my bass guitar work to ever be issued – with good reason! In the end, this project was mercifully abandoned – and I subsequently told Bill that we had come dangerously close to a lifelong career in motel lounges all across the Midwest."[10]

It is both strange and telling that Evans mixed acoustic and electric pianos for his last project with Verve/MGM and his first with Columbia – and that neither amounted to much. Indeed, that initial Columbia duo project was abandoned well before its completion, and it would wait until 1998 to be issued commercially. As if that were not enough, the second attempt for Columbia also involved electricity in the form of Evans's Fender Rhodes electric piano, set up alongside his normal acoustic grand. This was in effect the first time that the jazz world would sit up and pay attention to Evans's use of the electric keyboard, because *From Left To Right*, the final Verve/MGM project, also made with a Rhodes, had not been widely promoted and had registered virtually zero impact.

The second Columbia session has Evans confining the Rhodes to a supportive role as a "colouring" instrument, rather than boldly claiming it as a new extension of his expression and musicality. Tentatively still locating its most effective role in his existing set-up rather than trying to find a fresh setting for the instrument, he would only use it sparingly in the years ahead. Later comments suggest that he never took the electric piano seriously on its own terms, in contrast to younger jazz players then working with amplified music, such as Joe Zawinul and Chick Corea. "I've been happy to use the Fender Rhodes to add a little colour to certain performances," said Evans, "but only as an adjunct. No electric instrument can begin to compare with the quality and resources of a good acoustic piano."[11] Within a few years Keith Jarrett would be saying similar things as he permanently abandoned electric keyboards.

The resulting Columbia release, *The Bill Evans Album*, would go on to win two Grammys, yet it remains an odd experience for the listener more than 30 years after its recording. On paper it should have been a major event: a number of new songs were prepared, and reworkings were made of pieces that Evans had not often visited since originally recording them at the beginning of the 1960s. "As far as selecting the material," he said, "I had to think in terms of the type of vehicle that the three of us could play together. There were quite a few ballads and things that I had never done that I could have included, but I don't feel that it would have offered much in the way of creative potential. Mostly, I just wanted to find the best things that gave a little indication of what I might be into writing at this time."[12]

Certainly Columbia's publicity department treated the album as a triumph, trumpeting it in ads as a spectacular realisation of Evans's all-around abilities as a musician: the acoustic and electric pianist, the composer and arranger. In copy that manages to be even more embarrassing than Verve's latter-day efforts for the pianist, the Columbia ads read: "One day Bill Evans, who plays the Steinway, was discussing his next album with Bill Evans, who plays the Fender Rhodes electric piano. During the discussion someone suggested that Bill's next album contain only songs written by a writer occasionally used by Bill Evans. Lo and behold the name suggested was Bill Evans. And naturally Bill Evans the arranger also got involved. So there you have it: Bill Evans's first album for Columbia ... It's the first time these four guys did an album together. It sounds so good we don't think they'll ever break up."[13] No – the only people who broke up were the readers trying to work out what this ad's un-credited author was on at the time.

Any reasonably alert listener will notice Evans's unimaginative use of the Fender Rhodes on this record, given its potential as a source of colour and texture in his arrangements. He is happy to feature the instrument, and indeed the album kicks off with him playing it unaccompanied to introduce the theme for 'Funkarello', a tune held over from the old *Interplay* sessions. He solos on the Rhodes and, as the album progresses, switches regularly between acoustic and electric instruments. His first 'Funkarello' solo benefits from a dirty, smudgy timbre, and the switch to acoustic for the second solo, after Gomez's brief bass outing, provides an incisive contrast. To this extent the tune is arranged beyond the acoustic routine that Evans used normally with his trio. A nice touch comes at the end where, as the bass and drums finish, Evans turns to the Rhodes to execute a series of asymmetric embellishments on a fast blues-laden ascending run.

What Evans plays in his electric improvisations during these sessions is identical in conception to what he would normally play on acoustic piano. He makes no allowances for (and no moves to exploit) the unique characteristics of the instrument for his own artistic benefit. This must surely be because at heart he didn't believe in its intrinsic worth. There is also a conspicuous lack of double-tracking passages where the Rhodes could fill out or add another dimension to the sound of the acoustic rendering of a tune – for example on the pretty, bittersweet waltz 'The Two Lonely People'. This piece otherwise contains an exemplary Evans improvisation that arises with perfect pacing and logic from the initial theme statement, developing the ritardando and contrasts in dynamics that are inherent to the song's construction as it winds its way through a rapid series of typical Evans modulations. At the performance's close, Evans's unbroken improvisation – without bass or drum interludes – resolves seamlessly into a recapitulation of the theme, describing a perfect and simple parabola in its ABA form. The electric piano is not used on this track.

A similar construction is followed on the common-time 'Sugar Plum', with Evans moving from solo theme statement on acoustic piano to extemporisation. This time, however, a Gomez bass solo occurs at mid-point, and to accompany this Evans switches to Rhodes. The pianist solos on electric and acoustic keyboards after Gomez and then takes the piece out unaccompanied, once more on acoustic piano. The underlying harmonic organisation of the tune, which allows the players to improvise through all 12 keys, is explained in the album's liner notes. These reveal a typical Evans construction designed to stimulate his harmonic imagination. "The trio proceeds through the cycle of keys," wrote Fred Binkley in the liner note, "so that each time the melody is played it goes up a fourth or down a fifth, going through the cycle of fifths. Never mind, it all comes out where it should."[14]

'Waltz For Debby' closes side one of the original LP and is the first selection with electric and acoustic instruments played simultaneously. The rich acoustic piano sound achieved in the Columbia studios provides a pleasant contrast to so many of his albums for previous companies, and there is an agreeable combination of electric and acoustic timbres and textures. The performance is a relaxed one after another introductory solo piano excursion, with the arrangement once again asking for a Gomez solo to separate Evans's electric and acoustic solos. This time, however, the bass solo only serves to slacken the tension-and-release set in place by the rest of the arrangement, clouding the structure and diluting the piece's impact. Gomez cannot be blamed for this: the solo was simply allocated an inappropriate position.

'T.T.T. (Twelve Tone Tune)' starts as an out-of-tempo statement by Evans, completed in metre by the trio, and then moves into a medium-tempo duet between acoustic piano and bass. It then picks up momentum with the introduction of drums halfway through the chordal cycle. Evans devised the cycle by using a 12-tone scale. The 12-tone technique for composing had been developed in the early 1920s when composer Arnold Schoenberg codified the most widely-adopted 12-tone theories and practices. Conventional tonality is replaced with a system where all 12 notes of the chromatic scale are given equal importance. The notes are arranged by the composer in a particular order – the "note row" – on which the composition is then based. Evans was not the first to look into the idea of 12-tone jazz tunes – Leonard Feather had published one in the 1960s. But he was one of a small jazz minority equipped to develop his own personal take on the theory. Evans decided not to adhere too closely to the principles of 12-tone organisation, which included such rules as no note repetition before the full note row is used, no accidentals, and no attempt to reconfigure the tone row into a progression using conventional tonality. In this he was following the practice of many composers who "personalised" their use of the system in this way.

Bassist Gomez later pointed out that 'T.T.T.' was derived from a 12-tone row that Evans "harmonized so that it sounded tonal. We even considered trying to improvise using only the 12 tones of the row, but it was too difficult".[15] All three musicians play with conviction on the track, and it is exceedingly well organised – but the music does not communicate a great deal beyond a feeling of complexity and intellectual stimulation for the players involved and for people interested in unusual musical configurations. Evans's comment in the record's liner note suggests that he recognised the limited objectives of such a composition. "I think something about the row has some validity in music," he wrote, "but I wouldn't want to base a composition on it except as a challenge."[16] On this piece, the electric keyboard is used under Gomez's solo and for a series of exchanges with the drums before the acoustic piano's return.

'Re: Person I Knew' had been in the trio's performing repertoire for some time and was first recorded in Evans's Riverside days. He briefly states its initial theme here, unaccompanied on the Fender Rhodes, before bass and drums arrive. The underlying blues structure allows Evans to introduce occasional blues inflections and allusions, the subdued, "smoky" tone of the Rhodes being very effective in this idiom. During the Gomez solo midway through – apparently an inescapable feature of this Evans album – the pianos are switched again and the piece is completed with the acoustic. The last track on *The Bill Evans Album*, 'Comrade Conrad', is another Evans 3/4 ballad, originally instigated by a commission for a toothpaste commercial but developed more fully when it became a dedication to Conrad Mendenhall, a close friend who had died in a car crash. Once again the listener and the musicians are taken through all 12 keys in the course of the piece's harmonic journey, this device clearly stimulating the pianist's musical imagination and providing a defence against monotony and lack of contrast. The mood alternates between elegy and contentment. It is one of the briefer performances on the album, containing no bass solo, and it finishes with a perfectly executed, eloquent re-statement of the theme – initially unaccompanied, then with bass and drums for the hushed concluding bars. Another older Evans composition, 'Fun Ride', was recorded at the album sessions in May and June 1971 but left off the LP. It recently surfaced on the same Columbia compilation of Evans rarities that included the unissued piano-and-bass duets from 1970. A further adventure through the key signatures, it was perhaps thought too similar to others on an album already running over the usual playing length. Containing no electric piano work, it was an obvious candidate for omission, despite the cute unaccompanied piano ending.

The Bill Evans Album was clearly considered by Columbia as a major part of the campaign to reassert Evans's relevance and potency in contemporary music, but it was not welcomed without reservation on its release. In *Down Beat* Michael Levin praised Evans's unparalleled harmonic and melodic richness, but repeatedly expressed unease with his use of rhythm. "For some reason," wrote Levin, "when he starts to cook these days, Evans also starts to push – and in a trio above all other groups, that can be death to the beat. As a pianist, Evans is so far ahead of most others that it is bothersome to encounter this feeling of unease about time. On 'T.T.T.', for example, his inventions around the tonal row are interesting and pianistic but wobbly, even at times rushing."[17]

But during the summer of 1971 the sessions were successfully concluded and such tepid reactions were still in the future. Evans's health had improved and with it came a revival in his energies, so he enjoyed an active and diverse live career throughout 1971. As well as the usual clubs, he appeared in some unusual settings, including the early-summer American College Jazz Festival, held in the Kennedy Centre in Washington DC, and the July 24th "piano party" held at New York's Town Hall. His involvement in the College festival lasted two days as guest soloist with the University of Illinois Band, and he finished the first evening with a series of delicate and well-appreciated solos. The second evening he was billed alongside Clark Terry and Evans's old friend Mundell Lowe to perform with a bassist and drummer borrowed from the big-band; one observer thought this group was "the most musical of the festival".[18] The piano party was part of a series of Saturday night "Connoisseur Concerts" produced by Willis Conover, a Voice Of America broadcaster and long-standing promoter of jazz causes. The event occurred in the middle of a group of club bookings which included a return to the Top of the Gate. According to *Down Beat* Evans hosted a memorable event, where "Bob Greene played Jelly Roll Morton, Teddy Wilson (with Milt Hinton and Oliver Jackson) and Billy Taylor (with Bob Cranshaw and Bob Thomas) and Evans (Eddie Gomez, Marty Morell) played themselves, and Cecil Taylor, on solo piano, made some fantastic sounds".[19]

These unusual events, coupled with the increased promotion and better distribution available to a major company like Columbia, gave Evans greater sustained prominence – and this in turn led to improved record sales confirmed by higher positions in the year-end popularity polls. The trio finished up 1971 once more at the Village Vanguard before travelling to Europe for what proved to be an extensive tour in January and February of 1972 through Britain, France, Holland, Germany and Italy. Evans's partner Ellaine accompanied him for much of the trip. To judge from the collection of broadcasts which have subsequently been released on record, Evans was only intermittently inspired on the tour, and would sometimes spin out one idea over many bars with little effort at development. Most concerts followed the standard form, although a residency at Ronnie Scott's in London gave Evans an opportunity to unpack his travel bag and settle, if only briefly, into a daily routine. The pirate release from the Paris concert of February 6th, taken from an ORTF broadcast, concentrates for the most part on the minor-key section of the concert, with considered versions of 'Time Remembered' and 'Two Lonely People', although no startling conclusions are reached on the up-tempo 'T.T.T.'. But the trio combines beautifully on 'Re: Person I Knew', starting from an almost imperceptible whisper and moving into a medium-tempo trio exercise, Evans playing with that incredible, distilled depth of feeling unique to him. The piece's unity is disturbed by a somewhat frenetic solo from the otherwise impeccable Gomez, but there is still much to marvel at. The concert shows no signs of the Fender Rhodes, although other players of his generation, such as Ahmad Jamal, were appearing at festivals around this time with both acoustic and electric keyboards.

By mid March 1972 the trio were back in New York, in time for Evans to pick up his two Grammys for *The Bill Evans Album* and to perform 'T.T.T.' on the TV broadcast of the event. During April he was at the Village Vanguard for a series of dates, but by then was already deep into rehearsals and preparations for the recording of a major piece he'd commissioned some months earlier from George Russell. The composer and theorist had recently returned to the US to teach at the New England Conservatory after an extended stay in Europe that had lasted for most of the 1960s. With his old friend and colleague back in America, Evans turned to Russell when planning the follow-up to his Grammy-winning debut album for Columbia. Commissioning a work for big-band and soloist from another musician would not only put the resulting record in significant contrast to his first for the label, but would demonstrate to Clive Davis and others in the Columbia hierarchy that Evans had a keen ambition and was serious about expanding his music. After all, the *With Symphony Orchestra* album on Verve had proved to be durably popular and influential around the world, with Evans often being asked to perform some of its arrangements live.

Russell had most recently attracted wide attention following critical acclaim for his *Othello* ballet music of 1967 and *Electronic Sonata For Souls Loved By Nature*, premiered in Europe in 1969. The eight-part composition for big-band and piano trio that emerged for Evans was called *Living Time* and fits logically into the evolution of Russell's compositions and theories. Russell had at first hesitated about the commission, but decided that he could accommodate Evans's musical demands alongside his own. "Bill and I are both involved with modal music," Russell said at the time, "but we have sort of gone off at right angles from each other over the years. Bill is into more tonal playing. I haven't stayed there; I've been working in extensions, the outer reaches of modal things. But I love and respect Bill's playing so much that I really couldn't resist the challenge. As I saw it, the task would be to create a mode that enhanced his work without inhibiting my own."[20] This meant two things. First, Evans may have had his name first on the album's cover, but as with other such projects he functioned more as an improvising soloist playing against a musical backdrop that he is not normally associated with. Second, the dialogue between orchestra and soloist was set within a musical language devised by Russell. In this sense the project had distinct echoes of the relationship that Russell and Evans had enjoyed at the close of the 1950s. It also followed on directly from those recent works of Russell's.

Living Time is a continuous suite in eight sections, and preoccupation with rhythm is immediately evident. A top-notch orchestra was used for this daring and absorbing work, the producers taking advantage of many musicians' desires to work on a Russell project. Among the large cast of notables, apart from the Evans trio, are Snooky Young, Ernie Royal and Richard Williams (trumpets), Jimmy Giuffre, Sam Rivers and Joe Henderson (saxophones), Sam Brown (guitar), Ron Carter and Stanley Clarke (basses), Tony Williams (drums), Garnett Brown (trombone) and Howard Johnson (flute, tuba, bass clarinet). Evans plays both acoustic and electric pianos. Considering the forces at Russell's disposal and the composer's generally uncompromising stance in the presentation of his music, Evans was taking a high risk in producing such an album for a record company so geared to success. If the record was to fail with the critics and sell poorly, Evans and his management would risk being frozen out by Columbia.

Listening to the record again three decades or so after its creation, it's clear that Russell and Evans largely gave Clive Davis at Columbia what he wanted: *Living Time* is an extended work that employs sound and rhythm in thoroughly contemporary ways. At this time Miles Davis's electric *Bitches' Brew* album was in the shops and influencing people, as were records from Tony Williams's LifeTime group with guitarist John McLaughlin and the initial Weather Report album. The music on *Living Time* has an overwhelming sonic punch in several of its movements, and builds up to fantastic swirling climaxes of sound, usually augmented by electric instruments. As such it has few rivals in jazz outside Coltrane's *Ascension* and the dense forests of sound erected by Alexander Von Schlippenbach's Globe Unity group in Germany. There is a wild energy in this music that is immensely exhilarating, almost anarchic: listen, for example, to the driving backbeat of 'Event 6' being cut across by typically oblique Russell counterpoint and a half-valve trumpet solo from Snooky Young. There are long passages of lyrical and rhythmic continuity – 'Event 5', opening with an arpeggio that recalls Cecil Taylor's 1961 composition, 'Mixed', is particularly lucid against a strong rock backbeat and riff patterns from a Fender electric bass. We also arrive at sections which highlight Evans's reflective piano at its most beguiling, as on the closing measures of 'Event 5' and the opening of 'Event 6'. Other parts seem to have grown organically from Miles Davis's contemporary ideas and are then taken a few degrees further, such as the first minute or so of 'Event 2' that reflects the specific soundscapes of Davis's *Filles de Kilimanjaro*. The almost Moorish piano soliloquies in 'Event 4' are surrounded by driving rock passages and other more chaotic sections where great splashes of sound dominate, echoing Gil Evans and, more distantly, Duke Ellington at his most strident. Yet as much as there are echoes of existing music in *Living Time*, there are also anticipations of things to come. Much of the record has the specific electric/acoustic sound that would fascinate Gil Evans for most of the last two decades of his life as well as the heavy rock rhythms he came to prefer. Russell was also innovative in the way he used ostinato and other simple rock devices on which to hang so much of his music, especially in its most extreme sections.

Where does Bill Evans fit into all of this? To his credit he goes against his own readily identifiable style, adapting and moulding his strong musical personality to fit the score in front of him. He plays with concision and force, often using phrases that are found nowhere elsewhere in his recorded output. He assimilates Russell's musical language and moulds it to create a new type of keyboard eloquence, especially with the more astringent intervals and instrumental combinations that Russell prefers. This is nowhere more in evidence than the opening minutes of 'Event 8', the concluding section, where the score calls for dissonances closer to the extremes of Cecil Taylor, or Aaron Copland's 'Piano Variations' and 'Sonata For Piano', than the lush, romantic modality Evans normally employed.

This is a terse and extreme harmonic idiom, especially in the jazz world – and perhaps this was the biggest reason for the piece's general failure to make a popular mark. It is difficult music to absorb and listen to. Its length and musical architecture test the listener's staying power and provide few natural aural landmarks – there are no vocals and few easily-grasped melody lines; the motifs instead reside mostly in the various rhythm sections. But the greatest hurdle for the listener is probably the poor recording. There are simply too many problems evident in the balance of the various instrumental forces to list usefully here. If any major jazz album of the past 30 years or so needs a sympathetic remix, then this is a leading candidate. All its difficulties aside, this large-scale work was a major achievement for Russell and Evans, and one that is unjustly neglected both in the history of the pianist's overall career and the development of contemporary jazz in the early 1970s.

With its deep complexities and swirling textures, its deployment of many different rhythms including rock grooves, and its use of acoustic and electric instruments, as well as Evans playing concert grand and Fender Rhodes, *Living Time* left many observers of the time confused. Record-buyers simply stayed away in droves. With jazz increasingly polarised between purist acoustic styles and the rapidly-evolving jazz-rock or fusion factions, such a determinedly hybrid venture had no sure contemporary platform. It lacked the irony and textural clarity of contemporary works by Carla Bley, let alone the more orthodox use of rock elements as heard in her *Escalator Over The Hill*. The music was too difficult for quick assimilation by the average jazz-rock fan of the time, who was probably still reeling from the effects of the first Iron Butterfly album and the more subtly presented complexities of Davis's *Bitches' Brew*. *Living Time* was also too far away from Evans's normal ambit to appeal strongly to his regular fan-base. Nevertheless, both pianist and composer remained proud of the work. Evans would be happy to appear as soloist in Russell's presentation of *Living Time* at Carnegie Hall in 1974, while the composer would later name his own ensemble The Living Time Orchestra.

More immediately, however, Columbia did virtually nothing to promote the release or Evans himself in the winter of 1972-73. Russell, heavily committed to his teaching studies and increasingly taken up by further development of his Lydian theories, withdrew from composing for almost five years. Columbia left Evans to his own devices for a while before deciding not to renew his contract. The feeling by this time was clearly mutual, for Evans and Helen Keane were less than impressed by Columbia's lack of sympathy for an artist of his stature.

Evans worked hard through the summer and autumn of 1972. He made more TV and radio appearances in the US, including an appearance at Carnegie Hall in July as part of the newly revamped Newport In New York festival, broadcast by Voice Of America. He flew to Europe in June for a brief visit, with British drummer Tony Oxley appearing on drums as deputy for an unavailable Marty Morell. Evans and his manager began to look for their next recording deal. Nothing was resolved by the time Evans left the US in December 1972 for a tour that would take him first to France, in tandem with Phil Woods's European Rhythm Machine, then in January 1973 to Japan. Late in that month a concert at Tokyo's Yubinchokin Hall was taped and broadcast by a local FM jazz station. The technical and musical quality was high enough for Evans and Keane to sanction a release of selected tracks on Sony in Japan and CBS/Columbia in Europe, while North American rights eventually went to the Fantasy group of labels. So it was that in a single live date the past and future of Evans's recording associations were briefly combined.

CHAPTER 13

Rebuilding from the Rubble (1973-1976)

"I THINK BILL WAS VERY TOUCHED WHEN STAN GETZ WARMLY WISHED HIM A HAPPY BIRTHDAY AND PLAYED AN IMPROMPTU 'HAPPY BIRTHDAY' BEFORE AN AUDIENCE OF 7,000 PEOPLE."

MANAGER HELEN KEANE ON EVANS IN HOLLAND ON HIS 45th BIRTHDAY

The Tokyo concert of January 1973 found the Evans/Gomez/Morell trio playing an adjusted and expanded repertoire, even when compared to the concerts they played just a month earlier in France. There were many welcome arrivals: 'Up With The Lark' by Jerome Kern, 'T.T.T.T.', the second of Evans's 12-tone compositions, 'Mornin' Glory' by Bobbie Gentry, Clare Fischer's 'When Autumn Comes', 'Yesterday I Heard The Rain', and 'Hullo Bolinas' by Steve Swallow. There were old friends too: 'On Green Dolphin Street' and 'Gloria's Step' were once more regulars in the set. Not included on the released album but also played that night were 'Emily', 'Who Can I Turn To?' and 'Waltz For Debby', making for a fine balance between old

Evans and his new bearded look of the early 1970s

and new. The Tokyo concert reveals the trio functioning at a high level, with each member by this time able to anticipate whatever direction the music might take. Evans plays with restraint and controlled power, his touch superbly caught by the recording engineers, his mood buoyant. Gomez is at a peak. His extravagance of earlier years is more contained and his ideas more fully matured and developed, while his technique is no less forcefully deployed, but now more closely complementing Evans's. His ability to create and carry through a more vocalised approach to the instrument, even at speed, is much improved, and suits Evans better than his approach of the late 1960s.

There is also a new rhythmic ease from Gomez that comes close to that of Scott LaFaro: space and simplicity live meaningfully alongside complexity and drama. This allows a true counterpoint to exist, as is most excellently demonstrated during Evans's solo on the 3/4-time 'Up With The Lark'. Here each player toys with the metre in simple but delightful ways, moving phrases and notes between each other or setting up counterlines that effectively highlight the other's playing. Gomez is a more assured, much less frantic soloist, prepared to build a statement rather than rush in with a bag of pyrotechnics to knock the listener flat. In the midst of this relaxed, improved dialogue between piano and bass, drummer Marty Morell keeps the beat alive, remaining sensitive not only to dynamics but to the very nature of the basic pulse and avoiding the feel of a mere metronome.

Of the older material, 'Gloria's Step' comes off particularly well. Evans's ease with its augmented progression suggests that he may well have had fun had he ever tackled some of Eric Dolphy's compositions, the dense harmonic language and unresolved patterns of which would have brought him a different stimulus than the more familiar patterns of the popular song form. Of the new material played, the most technically challenging and musically intriguing is 'T.T.T.T.', the second Evans 12-tone composition, taking him a few steps further into this discipline and calling for all three musicians to dig even deeper into their artistic and technical resources. But the most subtly arresting is the beautiful Steve Swallow melody, 'Hullo Bolinas', played with consummate restraint and tenderness by Evans alone. Opening with an almost wistful theme statement, and its slow waltz time carrying echoes of works by Villa Lobos and Milhaud, the piece rises to an eloquent but muted climax before falling to a fragile, dignified pianissimo resolution. In the catalogue of Evans's later live recordings, this Tokyo concert occupies a definite high point. But with the uncertainty after the expiry of his Columbia contract, it had to wait until July 1974 for its official release in the US.

Evans and his trio were in high spirits and generally relaxed at this concert, partly explained by the improvement in Evans's personal life. He had met a young woman, Nenette Zazzata; at first he became infatuated with her, and later fell in love. This personal upturn was shattered by the reaction of his partner Ellaine after Evans told her the position when he was back in New York early that spring. Waiting until Evans left the city to play on the West Coast, she committed suicide by throwing herself under a subway train. This shocking and desperate act by someone who had been through so much with Evans since the beginning of the 1960s devastated him and all who were close to the couple. Gene Lees wrote, "I can barely listen to [Evans's] performance of 'Hi Lili Hi Lo' [from the album *Intuition*], [Ellaine's] favourite song. And I can only guess what Helen [Keane] went through at the time: Bill was out of town, and she had to identify the body."[1] It was several weeks before Evans was able to honour his professional commitments once more.

An appearance by the trio in spring 1973 at the Jazz Showcase in Chicago found the group in striking form but sticking to familiar grooves. Reviewer Jon Balleras observed: "Evans has devoted his musical life to finding ways of moving easily within the confines of the 32-bar song form. Appropriately, his group began their first set … with an up-tempo version of Evans's 'Very Early' … If I had had a camera with me this evening, the one shot that I'd have taken would have been of Evans not playing. While the uninitiated may think Bill is catching short naps as he bows his head over the keyboard during his sidemen's solos, he, of course, is actually listening intently to his cohorts." Balleras detected a difference in the playing. "Whatever happened to the unashamedly lyrical Bill Evans?" he asked. "Is it that Evans once took Miles Davis's remark that he doesn't swing hard enough too seriously?"[2] Before 1973 was over, Evans appeared across the country from Boston to Los Angeles (in the new Shelly's Manne-Hole) and made his first trip to South America, where in June he performed to an ecstatic audience in Buenos Aires. He also gave some broadcast recitals, including one at Alice Tully Hall for Newport In New York, and in July at Carnegie Hall as part of a special solo piano evening dedicated to Art Tatum. This event included the unaccompanied talents of Eubie Blake, Earl Hines, Art Hodes, Brooks Kerr, Ellis Larkins, Dave McKenna, Jimmy Rowles, George Shearing and Billy Taylor, with Evans playing 'I Loves You Porgy', 'Hullo Bolinas' and 'But Beautiful'.

By mid November, still criss-crossing continents, Evans was once again on tour in Europe, appearing in Denmark, Belgium and Holland among other countries. Back in the States by late November he was guest soloist at Alice Tully Hall in New York, playing his own compositions with the National Jazz Ensemble whose director, Chuck Israels, was an expert on Evans's requirements thanks to his own stint with the pianist. The performance was a highlight in a topsy-turvy year that also saw Evans marry Nenette Zazzata in late summer.

Evans and manager Helen Keane had by the end of the year come closer to a decision about which record company to sign with, but they intended to continue to make their own recordings for now and sell the edited masters to the eventual partner. They were talking about this constantly with Fantasy, the company that finally agreed to a US release of the live Tokyo recording (already released in Japan and Europe on Columbia). A recent deal had combined the back-catalogues of Fantasy, Riverside, Prestige and Milestone, and effectively took Milestone, Fantasy and other labels such as Galaxy into the 1970s. It quickly established the Fantasy group as the most active US specialist jazz company still concentrating on mainly acoustic "mainstream-modern" jazz.

The output of jazz from Columbia, Impulse!, Blue Note and Verve withered from 1972 to 1975, leaving jazz musicians confronted with stark decisions, mostly between recording for small labels in Europe and Japan or turning to relatively healthy independents (such as the Fantasy group, Lester Koenig's West-Coast based Contemporary label, Joe Fields's Muse label in New York, and Norman Granz's new label, Pablo). Evans's move to Fantasy was a sensible one, although for the first time in over a decade it placed him with a label that lacked the distribution and publicity muscle of a corporate-backed major such as Verve or Columbia. In the eyes of the music business, it put Evans back in the specialist field of "jazz pianist" with little crossover appeal. This may have been no bad thing for an artist burned by his recent experience with a major, but it further confirmed his relatively declining status in his own country. New generations of acoustic and electric pianists – Jan Hammer, Chick Corea and the like – had become the latest standard-bearers. The irony was that most of them were deeply indebted to Evans and happy to acknowledge that fact publicly.

Another significant factor with independent labels is that they have more limited recording budgets. Thus it is noticeable that none of Evans's sessions with Fantasy between 1973 and 1977 feature an ensemble larger than a quintet. While this is not a comment on the quality of the music he produced for the label, it is put in perspective when one considers Evans's album *Symbiosis*, made in February 1974. This had Keane producing, Claus Ogerman composing, arranging and conducting, and featured an orchestra of 35 jazz musicians plus a full string section. Recorded in Columbia's New York studios, it was commissioned and released by the German label, MPS-Saba.

In the months immediately before this major recording event, Evans and Keane had attempted two new records, both of them location recordings and both in anticipation of the Fantasy deal. Perhaps the coldness of a studio was more than Evans could face at this time. Perhaps he had no new material to offer at the conclusion of such a busy year: after all, he had spent most of it on the road in one way or another. Live recordings offered the least disruption to normal professional life. The first date, in November 1973 at the relocated Shelly's Manne-Hole in Los Angeles, had Orrin Keepnews as producer and used the forces of the well-established Evans/Gomez/Morell trio. They played a repertoire similar to the Tokyo concert of the previous February (at that point still unreleased in the US): here again is 'Hullo Bolinas' and 'T.T.T.T.' along with 'My Romance' and 'Mornin' Glory', but the fire is noticeably lacking in Evans's own playing, with even his ballads pushed along in a way that seems intent on avoiding any emotional depth. 'Quiet Now' is a case in point, where Evans rushes through the evocative melody and its accompanying harmony in an ill-conceived excursion in bright-medium tempo.

Keane and Evans shelved this session, leaving it unreleased during the pianist's lifetime. More recently, the Evans estate cleared for release on Milestone another early-November location recording of the trio, *Half Moon Bay*, made just days prior to the Shelly's Manne-Hole engagement, at a small Californian beach club called The Bach Dancing & Dynamite Society. An appreciative audience and good recorded sound deliver a warm and generally well-integrated set from the trio, but it contains few surprises. The repertoire, apart from Earl Zindars's two originals 'Sareen Juror' and 'Elsa', consists of Evans staples, including a dusting-down of his 1966 arrangement of 'Who Can I Turn To'. The pianist's flame continued to burn low.

The second official live date, this time at the Village Vanguard in January 1974 and produced by Keane herself along with Keepnews, suffered another delayed release, eventually appearing as *Since We Met* some two years later (in February 1976). A further collection from the same sessions, *Re: Person I Knew*, was issued posthumously in May 1981. Helen Keane explained in notes for the Fantasy boxed set that "extra takes from [this] date were originally put aside for later consideration, but because there were so many projects in the planning stages we never got to them".[3] Those takes eventually made up the posthumous issue.

The trio performs admirably and the crowd is sympathetic in its attention and applause, but the repertoire had not moved on appreciably from the superior Tokyo concert of almost a year earlier, and it is understandable that this session was sidelined at the time to make way for other projects. The most impressive aspect of these Vanguard sessions was the now effortless cohesion and unity of the trio. Gomez was able to play alongside Evans without having to stop and think about anticipating him. They had an entirely natural mesh. Morell, meanwhile, produced the precise rhythmic backdrop expected of him, remaining acutely attuned to the colours that drums could add to the trio's sound. Evans and his men may have been skating the surface until he was ready to re-engage on a deeper emotional and artistic level, but at least they were doing it in unison.

A month later, in February 1974, Evans made *Symbiosis*, the German-label recording in New York with Claus Ogerman and the large ensemble. Ogerman and Evans had a history of collaborative efforts stretching back to the pianist's very first Verve recordings and including the *With Symphony Orchestra* release of 1965. This new session is as fascinating for the logical development in Ogerman's writing as for the superb response from Evans and his trio. Ogerman composed all the music for the record, and explained the form of the work in detail in the liner notes for the original MPS release. "The composition is divided [into] two movements," said Ogerman, "[two] entirely opposed night pieces. The tranquillo of the second movement (largo) releases the inner tension of the first. However, both movements share one joint foundation: the second movement is almost in its entirety a (slowed-down) repeat of a fast 41-bar 16th-note woodwind/saxophone passage of the first movement … This transfiguration is preceded by two new largo themes for piano and accompanying orchestra. The piano concludes the piece by establishing the D-major theme of the first largo."[4] Such an analysis was unknown in liner notes for American-recorded jazz releases, and is valuable as a succinct guide to the general outline of the 40-minute work. Ogerman gave further valuable pointers: "This metamorphosis of material serves as a hint that, at times, another value may be hidden in places where one would expect it the least (as in first judgements of people). The piece is composed within the major-minor principles. Twelve-tone rows are used merely for coloration … My only desire was to somehow 'reach the listener'. Therefore the choice of technique in composition is a second-rate problem." Ogerman singles out Evans for deserved praise, commenting: "*Symbiosis* stands here for Bill's free playing and the binding, severe text of the score … We might not have succeeded without Bill's ease at situations that call for accommodation. He is – as no other player – able to create within any degree of musical tension."[5]

This last point is memorably borne out in the third section of the first movement of *Symbiosis*. While he also uses acoustic piano, here Evans is on Fender Rhodes, for five minutes improvising a freely-conceived and fast-moving right-hand arabesque over sustained, slow-moving string harmonies and a walking drum-and-bass jazz beat. Enormous tension is generated, Evans sustaining his invention to the natural resolution of the section in a series of unaccompanied descending phrases. Elsewhere, Evans works like a concert soloist with orchestra, articulating Ogerman themes and passages that reflect the classical repertoire of the first decades of the 20th century. Evans brings to the work the consummate artistry and sensitivity that occurs when he is stretched and stimulated. His rubato playing in the opening of the second movement – sometimes alone, sometimes in perfect unison with the strings – is both moving and immensely accomplished in a way that few other jazz or classical pianists could have countenanced. This is entirely due to Evans's training, his technical standards, and, as Ogerman pointed out, his ability to imply his own musical response rather than resort to exaggeration.

Additionally, Evans brings to the interpretation of his written part here a freedom and licence that is quite simply beyond concert pianists working in the classical tradition. He is thus the perfect man for the project and plays wonderfully throughout, whether with just his trio or the complete ensemble. It is one of his finest achievements within the confines of a recording studio. The composition itself is expressive, expertly conceived and avoids bombast and ostentation, so Ogerman too must take a proper share of the credit for the artistic success of the album. Evans noted: "With *Symbiosis*, I only wish to say that this recording is one of those events which happens rather infrequently but in which I'm most proud to have participated."[6] A record loved by hard-core Evans fans, it was barely noted on its release in the US and generally shunned by a record-buying public still trying to recover from the Evans-Russell *Living Time* LP of 1972.

During what was for Evans a quiet spring and early summer of 1974, an agreement was finally reached with Fantasy and *The Tokyo Concert* was prepared for US release. It appeared in July 1974, some 18 months after it had been recorded. Evans performed with his trio at the Newport In New York festival on July 4th at Avery Fisher Hall as part of an evening dubbed A Cool One by festival organiser George Wein and featuring the groups of Stan Getz, Gerry Mulligan, The Crusaders and Elvin Jones, among others (although the connection of the latter two to cool jazz seems tenuous to say the least). The Evans trio went through a typical concert set for the time, the only surprise coming with an unscheduled appearance by Stan Getz who sat in for a blues at set's end.

The success of that informal blues must have stuck in the minds of both musicians, for when they found themselves on the same bill a month later for festivals in Holland and Belgium they agreed to appear together for the concluding part of the Evans trio's set, rehearsing extensively before the first concert for a co-ordinated effort. Both concerts were taped by local broadcasters and not long after pirated – inevitably, in poor sound – by small European record companies. Years later, Helen Keane cleared some of the better moments to appear on a Milestone album, *But Beautiful,* in predictably better sound.

Not all went smoothly during the first concert. Getz had a mercurial temperament – he was once famously described by Zoot Sims as "a nice bunch of guys" – and could be unpredictable onstage, thriving in particular on the thrill of the unexpected, and thus the absolute opposite of Evans. Helen Keane later described an incident during the Dutch concert, held in Laren: "After the trio finished their set, Stan was announced. As he entered the stage, he called a tune they hadn't rehearsed. I was watching the performance on a television monitor in the audio truck and saw the angry expression on Bill's face as Stan began to play the unrehearsed 'Stan's Blues'. Bill played a little on the melody chorus, then took his hands off the keyboard and didn't play for the rest of the tune … Bill was a gentle person, but was very strong. Although he always worked well with other musicians, obviously Stan's behaviour really affected him."[7]

The later Milestone release preserves the take of 'Stan's Blues' that followed Getz's public faux-pas – and Evans's subsequent silence – along with just one other quartet title from the Laren concert, a fine but subdued version of an old Getz favourite, 'Grandfather's Waltz'. Ironically, Getz plays with confidence and verve on the offending blues. His sinuous lines and rhythmic ease underline his ability as the outstanding blues player his fans know him to be, although this is not so well known to the general jazz lover. There are also two trio tunes from Laren on *But Beautiful* – 'See-Saw', an Earl Zindars composition first recorded at the Village Vanguard six months earlier, and Evans's 'The Two Lonely People'. These are well integrated and swing happily, though they set no new standards for the trio.

The Antwerp concert with Getz in Belgium took place five days later, on August 16th 1974 – coincidentally Evans's 45th birthday. It finds all four players in good form and a more relaxed frame of mind.

An attractive version of 'But Beautiful' is perhaps the highlight, as well as an indication of what might have been achieved by Getz and Evans had they ever managed to sustain an equal musical partnership for more than such fleeting hours as these. Elsewhere, Getz finds it difficult to penetrate Evans's by now hermetically sealed treatment of 'Emily', but manages a warm and masterful version of 'Lover Man', his paraphrases and variations of the theme an object lesson in linear improvisation. Clearly inspired, he takes an opening solo which swallows over five minutes of a performance that lasted less than eight. Evans, stimulated by the saxophonist, takes a short, biting, highly blues-inflected solo. Both men cook on 'Funkarello', particularly Getz who positively swaggers, while Jimmy Rowles's ballad 'The Peacocks', then a Getz favourite, receives a reverential treatment from all four players. After this, Helen Keane related, "Stan warmly wished Bill a happy birthday and played an impromptu 'Happy Birthday' together with a few bars of 'I'll Be Loving You Always' as a segue into 'You And The Night And The Music' … I think Bill was very touched by Stan's birthday wish before an audience of 7,000 people."[8] Those melodies were played alone by Getz, and even heard now on the CD are moving performances. This up-beat concert was a memorably happy 45th birthday for the pianist, who was also enjoying a sustained period of greatly improved health. He had put on weight as a result, and his fuller face was now partly hidden by a copious beard that he'd grown during the course of the year.

On the group's return to America in summer 1974 they played a concert at Camp Fortune, Hull, near Ottowa in Canada, which was taped by the Canadian government radio network CBC. A semi-official release later revealed a group of tracks including 'Midnight Mood', 'A Sleepin' Bee' and 'Time Remembered', the last being the highlight. After Evans's death, Helen Keane acquired control of the tapes and authorised the release of a completely different selection, *Blue In Green,* on Milestone, part of Fantasy. That summer the trio was on the point of breaking up, and the concert found them in generally rakish and occasionally inspired form. Evans's own playing is more energised than on many of the previous year's live recordings, with an incisive touch and a poised rather than rushed rhythm. In fact it is Gomez who is most guilty of pushing the beat here; this is doubly unfortunate as drummer Morell articulates right on top of the beat, so there is often rhythmic daylight between bass and drums, leaving Evans exposed. This is notable on the medium swingers, such as the opener, 'One For Helen', and the classic that Evans had helped to create back in 1959 for *Kind Of Blue,* 'So What', but a tune he rarely revisited.

There is from Evans an air of subdued joy about these performances: he clearly enjoyed the group's internal rapport and its unusually attentive audience that evening, though he complained to the concert's organiser after the event of being too cold to completely free up his fingers. "My brain knew what it wanted to do," he said, "but my fingers refused to co-operate."[9] The standout that evening was the tenderly handled Tadd Dameron ballad 'If You Could See Me Now', a tune Evans knew well and cared for deeply. During its almost four-minute length the trio once more intertwine seamlessly and plays to its true unified potential. Again reaching back to *Kind of Blue*, Evans gives an uncluttered, concentrated rendition of 'Blue In Green' as an inspired Gomez delivers his best playing of the evening.

Shortly after the group's return to America drummer Marty Morell gave notice to quit, wishing to return to Canada and settle there once more. Evans, now so far out of fashionable critical favour that he was not even listed in the August 1974 *Down Beat* International Critics' Poll, began the task of finding a replacement. On a more positive note, Morell's departure created the opportunity to make a duet album with Eddie Gomez. *Intuition*, as it would be titled, was made at Fantasy's studio in Berkeley, California. Helen Keane felt that "it was the perfect time for this beautiful record to be made" because the seven-year relationship between Evans and Gomez "had reached a pinnacle musically".[10] It was Evans's second release on his new label and would appear in March 1975.

There are limited precedents for a piano-and-bass duet record. The first was the famous Duke Ellington-Jimmy Blanton collaboration of 1940, followed by Duke's follow-up album of 1972 with Ray Brown, *This One's For Blanton*. Herbie Hancock and Ron Carter had cut some duets in the mid 1960s. Pianist Kenny Drew made a duet album with Niels Henning Ørsted Pedersen in 1973, as did Paul Bley. Looking ahead just two years, bassist Charlie Haden was about to begin a series of duets with various pianists, including Keith Jarrett,

Alice Coltrane and Hampton Hawes. But Evans's use of a slightly modified Fender Rhodes on two tracks of the Gomez album most strongly brings to mind a different but nearly contemporary session by Bley with his trio, *Scorpio*, featuring Dave Holland on bass. Evans is considerably more conservative in his application of amplification to the music, but the parallel in lyricism is notable. By contrast, Bley's acoustic duet LP with Pedersen fully explores the timbres, textures and sonorities of the respective instruments in a way that Evans never even considered, although Gomez had recorded and played with Bley in the mid 1960s and so was aware of the potential in this freer yet still tightly controlled and highly idiosyncratic approach to improvisation.

Evans and Gomez had long before resolved the problems of sequence and balance, each being well accustomed to the other's characteristic musical patterns. As with Evans's earlier dialogues with guitarist Jim Hall, there is an intimacy between the two musicians on their duet album that becomes spellbinding once the listener too is absorbed by the mood. Gomez perhaps even more than Evans finds constant points of inspiration and plays with a combination of force and lyricism new even to him. It helps that, for once, he has no need to balance his sound and note-placement between piano and drums. For much of the time Evans seems to be playing by memory and enjoying what Gomez is doing, letting him stretch as far as he dare. Only in the gentler, slower numbers does his romanticism take over and a more unified conception prevail, imparting to them a new identity in the process.

This is most evident on their treatment of the standard 'Hi Lili, Hi Lo', subtitled by Evans 'For Ellaine' and made into an elegy for his partner's tragically ended life. There is a degree of tenderness mixed with regret here that is unusual even by Evans's standards. The halting, haunting arrangement has every verse ending in a pause, after which the key is raised by a fifth and the intensity heightened a notch. Gomez is well aware of what is unfolding before him and sticks to the most elementary accompaniment so as not to detract from the completeness of the performance that Evans is constructing. While this singularly affecting recital is perhaps the highlight of the *Intuition* album, the subsequent number, 'Gone With The Wind', suggests an oblique commentary on what has just concluded. The long solo introduction from Evans works as a bittersweet summation before he moves into a more assured, comfortable, medium-tempo improvisation, with Gomez accompanying in classic LaFaro style. Further use here of Fender Rhodes electric piano against stabbing acoustic chords and a strong walking bassline underlines Evans's determination to put the past firmly in the past. Meanwhile, the Christmas season and the new year of 1975 brought nothing novel to his career. The slip in fashionable popularity in the US was confirmed by a placing in *Down Beat*'s Readers' Poll below McCoy Tyner, Keith Jarrett, Chick Corea and Oscar Peterson. Perhaps this reflected his lack of record releases for such a long period of time rather than any waning in the appeal of his live appearances. His regular winter jaunt to Europe, once again beginning in February, proved as popular and as successful for his audiences as previous years. Fans in Switzerland, France, Belgium, Holland, Britain, Denmark, Sweden and Norway had the chance to see the new line-up of the trio, with young New Yorker Eliot Zigmund replacing Morell.

The group had not had a great deal of time to prepare for the tour. They had played a club in Atlanta, Georgia, in mid January 1975 and then spent a week at the close of the month at the Village Vanguard (a fraction of which can be heard on *The Secret Sessions*, from January 26th, with entirely familiar repertoire: 'Turn Out The Stars', 'Quiet Now', 'Waltz For Debby' and 'Sugar Plum'). Zigmund's youthful zest took the trio further in the direction they'd been heading with Morell and he swung more assertively as the gigs went on. During that tour of winter '75 he explored the dialogue between Evans and Gomez and, following his own instincts, cut loose a little more than most Evans drummers. Bootleg and broadcast recordings from the tour show a renewed alchemy – even if the repertoire remained where it had been for close on two years.

A major event occurred in Hilversum, Holland's main television and radio broadcasting centre, on February 13th 1975 when the Evans trio combined with The Metropole Symphony Orchestra conducted by Dolf van der Linden for a broadcast performance of Claus Ogerman's *Symbiosis*. The other unusual musical event on this particular tour was a further meeting with Evans's old friend, singer Monica Zetterlund, at the Konsthallen in Lund, Sweden. A bootleg reveals the trio segment following the normal curve of an Evans performance and finds him in good spirits, playing with commendable imagination on 'Sareen Jurer' even though he is battling a piano painfully in need of a tuning session. Then Monica Zetterlund is introduced, with 'Come Rain Or Come Shine', accompanied for the first verse by piano alone. After that, she is supported by the trio. Her intonation is generally flat, but she has an attractive timbre which had deepened during the years since she had last recorded with Evans. Her expressive warmth seems to stimulate the group to sympathetic and consistently creative accompaniment. This was a pleasant night for all concerned, but it is questionable whether the bootleg of the concert reveals anything of musical import.

Coincidentally the next studio recording project, which took place in Berkeley in June 1975, featured Evans in duets with another singer, but this time a male singer: Tony Bennett. Evans explained later, "We had been friendly for many years and Tony was a big fan of mine. I must confess I didn't like his voice when I first heard him … However, he kept saying that we would make an album together one day, and finally we met up in London and agreed the date and the outline of the music. Now, I like Tony's singing."[11]

It was Helen Keane's idea to make the album, and it was heartening for her when both men "agreed immediately", as she put it. "The four or five days we spent in San Francisco were wonderful," she said. "We worked hard, we had dinner together every evening after recording, [and we] laughed a lot."[12] Evans evidently enjoyed the experience but, characteristically, he felt that his own playing left much to be desired. "I wasn't too happy with my contribution to the album," he said later. "I should have spent a little more time and taken more care."[13] Although it is often prudent to take Evans's public assessments of his own work with a pinch of salt, there is something in what he says here. Keane recalled that Evans quite correctly regarded the accompaniment of singing as a highly specialised art, and one where very few pianists achieve greatness, whether jazz or classical.

By these standards Evans fails on this album, for while generally he is entirely sympathetic and never plays incorrect or inappropriate chords and phrases, he is constantly trying to turn the duet into a dialogue – the most difficult thing to do between singer and accompanist in any musical genre. Such understanding usually takes years, and it is arguable that Bennett wasn't the most obvious choice of singer with whom Evans might achieve it. Only fleetingly is that level of musical telepathy reached on this June 1975 recording. As is to be expected, Evans excels on introductions and codas and his voicings are crystal clear. But his rhythm and phrasing are rarely more than approximate to Bennett, while his fills between and under Bennett's melody are too often those of a soloist rather than a player keen to blend into the broader sweep of the singer's meaning and line. Working over a long period with a singer leads a sympathetic pianist to shorter fills, closer phrasing and a better match of dynamics: precisely the aspects that one finds largely absent here. But there are some occasionally questionable choices of key that leave Bennett straining in a rather ungainly fashion for his upper register, or pushing notes and phrases when the lyrics suggest pianissimo or some other form of restraint. This is emphasised by the natural technical decision to give the vocalist a slight prominence in the mix, making any imperfection or strain immediately apparent, especially as the recording is also given a rather "dry" sound with a low level of reverb (artificial ambient echo), leaving it in sharp and close focus. 'The Touch Of Your Lips' encapsulates many of these problems in its final verse where Bennett is straining to give proper control to his high notes and Evans is pounding away with both hands in an off-beat rhythmic pattern, its unvarying dynamic and shape leaving the vocalist with nowhere to go. Generally the slower material is better handled, with Bennett's diction as ever a dream and his gritty timbre usually a real bonus and Evans's accompaniment open to the small changes in dynamics and tempo which make such a duet gel. 'Some Other Time' is a good example.

Clearly both men enjoyed recording together, for almost exactly a year later they appeared at Carnegie Hall as part of Newport In New York '76, and that September repeated the studio experience in San Francisco for a second duet album, *Together Again*, this time for Bennett's own Improv label. The Newport gig, although immensely enjoyable for the artists, was not without its critics. Arnold Jay Smith, reviewing the concert in *Down Beat*, found the format perplexing and, finally, infuriating. Billed as an evening with Evans and Bennett, the two in fact only appeared together on two bookended songs, the rest consisting of the Evans trio alone followed by Bennett with his own orchestra. The *Down Beat* man considered 'In Your Own Sweet

Way', the final waltz of the night, as Evans and Gomez at their finest. "Eddie double-bowed his arco solo to perfection," wrote Smith, "while Zigmund pushed Evans through some fine exchanges … [but] Bennett's set was Las Vegas from opening to close."[14]

In July 1975 Evans crossed the Atlantic for the second occasion that year, this time with Gomez only. Their bass-piano duet album had been released in the US in March and distributed in Europe soon after; manager Keane felt it appropriate for the duo to play live and that a recording at Montreux again made sense. The duo appeared at the Swiss festival in July to a tremendous reception, as in Paris the same month. The Montreux concert was recorded by Fantasy and would appear as *Montreux III*. The two French concerts on July 21st at the Antibes Festival were also recorded for broadcast by French radio and television. The sets on all three occasions were very similar, the only new addition being the Brazilian piece 'Minha' ('All Mine'), although John Lewis's 'Django' had not been played for some time and his 'Milano' was a relative rarity.

At Montreux Evans sounds at ease with an audience he knew had come specifically to revel in his own special qualities. Despite an out-of tune upper register on the acoustic piano – he also uses electric on a couple of tracks – Evans plays with none of the indifference that often clouded his concert performances during the 1970s. On the waltz 'Elsa' his tempo is not rushed, his touch not too driven, his phrasing beguilingly long-breathed and connected, with each cadential moment often addressed as a point in the music where both the player and the listener reflect on the phrase just shaped and on the one now appearing. In all this Gomez is a perfect and settled partner, not pushing too hard when Evans is in full flight but offering enough musical substance to continually influence the direction that the performance might take at any moment. 'Milano', on the other hand, brings out the conservative in Evans. His embellishments and paraphrases oddly echo the sparse style of the tune's composer and he sticks closely to a conventional ballad performance. With the continual modulations of the triple-time 'Venutian Rhythm Dance', Evans plays in his more distracted, chopped-up fashion, the ideas not running smoothly or freely, and he seems more concerned with the harmonic movement than a unified performance. Evans uses the Fender Rhodes to accompany Gomez's brief bass solo and to close the song, bringing a needed contrast to the performance.

The duo's version of 'Django' doesn't make a great deal of sense, the theme stated in a rather grandiloquent way with a raft of chord alterations that stamp Evans's personality on the piece but bring no special insight. After this, a rather rushed tempo is set and Gomez settles in for a long solo, dissipating any mood that might have built up from the opening. The following piano solo is Evans at his most perplexing, his fingers dancing through the changes with facile ease, his playing stuffed full of his own pet phrases – and none of it bearing much relationship to John Lewis's composition. Only the short, near-funereal ending brings a sense of what Evans and Gomez could have achieved here.

'But Beautiful' is pretty but has little new to offer, while 'Minha', written by Francis Hime, is an affecting ballad with a typically Brazilian lilt. Evans and Gomez interpret it in an almost recitative fashion, stretching bar-lines and tempos past breaking point, fashioning a statement which is both touching and dangerously close to lugubrious. 'Driftin', a loosely swinging tune by Dan Hearle, proves much more suitable than 'Django' for Evans to hand over to Gomez straight after the theme statement, the bassist playing a coherent and swinging solo full of technical wonders and real melody. Evans's Fender Rhodes improvisation is similar in its light-hearted jauntiness to that which he had played in 'Django' but this time it is much better suited, his agility and poise transformed into grace and eloquence, swapping between right-hand Rhodes and left-hand acoustic comping.

Michel Legrand's 'The Summer Knows' gets an appropriately bittersweet rendering, including some spot-on bowed playing from Gomez, while the final number, 'In A Sentimental Mood', a tune appearing for the first time on an Evans record, is played at a tempo suited to its wistful personality. Evans's solo is full of well-sustained ideas and sound construction, including some typical modulations to catch the listener by surprise, and is a fine way to end an uneven but intriguing concert. The *Montreux III* album, issued in October 1976, received extensive critical coverage. *Down Beat*'s reviewer Chuck Berg noted: "Throughout, the special Evans-Gomez chemistry is at work. Their intertwined exchanges, their ability to elaborate on and extend each others' ideas, and their overall musically supportive empathy form one of the most productive feedback loops in improvised music."[15]

In September of 1975 – a year in jazz marred by the premature deaths of two of Evans's old colleagues, Cannonball Adderley and Oliver Nelson – his wife Nenette gave birth to a son, Evan. This was a happy and important event for the father, who for some years had longed for a family. Mike Hennessey wrote later that Evans "was certainly convinced that a more normal family life in a new home would bring more contentment and happiness".[16] Not that Evans was at home much, what with tours and his other commitments. That same month saw Fantasy release the Tony Bennett/Bill Evans duet album, advertising it widely with pictures of Evans that emphasised the weight he'd gained in the past two years. Indeed his bearded face and figure were for the first time in his adult life filled to a point not far short of obesity.

That busy September also saw Evans's second appearance at the Monterey Jazz Festival (the first had been in 1970). In a *Down Beat* report on the festival, Len Lyons wrote: "The Piano Playhouse featured an interesting combination of players, though none of them were on long enough to be fully appreciated. Marian McPartland opened unaccompanied with her own ballad, 'Afterglow', and a lively 'Close Your Eyes'. Bill Evans said she sounded so good that it started him thinking about a similar format for himself. Evans himself played next in duo with bassist Eddie Gomez. His new drummer, Eliot Zigmund, was supposed to have been on the set, but he claimed that lack of time and stage co-operation kept him from setting up. By Sunday he appeared rather piqued at having spent the weekend 'hanging out and overeating'. Bill, whose first child … was born days before the Festival, played well-defined, energetic lines. Unfortunately, a beautiful ballad recently added to Evans's repertoire, 'All Mine', was too delicate to survive the enormity of the Fairgrounds Arena, but his own 'T.T.T.T.', sort of a 12-tone bop tune, was strong enough to knock everyone out."[17]

Patrice Rushen, who had progressed through Monterey's high school competitions of previous years, played a duet with Evans on 'Autumn Leaves'. She was evidently overawed and nervous, although both pianists played well, Evans in particular rising to the occasion. Not content with these pianistic complexities, the Monterey organisers next presented John Lewis and Marian McPartland in duet on 'How High The Moon', followed by all four pianists for an eight-handed finale on 'Billie's Bounce' that, according to Lyons, "was gimmicky but fun".[18] The performance was recorded and broadcast by the local radio station KJAZ, while the finale was filmed for television. Evans spent a good deal of time soaking up the atmosphere at the various concerts, staying backstage on Saturday specifically to hear Chuck Mangione's group. He appeared on the Sunday afternoon as guest soloist with the Oakland Youth Symphony Orchestra, as on his first appearance at the Festival, this time playing another performance of Ogerman's *Symbiosis*, conducted by the orchestra's director Denis de Coteau. It nestled between a reading of John Lewis's *In Memoriam* (with Lewis conducting) and Benny Golson leading the All-Star High School Band through an expanded arrangement of his 'Killer Joe'. Unfortunately this afternoon's programme was the most poorly attended event of the Festival, confirming the usual suspicions that, even with stellar guests on board, people will rarely pay to watch promising young players unless the youths in question are their own children.

That encounter with Marian McPartland's solo performance at Monterey stayed with Evans. While he fulfilled his normal quota of appearances in the autumn of 1975 – appearing again with Tony Bennett, this time on the Johnny Carson Show – and spent what time he could with his wife and newborn son in New York, he allowed Helen Keane to persuade him to make his next recording project a solo album. He had long been reluctant to do so, despite the public acclaim for *Alone*, released on Verve five years earlier. Keane felt that it was "probably the only area he felt insecure about musically, and the fact that he got a Grammy for *Alone* didn't help. Convincing him to do a second solo record was no easy task … There were no takes slated and the tape rolled until Bill wanted to stop".[19]

The resulting album, *Alone (Again)*, would be released by Fantasy in November 1977, two years after the sessions. It is a curiously intimate recital; curious because on many of the interpretations Evans's playing suggests that is he unaware not only that he is in a studio but that there might be any kind of audience at all to communicate with. While this was not the first time such a feeling had been generated by an Evans solo recording date, it still comes as a surprise to the unsuspecting listener. For the most part the artist communes with himself, trying out ideas and combinations to see how they sound to his ear. Keane and Don Cody, her regular engineer for Evans sessions, had painstakingly created an atmosphere in the studio that succeeded in freeing the pianist from temporal concerns – though perhaps in ways they had not entirely anticipated. For example, with 'All Of You', an item in his repertoire since the 1961 Vanguard days and beyond, there is a torrent of improvisation, much of it familiar Evans licks, turns of phrase and harmonic ingenuities. But when it comes to wrapping up the performance, Evans rushes through the recapitulation as if he no longer has the time or interest in presenting a fully-rounded portrait of the song. It is doubtful that he would have been so cavalier in concert. 'In Your Own Sweet Way' loses virtually all of its insouciant charm, the loping melody flattened out while Evans concentrates on some mannerisms. 'What Kind of Fool Am I' receives a no-nonsense beginning that bears little relation to the mood of the lyrics until the theme recapitulation. At this late stage Evans apparently recalls the song's meaning, pauses, and moves into a lush, romantic treatment which, with a little mid-tempo embellishment thrown in, is maintained to its end. The sparkling filigree runs at the close are perfectly judged. Elsewhere, Evans seems to be paying some sort of private homage to personal heroes: 'Isn't It Romantic', part of a medley, is close to the treatment Art Tatum might have given it, while 'Make Someone Happy' has hints of a range of pianists who were at their peak in Evans's youth.

Judged by Evans's own criterion from the liner notes of *Alone*, where he suggested that the length of a performance tended to suggest how deeply he had got into a particular solo piece, the most successful performance on *Alone (Again)* is the Bacharach-David song, 'People'. Yet this strange 13 or so minutes consists for the most part of a continual re-stating of the theme in a loosely non-metric way. For the first five minutes Evans seems to be giving an impression of how the song might have sounded played by Brahms, with endless left-hand arpeggios dressing the chordal theme statements of the right hand. At this point he seems about to conclude the performance, but instead modulates. For the next few minutes he intersperses rather Tatum-like daintiness with a more torrid style that intensifies the Brahmsian, windswept mood into a darker melancholy more reminiscent of Rachmaninov. Three minutes later the piece once more comes to a stop, yet Evans refuses to conclude and modulates again. He modulates a further time at the ten-minute mark, only now allowing the turbulence to largely subside in order to pick out the tune with tender simplicity while his rich harmonic substitutions cloak the theme in brilliance. As in the (rather longer) *Piano Fantasy* by Aaron Copland, it is almost as if Evans has had to work through the storms in order to arrive at a settled and balanced conception of the composition's message.

In all this there is no sense that Evans cares whether anyone else might ever hear this music. He could be at home playing in his lounge for his own pleasure and interest, with the listener being the intruder. It's an off-centre performance in both its content and emotional attitude, but of interest because it is so untypical of Evans's output. A review did not appear in *Down Beat* until April 1978, written by Mikal Gilmore. It praised Evans's integrity and depth, but found the record ultimately wanting. "He plays like a man caught up in personal epiphany," wrote Gilmore, "almost a conduit for forces and emotions that pure intellect would be helpless to transcribe. But to sustain such an acute level over a generation of performing and recording is an extraordinary task, and Evans – always a meticulous structuralist – has grown more interested of late in the complexities of edifice than in the laurels of introspection … *Alone (Again)* is impressive for its dextrous constructions. But like the best devices of artifice, it reveals little about the burden – or secret joy – of its maker."[20]

Despite the release of two new albums in 1975 and a good showing at live performances, Evans continued his poor run when the end-of-year polls were published, slipping behind Cecil Taylor in the acoustic piano section of the *Down Beat* Readers' Poll, while in sixth place on electric piano in the same poll he sat between Bob James and Jan Hammer. Yet the work continued to pour in. Evans remained in demand, able to work as hard as he wished or needed to. By the end of January 1976 he had toured Japan and made a well-received appearance in Los Angeles at the Concerts By The Sea series. He also agreed to a further *Down Beat* Blindfold Test, to be done at Leonard Feather's Los Angeles home, this time in tandem with the great swing-era pianist, Teddy Wilson. It was a highly agreeable way for Evans to start another year of change.

CHAPTER 14

The End of the Gomez Trio (1976-1977)

"HE PLAYED SOME ABSOLUTELY CLASSIC SOLOS. IT DIDN'T HAVE TO BE BASS FIDDLE, IT COULD HAVE BEEN ANYTHING – JUST SOMEBODY EXPRESSING THEMSELVES IN A BEAUTIFUL WAY."

BILL EVANS ON EDDIE GOMEZ

The pattern of Evans's professional life in 1976 deviated little from the previous year. He made two separate trips to Europe, in the spring and autumn, played a variety of jazz clubs from Boston to New York to the West Coast, appeared a number of times during the summer festival season in New York, and squeezed in another trip to South America during late spring. By May 1976 it was also time to make another record for Fantasy.

On this occasion Evans and Keane felt that it was important to get away from the trio format. He had already tried duets and solos, and the last solo album had not yet even been given a scheduled release date. Evans liked the idea of an expanded group but it was Keane who made the main suggestions

Eddie Gomez in the 1960s at the start of his time in the Evans trio, with Joe Hunt on drums

of personnel for what became *Quintessence* (a title typical of Evans's penchant for wordplay). "*Quintessence* developed from an evening I spent at Donte's in LA," said Keane, "where [tenor saxophonist] Harold Land was playing. I spoke to Bill about doing a date with Harold and [guitarist] Kenny Burrell. Bill suggested adding Philly Joe [Jones on drums] and [bassist] Ray Brown."[1]

They had in effect arrived at a mirror of the quintet instrumentation for the second *Interplay* session of 1962, and it is highly unlikely that this was by chance. Indeed, a blues such as Kenny Burrell's 'Bass Face' on *Quintessence* draws close parallels with the loose, relaxed feeling of the first *Interplay* date of 1962 featuring Freddie Hubbard, as Evans indulges in some of the most down-home blues playing of his career, sounding completely at ease. Equally, the group's evident poise in their rendition of Kenny Wheeler's waltz-time 'Sweet Dulcinea' can be traced back to the arrangements for that long-ago second *Interplay* session with Zoot Sims and Jim Hall.

Land was an inspired choice and credit for that must go to Keane. His style of playing had shifted since his early days as a national figure in jazz during the late 1950s. The saxophonist's long tenure in groups with vibes player Bobby Hutcherson and his continuing fascination with the music of John Coltrane had given him a broad view as a player and developed his harmonic sense so that he was comfortable with any material put before him. His tone gave his playing a uniquely expressive edge: keening, vulnerable and winsome on ballads but strong and incisive on faster numbers. Ideally for Evans, he preferred to be a group player rather than someone rallying the troops for battle. The presence of Burrell allowed the pianist to arrange the music so that guitar and piano alternate as accompanists on some numbers; elsewhere there are passages where both lay out, leaving just Brown and Jones to supply the forward momentum and harmonic signposts.

All this variety is welcome in a recorded programme which, in Evans's small-group incarnation, had become dangerously monotonous and formulaic over the past few years. Evans's own playing on the date is apposite and happy but not especially inspired. He seems mostly concerned with being a pianist within a group rather than leading it by example, and the resulting album sounds very much a co-operative effort. Evans said later to Mike Hennessey, "When I do an album with a couple of horns, or any front line, I try to put out of my head how we approach the music in the trio. I tell myself that we are doing a straight-ahead date which has to be more physical and outgoing. Things take on a different character and different disciplines are involved."[2] Evans is relaxed and communicative when he solos on Jimmy Van Heusen's 'Second Time Around', with Brown and Jones swinging mightily behind him, but nothing he plays is particularly fresh or arresting, however much fun it might be. Perhaps his best and most concentrated playing comes on Thad Jones's ballad 'A Child Is Born' where he presents the first three minutes of the performance as a piano-trio arrangement, including a piano solo, before Kenny Burrell's entry for a subdued solo. It's followed by Land, whose tender playing here is a highlight. The tune ends at the theme again, presented as a hushed trio statement.

Quintessence hardly redefined the boundaries of jazz or set out to make a Significant Statement, but it was a relaxed and rewarding quintet session and one of the highlights in Evans's later recording career, proving something of a breath of fresh air. It was released in May 1977, twelve months after its recording, and made scant popular impact in America at the time, though it subsequently proved to be one of the pianist's own favourites from this period.

In June 1976 Evans appeared at Carnegie Hall on the opening night of the Newport In New York festival alongside Tony Bennett. The two had greeted the audience at a noon launch of the festival at the Rockefeller Center featuring the Joe Newman Jazz Interactions Orchestra. At Carnegie Hall, where the programme was titled Schlitz Salutes An Evening With Tony Bennett, there were two performances. According to an observer, "Pianist Bill Evans accompanied Tony on 'My Foolish Heart'. Then, surrounding himself with a 32-piece orchestra that included everything from strings to a harp and tympanist, Bennett belted out over a dozen standards with some medleys … included. It upset someone in the centre of the orchestra seats, who stood up shouting, 'This is supposed to be a jazz festival; bring back Bill Evans!' Evans, slumped over his keyboard, head buried in his chest, played well, but seemed quite out of place in the role of accompanist on that large stage."[3] The trio also delivered a set of their own that evening, playing such staple Evans repertoire as 'Someday My Prince Will Come', 'Sugar Plum' and 'T.T.T.'. 'Someday' reappeared in the set when Evans played again during the festival, this time at Radio City Music Hall in a broadcast concert that united his trio with the horns of ex-Tristano sidemen Lee Konitz and Warne Marsh. It was perhaps the success of this unusual yet logical musical pairing that led to a studio quintet recording with the two horn men the following spring.

The slow decline in Evans's critical and popular standing was finally arrested in 1976, aided no doubt by the accelerated release schedule of his Fantasy albums and his close association with Tony Bennett over the year's course. The *Down Beat* Critics' Poll in August awarded him fifth place on acoustic piano and even placed him sixth on electric piano. Meanwhile he kept up his busy schedule, crossing the Atlantic twice and fitting in the second duet album with Tony Bennett in San Francisco that September.

On the second trip to Europe, as part of George Wein's "Newport à Paris" package, the trio appeared for a broadcast concert and the recording quality proved to be exceptionally good. The tapes remained unreleased (and unbootlegged) until the 1989 issue of the Fantasy boxed set and *The Paris Concert*. The extra drive and power brought to the group by drummer Eliot Zigmund – a player who had listened closely to Elvin Jones and Roy Haynes in developing his style – is very evident on the medium-tempo swingers such as '34 Skidoo' and, after its free-time start, 'T.T.T.T.', where a considerable head of steam is raised. The delighted audience response seems to make the trio determined to sustain this kind of pace for the duration; indeed some of the tunes suffer from a creeping acceleration. Even 'Turn Out The Stars' becomes something of a gambol during the pianist's solo. It is also noticeable during this particular rendition of 'Stars' that Evans is altering the chords to change their emotional impact, turning from the minor and from dissonance and letting in lighter colours and clearer feelings. This happy concert in front of an appreciative crowd effectively marked Eliot Zigmund's recording debut with the band.

Evans continued to work hard as 1977 arrived. He appeared at the Village Gate just after Christmas, opposite the Kenny Burrell Quartet, at the Jazz Showcase in Chicago in late winter, and once more joined up with Stan Getz, this time at the Macky Auditorium in Denver in late spring. By then his next recording project was in the bag, made on a number of dates in late February and early March 1977. This was a quintet date, later given the title *Crosscurrents*, featuring alto saxophonist Lee Konitz and tenor man Warne Marsh. It was a problematic session in a number of ways. Helen Keane's recollection certainly had a note of regret: "Bill was playing the Great American Music Hall in San Francisco the weekend after the record date and Warne came by to sit in. I often wish we could have recorded that set."[4] Listening to the missed opportunities on *Crosscurrents*, one can only agree. The two saxophonists had come to fame in jazz circles at the end of the 1950s when appearing and recording with pianist, theorist and teacher Lennie Tristano. After that there was an occasional recorded meeting, including a session for Verve in 1959 with Jimmy Giuffre that had featured both Marsh and Evans as sidemen. This was followed by a live session the same year at the Half Note in New York City where Konitz and Marsh were supported by Evans with help from bassist Jimmy Garrison and drummer Paul Motian (and that music remained unreleased until 1993). Afterward, both saxophonists had largely gone their own ways, with Konitz spending time increasingly in Europe. Konitz and Marsh had never been particularly close on a personal level, but in former days their tones and musical conceptions had combined memorably.

That was not the case on *Crosscurrents*, where Konitz – by 1977 a much more angular, multi-faceted and unpredictable performer than 20 years before – seems a lot of the time to be matching Marsh for wilfulness and oblique strategies. Their unison playing is studiedly vague, their intonation equally personal. Both had long made a virtue of extreme variations of pitch on any given note, pushing it up or down from the standard tempering of any accompanying pianist in order to get extra emotional or dramatic edge. Konitz tends to favour playing sharp, where Marsh is happy to play both sharp and flat (as well as occasionally in tune), depending on the musical or emotional needs of the moment. On this record both men sound generally and determinedly oblivious of the other's pitch, asserting their own version of events at every turn.

Bill Evans

Given this rather intractable problem, the best sax playing comes mostly during solos or solo horn statements – for example Konitz's opening of 'When I Fall In Love' where his habitual sharpness seems part of his overall style and strategy, providing a winning wistfulness. On the unaccompanied mid-tempo duet opening of 'Night And Day' the old Tristano rules of counterpoint and melodic line hold good for the minute or so of its presence. Although the Evans trio then enter at a different tempo for a piano-and-rhythm workout on the changes before each horn in turn takes a solo, the arrangement works and good ideas are presented by all three major soloists. The ending, however, demonstrates again that neither saxophonist will play the melody. Both instead want to embellish a lead presented in the manner of a no-frills trumpeter. With the two merely embellishing and nobody leading, the overall impression is of dissipation and wasted opportunities.

Konitz and Marsh individually are experts at studied inaccuracy, but together, with both playing the same musical game, the result is frustration. Nonetheless they do manage a unified and in-tune rendering of the opening melody to Steve Swallow's minor-key 'Eiderdown'. Konitz gets off a particularly well-wrought and urgent solo here, as does bassist Gomez straight after him. Marsh's more oblique solo builds well to a satisfactory conclusion, while the tenor player's feature ballad, Cole Porter's 'Every Time We Say Goodbye', is played with evident passion, though it is not one of his best on record. The performance closes to diffident pathos rather than tenderness and thus fails to reach out to the listener. Perhaps the low point of the record comes on Clare Fischer's beguiling Latin-flavoured 'Pensativa', once part of the Jazz Messengers' repertoire, where both saxophonists seem stylistically at sea and not especially interested in being rescued.

The Evans trio itself plays with flair, sensitivity and remarkable cohesion during the course of the date, their consistency and deftness making it doubly unfortunate that the front line, offered assiduous support, is so inconsistent in delivering the heavyweight quality of which it is capable. Evans seems to enjoy his role as leader-cum-accompanist, his solos brief and effective, his arranging mostly bringing out new twists in a piece or allowing clichéd constructions to be avoided. A pity, then, that this opportunity for old colleagues to shine together was not fully realised.

Evans missed Newport In New York for 1977 but was constantly working his group, appearing (among many other places) at New York's The Bottom Line in June for a week. His manager was also negotiating the end of the current record deal with Fantasy and a change to Warner Brothers. Under Tommy LiPuma, Warners had reactivated a jazz programme that had last been in operation in the late 1950s and early 1960s when Chico Hamilton and Paul Desmond were the label's hottest jazz acts. All jazz activity at Warners had stalled by the time Frank Sinatra had set up his Reprise label under the aegis of Warners in the early 1960s, and a number of noted jazz talents were nurtured there while Sinatra retained an active involvement in recording policy. But since their link up with Atlantic and Elektra at the close of the 1960s, Warners had left jazz and related music to its sister labels in the WEA group. Thus when LiPuma was given the chance he went for jazz players who had track records, active performance schedules and a worldwide following. Evans was a sure example, as was Dexter Gordon.

As a major company, Warners could afford much more to secure its artists and pay for their sessions than an independent such as Fantasy. Even though Keane and Evans may have come to miss the friendliness and intimacy of working with a small and integrated team, the move made financial sense. In fact, according to Keane, it was not only sensible but "an offer we couldn't refuse".[5] Evans noted that "Fantasy was a nice, congenial atmosphere and, of course, they had all my old Riverside catalog as well. I've known and loved Orrin Keepnews for many years but, frankly, the production budget isn't there. If you want to do a larger thing, it's hard to get it done. Basic money isn't there for recording and I just got a vastly better contract at Warner Brothers. They wanted to start a jazz catalog and I was more or less the start."[6] To finish the pianist's commitments to the old label, a studio date for the trio was arranged for mid May 1977 – and remarkably enough was their first such session for Fantasy. It yielded the *I Will Say Goodbye* album, which would be held back from release until January 1980 – though not because of any doubts about its quality. Not only did it win a Grammy that year, but it is also one of Evans's most consistently inventive and involving latter-day trio albums. He was content to set easier tempos, not to push the rhythm so much, and generally avoid regular items from the trio's live set. Drummer Eliot Zigmund was playing his first studio session with the trio, despite having been with Evans for two years. He later offered an insight into how Evans chose pieces for recording at this stage. "When we would do record dates," said Zigmund, "the tunes were always brand new. And Helen would give Bill some sheet music, and he'd sit in the studio and just whip together one of these arrangements. So within 15 or 20 minutes the tune went from being a standard to a Bill Evans arrangement of the standard, which a lot of times became the definitive thing. It was really far out to hear it happening."[7]

Repertoire receiving the Bill Evans touch in May 1977 included songs by Burt Bacharach ('A House Is Not A Home' at last), Michel Legrand ('I Will Say Goodbye', which became the title track, and 'Orson's Theme'), Herbie Hancock ('Dolphin Dance', a piece which itself seems to hark back to the Evans-LaFaro-Motian trio) and Johnny Mandel (the romantic 'Seascape'). Evans's approach to this diverse and mostly contemporary repertoire is less formulaic than in the recent past, his own playing paradoxically more pianistic, in the sense that he is more prepared to try techniques and devices closely associated with other pianists. In fact, the ghosts of Garner and Tatum both seem much closer on this record than anywhere else (Garner had died in January 1977), especially in their guise as rhapsodic romantics and in the consummate way they shaped the material of others. Zigmund again: "The compositional thing started to become part of the technique, or part of his approach, to the trio playing. It became less freewheeling, and it became more refined. He always had an architectural sense of the shape of the tune, and from night to night you knew where the improvisation was going. It wasn't as freewheeling as it might have been when he was younger, playing with Paul [Motian] and Scott [LaFaro]."[8]

On Evans's last session for Fantasy the most freewheeling performance is of his own composition, 'The Opener', which had previously appeared as part of a medley on *Alone (Again)*. Here everyone stretches out on the longest track of the session, sounding for all the world as if they are playing in front of a packed concert hall in Paris, New York or some other major city. Zigmund's tradings with Evans after his own short solo are a highlight and also a throwback to the excitement of the shortlived 1967 trio with Philly Joe Jones. Elsewhere, a more elegiac though hardly bittersweet approach is evident, as on Earl Zindars's ballad 'Quiet Light', played here with delicate blue translucence and perfect control of form. 'A House Is Not A Home' opens with a restrained but exquisite solo piano rendering of the Bacharach theme, its harmonies subtly shifted and altered, the form of the piece being re-shuffled to introduce the short bridge later, finally discarding it altogether in the short improvised passage where Gomez and Zigmund accompany.

The two Legrand themes demonstrate that writer's ability to conjure attractive melody from what amounts to little more than a simple germ of an idea, as well as demonstrating his thorough mastery of the difficult art of writing for films by producing musically successful material rather than mere screen fodder. 'I Will Say Goodbye' is a melancholy fragment that Legrand winds through a stimulating series of chord changes, in places echoing 'My Foolish Heart'. Evans handles this beautifully, bringing the trio to a complete stardust-scattered halt at the end of the first statement of the theme. 'Orson's Theme' is based on a falling-fifth interval taken through a succession of harmonic twists to add colour and flavour, all at a slightly dizzy but entirely poised fast waltz tempo. That interval may be the same as on 'Flamenco Sketches' but it is put to an entirely different use here, the related majors being emphasised rather than the minors. Combined with a rhythm reminiscent of a soft samba, this gives the tune a carefree feeling that Evans builds upon convincingly. It has a fresh, youthful feeling, as if the players had found new inspiration through their ability to step aside from their usual practises together. In fact this feeling pervades the whole session, underlining a relaxed and open atmosphere. Such an upbeat feeling would remain for the first Warner Brothers session, held just three months later and with the same trio – the last time these three would record together. It took place over three days in late August 1977, just a week after *Down Beat* had given Evans some sort of critical rehabilitation by placing him fourth in the acoustic piano section of their Critics' Poll – behind McCoy Tyner, Cecil Taylor and Keith Jarrett. The fickle winds of jazz fashion were perhaps blowing in Evans's direction once more.

The Warners trio album would be titled *You Must Believe In Spring* on its release in 1981, just a few months after Evans's death, and in many ways it complements the last Fantasy session. It has the same musicians, the same approach and the same balance of repertoire, along with a similar feeling of elegy and restrained ease. Beautifully recorded at Capitol studios in Hollywood, the LP documents a trio completely at ease with each other and allowing the music to flow in the most natural but refined way. One may wonder just what Warners' motives were for starting their new deal with Evans with such a project, but the quality of the music is not in doubt. The disbanding of the trio later in the same year resulted in the album being quickly shelved in favour of subsequent projects. This is not a criticism of the music's worth: Gomez and Zigmund in particular shine at every opportunity. The bassist lavishes some of his most composed and insightful playing upon the listener, while Zigmund stokes the fires at every opportunity. Gomez, long past blitzing the listener into admiration for his playing, blends his solos and accompaniment beautifully into each piece.

Evans's role is more equivocal. As with the previous Fantasy date, he takes a step forward by choosing contemporary music – the title track is another Legrand theme – as well as supplying two new tunes from his own pen. He also registers some of the most thoughtful and carefully constructed playing of his later years. But his improvising, though emotionally charged, is neither rhythmically nor melodically fresh. It is almost as if his attention is no longer on the horizontal movement of linear improvisation but has more to do with the adaptation of the song's vertical patterns, both on a specific and a larger scale. Evans is now more than ever obsessed with form over any mere details.

On *You Must Believe In Spring* the pianist is concentrating on looking back and reflecting. The opening piece, his own 'B Minor Waltz', is subtitled 'For Ellaine', and is a contemplative ballad waltz full of muted regret and tenderness. It is also the first of four triple-time compositions on the album, accounting for over half the record's repertoire. With Evans's well-established penchant for 3/4 time to articulate the more tender and ruminative side of his artistic character, such an imbalance here tells its own story. The choice of the late Gary McFarland's minor-key 'Gary's Theme' suggests further glances into the past, for Evans had many reasons to remember McFarland fondly, and this tenderly melancholy waltz neatly avoids the coarseness of sentimentality. The expertly transposed minor thirds of the melody's recapitulation are a particular treasure. A similar outline can be sketched for the more fully explored piece 'The Peacocks', a memorable Jimmy Rowles ballad that Evans first tackled while playing concerts with Stan Getz some three years earlier. McFarland's 'Gary's Theme' has a similar air of soundtrack writing – of a scene being articulated, a landscape of memory being recalled – to Legrand's 'You Must Believe In Spring', which comes immediately before it in the record's sequencing. Sergio Mihanovich's 'Sometime Ago' deals in similar emotional and musical currency, although during the improvising section Evans allows himself to push at the song's fabric a little less respectfully than elsewhere before acceding to a flowing, lyrical bass solo from Gomez. This is part of the shape of the record's programming, with the final two selections bringing the listener gently out of the nostalgia and remission of earlier performances and into something more life-affirming – notwithstanding the 'Suicide Is Painless' subtitle of the final piece, 'Theme From M.A.S.H.'.

That takes us back to what seems the album's central theme of death and rebirth – although if that had been Evans's intention at the time, it was not self-referential. 'We Will Meet Again', one of the 3/4 pieces on the record, was written by Evans for his much-loved and admired brother, Harry, and it carries a balance of hope and quiet celebration within its complex emotional character. It echoes the sometimes blithe, sometimes nostalgic feelings evoked by Legrand in the title song, similarly moving between major and minor. The song's original title at that 1977 session is unknown, but two years later, before the album was given a firm release date, Harry Evans committed suicide. The impact on his younger brother was immediate and deep. It was during the interim that Evans gave it the title 'We Will Meet Again (For Harry)', before the piece was heard by the world at large on the album's eventual release in 1981.

In the immediate aftermath of that first Warners session of August 1977, Eddie Gomez and then Eliot Zigmund handed their resignations to Evans. For Gomez it was a matter of making a change after more than a decade playing in the same group – just as Ray Brown had done some dozen years earlier when he moved out from under the giant presence of Oscar Peterson in that pianist's trio. It was simply time for a change.

Evans was deeply appreciative of what he and Gomez had managed to do together, and of the bassist's crucial role in his own continuing musical development. A year or so later, during an interview in November 1978, Marian McPartland told Evans that Gomez, who had moved from her group to his, had as a young player wanted nothing more in the world than to work with Evans, and was the happiest man in the word when it happened. "So was I to find him," replied Evans, "and we had 11 wonderful years together. In fact there are a couple of unreleased trio records which I think illustrate the maturity of his playing – and, perhaps, our playing together – perhaps more than any other record. One is an unreleased trio record on Warner Brothers, and the other an unreleased trio record on Fantasy. But especially the one on Warner Brothers … he takes a couple of solos that are to me just absolutely classic, beautiful solos. It doesn't have to be bass fiddle, it could be anything – just somebody expressing themselves in a melodic and beautiful way."

McPartland pushed Evans to compare Gomez with Scott LaFaro, but the pianist resisted. "Some things you think are maybe once in a lifetime," he said, "and there's no way to compare with Scotty – that was a once in a lifetime thing. But I have had marvellous experiences with other bass players – with Eddie, certainly, for 11 years."[9] It was a fitting epitaph to a long and consistently creative partnership – and to the trio that had disintegrated in the autumn of 1977, leaving Evans in search of a new band.

CHAPTER 15

New Hope, Last Hope: The Final Trio (1978-1979)

"I FOUND OUT LATER THAT BILL HAD NO PRECONCEIVED IDEAS OF WHAT YOU SHOULD DO, AND THAT HE WAS DEFINITELY NOT LOOKING FOR PEOPLE TO EMULATE HIS EARLIER GROUPS."

THE EVANS TRIO'S LAST DRUMMER, JOE LABARBERA

In his 1978 radio interview with Marian McPartland, Evans expressed delight with the eventual replacement for Eddie Gomez. "I've now found a new young bass player," Evans told McPartland. "He's got it all going and has a wonderful sound. His name is Marc Johnson. He was playing with Woody [Herman], he's 24 years old and he's from Dallas, Texas, and he's just gorgeous. Percy Heath … and Thad Jones were in the wings when we were doing Tokyo recently and when we came off, Percy came over and said, 'You keep pulling them out of the woodwork!', talking about Marc, because it is remarkable. I looked very hard when Eddie left, because there's no way you can replace him, but I needed a certain kind of musician and after about four

Evans at the piano in his final years

or five months of searching, Marc did appear and he was absolutely the one."[1] Johnson might have been "the one" but he had not come easily to Evans, who spent the autumn and part of the winter of 1977/78 using temporary personnel and auditioning in New York. For a time before drummer Eliot Zigmund left, Evans had his old friend and colleague Chuck Israels once more on bass, moving his repertoire accordingly back into the mid 1960s so that Israels had a firm basis on which to play and didn't have to struggle so much to catch up with the newer material introduced to the set over the course of the 1970s. At other times Evans had used what he later recalled as "six different bass players. Some were very good, others were committed elsewhere or didn't want to travel".[2] One of those was Michael Moore, who played with the Evans trio for a while but ultimately found it uncongenial. According to a musician friend of Evans's, Bill Kirchner, "[Moore] told me that he stayed for a couple of months but apparently Philly Joe [Jones], he said, was rushing like mad."[3] There are many stories about Jones's prodigious refuelling habits in his later career, prompting the thought that his previously impeccable timekeeping had deteriorated at least in part because of a physical decline.

Evans had turned to Jones in the aftermath of Zigmund's departure at the end of 1977. Although still an Evans favourite, Jones no longer had the metronomic time of old, which made his always assertive playing hard to take now – especially for a new bassist with concerns of his own. Interviewed in *Down Beat* in late 1979, Evans mentioned the holding role the drummer had played. "Philly Joe Jones came in for a year," said Evans, "and I must have had four or five different bass players. [I was] more or less searching and also giving these bass players a chance to try the music and decide whether they wanted to make a commitment … I feel like all that trauma of about a year looking for the trio that I finally ended up with was probably one of those necessary transitional things that allows you to arrive at something which is special."[4]

Another of the bassists given the opportunity to "make a commitment" to the new trio while Jones was there was George Mraz. Playing with Evans in New York ostensibly in a depping role, he was casually told by Evans about the next string of club dates right across the US. Realising that he was being offered the position, the in-demand bassist, who was committed to staying in New York City, gracefully declined. Given such contingencies, Evans fulfilled engagements the best way he could. For an appearance at Boston's Jazz Showcase club in late January 1978 the billing was "Bill Evans and Eddie Gomez", while in March he had a trio adding Jones on drums for a week at Chicago's Amazingrace nightspot in Evanston. After that the Evans/Gomez/Jones group moved west for a spot at Concerts By The Sea at Redondo Beach in Los Angeles that took them into April 1978.

By this time Johnson and Evans had finally managed to arrange an audition after many phone calls while Johnson was out on the road with Woody Herman. Appropriately enough the audition took place at the Village Vanguard, and the bassist was quickly hired. "A friend recommended Marc," said Evans, "and [he] sat in. We only played one number but I felt he showed more potential than anybody else. I'm sure there are ten other bass players who could do the job, but that's just the way it goes."[5] Johnson later commented, "I was prepared for the Evans experience by Woody Herman. Being on his band was marvellous; he's such a great teacher. And then Bill and [Philly] Joe spoiled me; they were so musical all the time. Bill could take you places that previously were impossible to reach."[6] Both men were clearly ready to work together. The Jones/Johnson line-up would provide Evans's basic working unit until November 1978 when Jones dropped out and the hunt for a permanent drummer began.

This period of uncertainty about personnel as new members settled in coincided with the commitment to record a second album for Warner Brothers. Taking advantage of adversity, Evans, Keane and the record company agreed to revisit the idea of parallel improvisation, as Evans had first done back in 1963 on *Conversations With Myself* and expanded in 1967 with *Further Conversations With Myself*. So while this was not a new idea, the layered-piano approach was to be given a fresh twist. Evans added what the record sleeve lists as "electronic keyboard" though it sounds like his normal Fender Rhodes fed through varying effects treatments in an effort to spread the tonal and timbral palette. During his interview with fellow pianist Marian McPartland later in 1978 Evans reaffirmed his preference for solo performance, but with a qualification. "I don't have the dimension to really be a solo pianist entirely," he said. "I just haven't expanded that part of my playing that much. But the feeling of playing solo is a marvellous feeling, as you know. You have complete control of the nuances and the rubatos and so forth, and it's a marvellous personal kind of expressive feeling."[7]

Evans was well aware of the duties of a solo pianist, in that same interview noting the advantages of playing in a trio format, especially when it came to "some of the functions that you must perform as a solo pianist – keeping the time or the bass or … playing voicings so full, [and] maintaining a fundamental structure". That this concern with structure was central to Evans's music was demonstrated time and again on these new multi-tracked recordings from January and February of 1978. "Keeping the structure going and more or less just following your own feeling and the movement of the time … playing rubato is one thing," Evans continued, "but playing in tempo is another. What I think the student should keep in mind is having a complete picture of the structure … as he wants to indicate it, [by] pre-planning a basic structure. I always have, in anything that I play, an absolutely basic structure in mind. Now, I can work around that differently or between the strong structural points differently, or whatever, but that must be. I find the most fundamental structure and then I work from there. I'm talking about the abstract architectural thing, the theoretical thing."[8] As a way of summing it up, for himself and other players, he concluded: "Intuition has to lead knowledge but it can't be out there on its own. If it's on its own you're gonna flounder sooner or later … Knowing the problem is 90 per cent of solving it, and the problem is to be clear and get down to basic structure."[9]

The album, given the title *New Conversations*, opens with a new tune for his manager, 'Song For Helen', in a manner very much in keeping with the sweeping multi-tracked arpeggios to be found on the 1963 efforts. It then falls into a thematic statement on solo piano. As Evans observed to Nat Hentoff, who wrote the record's liner notes, "This song is based on a very simple three-note figure, and its shape only changes twice."[10] The improvisational section is taken at a fast-medium tempo with a strong left-hand bass harmony kicking the rhythm along while there is a right-hand dialogue between acoustic and electric piano tracks. The electric piano does not sit so cleanly as would a second acoustic line, being better suited on this piece to supplying colour and additional harmony and melody to the concluding theme statement, which is played rubato (in a rhythmically flexible and expansive manner).

A similar pattern is followed for 'Maxine', another Evans original in triple metre and intended as a portrait of his 11-year-old step-daughter. The middle section, once again fast-medium, has three separate piano lines, one of them electric, but things fail to gel. The electric instrument sounds like a gawky me-too cousin loping along after two rather more elegant and surefooted twins. On the standard 'No One Else But Me' Evans plays an entrancing and astonishingly fleet, butterfly-like obbligato line behind the opening theme, but again it is on the electric instrument, its elegance hampered by the diffused tone of the instrument. Later, in the mid-tempo improvisation, the walking bass from the electric keyboard sounds like someone filling in for a bassist who failed to show up. Happier things occur when the interpretation turns bluesy and Evans uses the electric piano in a funkier way, bringing gusto and a touch of soul to an otherwise pedestrian outing, despite the immense sophistication that Evans brings to his arrangement.

Completing a series of family portraits on the first side of this album is 'For Nenette', a dignified ballad for his wife. Evans described it to Hentoff as "more of a gift than an attempt at a portrait".[11] The music is curiously restrained, as if pulling back from a fully romantic expression of feeling, much in the manner of Elgar's dedications and portraits. Evans was certainly aware of the desire for restraint on this number. "There was a danger," he said, "of the melody being too sweet, and so I worked on this with a great deal of control and thought. The result is, I hope, a delicate balance of romanticism and discipline."[12] The performance almost entirely consists of renderings of the theme with various amendments, interpolations and shifts in accompanying rhythms, styles and harmonies. The piece itself has a rather uneasy balance between sentiment and caution, or reserve, and perhaps hints at the increasing complexity of Evans's feelings for his wife in a relationship which at the time was under stress and going through changes. Only the final chords suggest unalloyed beauty and love in what may be a final attempt to resolve the equivocation that riddles the whole performance. As if aware of this, Evans throws himself into Cy Coleman's 'I Love My Wife' (the opener for side two of the original vinyl release) and relives the intense high spirits found on many of the 1963 multi-tracks. There is no doubting his mood here, nor his ample inspiration, but all this is disappointingly offset by his inability to find a fresher musical framework into which to pour all this creativity. Even the dashing, breathtakingly executed and technically impressive obbligato running behind the melody is borrowed from his 'Love Theme From *Spartacus*', re-cast into this new mould. This robs the performance of the impact it would have made had it been the first time – or even the second or third – that Evans had come up with these ideas, phrases and conceptions.

'Remembering The Rain', a final Evans original, uses his favourite vamps and a dignified, melancholy melody over chord changes which at one point suggest that part at least of the underlying harmonic structure originated long ago in Berkeley Square when nightingales sang there. Once again Evans sticks more or less to theme and variations. Much more expansive is his treatment of a Cole Porter tune, 'After You'. Evans said he had been introduced to its fascinations by pianist Pat Smythe: "The melody line is unique and unusually graceful. Listen to the way the phrases end, each time climbing up farther. It's masterful."[13] Evans takes the exposition in the key of G, modulating up to C for the solos, and takes one of his most cogent single-line flights over the charging two-handed rhythm of the first piano track. The central section is short (just one verse) before heading back to a full treatment of the tune in Evans's most cod-Rachmaninov fashion. Then comes the resolution through a sequence of diminished chords that is pure Bud Powell (though Powell himself never recorded the piece). This is a pleasing tribute in passing to two of his early heroes.

Evans claimed that he rarely played anything in the key of D. He found the resonances and overtones inherent to E and A somehow more appealing. However, he had fallen in love with Duke Ellington's 'Reflections In D', a composition inescapably in D. It had first appeared on Ellington's piano trio album made for Capitol in 1952, *The Duke Plays Ellington*, though Evans discovered it on a Tony Bennett recording. His comments to Nat Hentoff about the piece suggest that he was not aware of Ellington's own recording, but his interpretation sticks closely to the original conception. "I can't imagine," said Evans, "something this beautiful not being better known if it had been around for a long time."[14] This is another of those melodies that Evans clearly loves so much that he sees little need to improve – or improvise – upon it. "I don't do a lot to this song," he admitted, "because it stands so much on its own that I pretty much play the melody throughout and interpolate some voicings and things like that ... There are some things you just don't [change]."[15] The unadorned eloquence of the piece lends itself to the Evans touch and treatment, allowing the pianist that special combination of passion and restraint that so often delivered him (and his listeners) the greatest musical dividends.

Evans pronounced himself happy with *New Conversations* – a rarity, since he was hypercritical of his own efforts once they were released on record. The album was impeccably produced and packaged, with a special extra page inserted of the album notes by Hentoff. Evans mentioned later to Mike Hennessey that his only disappointment with the record came when Warners failed to get behind promotion and distribution on its release later in 1978. Considering it was the artist's first release on the label, if not his first recording for it, he was entitled to be disappointed. After all, Warners was (and is) a huge presence in music and was moving into jazz in an ambitious way. If it could not score a sales and marketing success with one of its major jazz signings, then the immediate future of the company's jazz investment was surely in question.

The rest of Evans's professional life was continuing in good order. He worked steadily during 1978 with his new trio, playing at Carnegie Hall in June accompanied by Johnson and Jones, then took off for the summer festival circuit in Europe, appearing at Nice, Montreux, Nimes and Terni in Italy before finishing the tour with an appearance at Middlesborough football ground in England in late July. For almost the whole of this European season Evans had saxophonist Lee Konitz with him, while at Nice, Stan Getz and trombonist Curtis Fuller sat in for a set on the fourth night of the festival, along with Christian Escoude on guitar. At Montreux the guest was different again; this time it was Evans's old friend Kenny Burrell. Konitz came back to the trio's tour in Nimes and Terni, while in Middlesborough just the trio appeared. At the end of this extensive jaunt around the major summer festivals Evans had successfully integrated his new bass player,

Marc Johnson, and was picking up plaudits from his ever-appreciative European audiences and commentators. His loyal Japanese fans were also rewarded by a visit this year. Back in the US in August 1978 he found his critical rating had continued to rise, with his placing in this year's *Down Beat* International Critics' Poll edging up to third, below Cecil Taylor and McCoy Tyner.

This critical rehabilitation fitted with the general course of jazz at this time. Jazz-rock fusion had begun to run out of steam and the avant-garde players of the previous decade had generally dispersed to seek ever more disparate goals. Some younger European musicians – for example Jan Garbarek and John Surman – were making their presence felt internationally. Many of these, along with a fresh crop of acoustic players in the US such as Richie Beirach and the phenomenally successful Keith Jarrett, were in part using Evans's theoretical and stylistic innovations of a decade or more ago to help build their own approach to jazz and improvised music. Others like Sun Ra, David Murray and The Art Ensemble of Chicago on the more avant side of the music were finding new sources of inspiration, not by pushing forward into previously unimagined sonic areas, as some of the late-1960s radicals had done, but by reinterpreting jazz's past and following the various strands of a fascinating hybrid. This would later lead to a chain reaction of artistic reassessments which continue to this day on both sides of the Atlantic.

For Evans the simple fact was that, like Sonny Rollins, Miles Davis, Dizzy Gillespie and a select few others, he had survived, physically and musically, where so many others had simply not made it. This group of older innovators was entering a period when at least one generation of musicians who had grown up under their spell had now moved into prominence – and had used that prominence to pronounce their debt to and respect for their still-active heroes. Evans along with his surviving peers was ripe for rehabilitation, and his enduring strategy of taking care of the music above all else had begun to bear fruit. Indeed, had he lived longer, Evans would have enjoyed a long career at the peak of his profession as a recognised giant in the music. But by the late 1970s he had already begun to push the personal self-destruct buttons that would ensure his early death. His long dependency on heroin, as well as the attendant illnesses associated with such addiction, had already seriously harmed his long-term health and inflicted irreparable damage. In the early 1970s Evans had switched to methadone, a cheaper synthetic drug intended to "cure" heroin addicts. It had limited the appalling long-term impact of heroin and arrested the speed of his deterioration, allowing him to eat and live more normally than he had done for many years.

But in the last years of his life Evans discovered the kick of another expensive and damaging drug, cocaine. At the time, coke was fast assuming the role of "fashionable" drug for America's monied classes and their wannabe hangers-on. The effect on Evans's appearance gradually became more marked: the weight he had gained slowly dropped away, his features again became gaunt. This self-destructive pursuit of drugs also led to a crisis in his second marriage and to him living alone when not out on the road with his trio. Whatever the tensions surfacing in his relationship with his wife Nenette, he must have found it hard to bear the necessary distance this created between him and his son Evan, regardless of his behaviour or condition. There are many stories of Evans "out there" on cocaine on social occasions in his later years, none affording him much in the way of dignity.

In public, Evans made light of this impossible balancing act, saying to interviewer Lee Jeske, "I think I'm more satisfied to be myself now than ever before. You know, in the Bible it says you change every seven years, and I've gone back and looked at that in my life and I can see, within a year on either side, where major changes have taken place. I'm 50 now, so that's the beginning of a new period … I have a family, a young son and a 12-year-old stepdaughter, and that probably has something to do with it. Part of it is that I'm at a certain period in my life where I'm coming into a good period of creativity and, I don't know, just a freshness."[16] This of course glossed over his private life, but then Evans had every right to do that. He had a career that he was trying to control, a group to run, commitments to meet, and professional engagements to fulfil. He picked up on the collaborative ideas that had dominated his recent European tour and, concerned about recording with a trio that was by no means permanent, opted for another quintet album. This time, however, he would include pieces arranged for different sized ensembles, from duet up to quintet. The guests in the front line were Belgian harmonica-player and guitarist Jean "Toots" Thielemans, composer of the popular 'Bluesette', plus the young saxophonist Larry Schneider. Eliot Zigmund was asked to guest on drums. The session took place in New York City on the last two days of October and the first two of November, 1978. Evans was excited because, as he explained later to Brian Hennessey, he had long been an admirer of Thielemans. "Toots and I talked several times about doing this album, but Toots is always so busy," Evans said. "He is the only harmonica player in jazz and I just love his whole feeling for music and melody. How he does it, nobody will ever know. I have stopped trying to figure it out."[17] Evans had heard Larry Schneider playing with the Thad Jones/Mel Lewis Big Band in Tokyo. "I made a mental note that I'd like to do an album with him and, fortunately, when the time came, he agreed."[18]

The repertoire for the *Affinity* LP was drawn from wide sources, from Michel Legrand ('The Other Side Of Midnight') to Paul Simon ('I Do It For Your Love') and Evans himself (another run at 'Blue In Green' with Thielemans in soulful mood). Other material includes a Thielemans favourite 'The Days Of Wine And Roses' and the standard, 'Body And Soul'. Generally, Thielemans's unabashedly emotional playing and his forthright approach spurs Evans into some of his most assertive piano playing on record. Evans's natural inclination to follow the lead on a quintet session gave him space to capitalise on Thielemans's confident projection. The harmonica and (electric) piano duet together on 'The Other Side of Midnight' and 'Jesus' Last Ballad', the latter track, according to drummer Eliot Zigmund, only being a duet by accident. After a number of takes, he said, "I eventually just got up and went out … and they ended up recording without drums. I just needed a break, and they finally got a take that [Evans] was happy with."[19] Thielemans is at his most persuasive on 'Body And Soul', using his full, lush tone, and Evans is strikingly imaginative in his accompaniment. Saxophonist Schneider plays warmly in his solo spots on 'Sno' Peas' and 'Days Of Wine And Roses', while his doubled tenor and flute work on 'Tomato Kiss' – where Evans is once more on electric piano – is a highlight on a generally satisfying, committed session. Kept in the background throughout, Johnson and Zigmund loyally do their duty and deliver an unerring musical base for the others.

Just four days later Evans recalled this session with warmth while being interviewed by Marian McPartland for her radio show recorded in New York for the National Public Radio network. With a piano to hand, Evans was asked to play 'This Is All I Ask' by Gordon Jenkins, and he mentioned that he'd never played it before the *Affinity* session. His performance in duet with McPartland echoed the legato phrasing which is a trademark of the Thielemans approach to melody. The interview – one of a great many McPartland has made with a huge array of jazz talent over the years, from Alice Coltrane to Dizzy Gillespie and Jay McShann to Roy Eldridge – is justly celebrated in jazz circles as one of the most intelligent and sympathetic discussions on jazz and the business of creating jazz.[20]

She persuaded Evans to disclose many of his theories, ideas and musical practises and demonstrate them on piano, either solo or in duet with her. Some of his most revealing statements came in spontaneous response to something she had just played. It is a fascinating portrait of a totally committed musician who thinks unusually deeply about the art in which he is involved. It is also an unerring portrait of the complex and vulnerable character behind that rigorous intelligence. McPartland later commented, "I think Bill was surprised by my playing. I felt very proud of that show with him. I don't think he realised I was such a keen student of his – I know all his tunes … I learned all the ballads like 'Time Remembered' and 'B Minor Waltz'. Some of his things are quite hard, like 'Twelve Tone Tune' [T.T.T.]. I love to play them, they're wonderful tunes and so unusual in structure."[21] That Evans responded to such genuine warmth and interest is clearly evident. The recording is now part of the Fantasy boxed set of Evans recordings.

In the opening month of 1979 Evans finally found a permanent replacement for Eliot Zigmund. Guitarist Joe Puma, a friend with whom Evans had recorded many years ago, tipped him off about the young drummer in his trio at the time, Joe LaBarbera, telling Evans he was unusually receptive and musical. LaBarbera came from a family steeped in music, his father giving both him and his brother, saxophonist Pat, their first lessons. Joe studied at Berklee College in Boston and first made an impact with Woody Herman before joining Chuck Mangione's band in the mid 1970s. Evans would have heard him with Mangione at the 1975 Monterey

Festival. LaBarbera remembered, "Joe Puma and Bill had been pals for years, and used to go to the racetrack together. I had been doing Monday nights at Jimmy Weston's with Joe and Bennie Leighton. When Bill and Helen [Keane] finally caught up with me, I was at Hopper's playing with Toots Thielemans. The next day I got a call to come down to the Vanguard and audition. Bill's audition process, like many bandleaders from the 1960s, was to play the Vanguard for a week and invite different guys in on different nights … For me, it fit like a glove immediately. Bill remarked, 'Have you been checking out the book? It just feels right.' I just had a feel for what he wanted, and it seemed to work."[22]

LaBarbera was quickly given the opportunity to join on a more permanent basis: he accepted and found himself immediately out on the road with the trio. His hopes were high and ambitions unlimited. As he explained, "My opinion was that the only stigma placed on a member of Bill's band was on the bass player, because of Scott's legacy. Bill had great drummers over the years, but they never shaped what the trio was doing the way Scott did. I wanted to be Scott LaFaro … I wanted to have that thing going with Bill in every possible way, to have some of that thing for me. I found out later that Bill had no preconceived ideas of what you should do … He was definitely not looking for people to emulate his earlier groups."[23] Drummer LaBarbera and bassist Marc Johnson quickly began to make their mark together on the music in their own enthusiastic and characteristic ways. The final luxuriant bloom of Evans's jazz-trio creativity was about to appear.

CHAPTER 16

Suicide is Painless (1979-1980)

"SOMEBODY AT THE END OF THEIR CAREER MAKING SERIOUS MUSICAL STRIDES IS ALMOST UNHEARD OF. GUYS USUALLY FLAME OUT, BUT ALL OF A SUDDEN HE WENT INTO OVERDRIVE."

PIANIST MARC COUPLAND ON EVANS'S FINAL CREATIVE EFFORTS

I n January 1979 the new Evans/Johnston/LaBarbera group played a concert at The Maintenance Shop in Ames, Iowa, which was taped, filmed and broadcast by the local Public Radio & TV station. The TV broadcast was later transferred to video in the US and the audio has been made available privately as well. The video shows a very different Evans from the one seen on BBC television back in 1964. Fifteen years later, Evans now talks to the audience and even scolds a rather below-par piano. During the recital the new group members are eased into a mixture of old favourites, such as 'Who Can I Turn To', 'Someday My Prince Will Come', 'Nardis' and 'My Romance', and newer additions to the Evans repertoire like 'Gary's Theme',

In Norway in August 1980, and very near the end

'I Do It For Your Love' and 'Theme From M.A.S.H.'. Evans slowly warms himself up and gives a professional show that brings together group and audience. His evident excitability and occasional waspish comments to those present may have been spurred as much by cocaine as by genuine ill-humour.

The Iowa gig was part of an extensive tour of North America planned for spring 1979, but it was interrupted by the news of the suicide of Evans's brother Harry in April. As had been the case following the deaths of bassist Scott LaFaro and Evans's partner Ellaine, Evans cancelled his immediate commitments and grieved privately. He had always been close to his brother and so the loss would have been hard to bear even without the added distress of suicide. He spent the rest of that spring away from the public.

By July 1979 Evans was ready to resume engagements, despite his now visibly deteriorating physical condition. Paradoxically, he was playing with more inner forcefulness and purpose than at any time since his earliest years on the jazz scene. He used the summer jazz programme in New York to ease himself and his trio back into playing, providing the framework to begin preparing for the next album for Warners, *We Will Meet Again*. This was a quintet date featuring a conventional front line with the brilliant and highly lyrical trumpeter Tom Harrell and saxophonist Larry Schneider. Made on four consecutive days in early August, it included a new (solo) version of the title piece, written and recorded two years earlier by the previous trio for *You Must Believe In Spring*, which still languished unissued on the Warner shelves. The rear of the new record's sleeve carried the line: "In loving dedication to my late brother, Harry L. Evans 1927-1979." The photograph of Evans chosen to accompany this dedication shows him smiling warmly, but also makes painfully clear his alarming physical decline.

Evans had first used saxophonist Schneider on *Affinity* alongside Toots Thielemans, having come across him some years earlier. "Oh, he's just marvellous," Evans told interviewer Lee Jeske. "I had heard him with the Thad Jones/Mel Lewis Band … in Tulsa and I was so impressed that … later I told Helen [Keane] to try and locate him. It was a matter, again, of a musician impressing himself upon me."[1] While Schneider may have impressed Evans with his abilities, his playing on *We Will Meet Again* is competent but undistinguished. His light tone and legato phrasing on both soprano and tenor echo Wayne Shorter and John Coltrane in a way that was fashionable at the time. He improvises tidily, but the ideas and their expression are not arresting. This is a shame considering the thought that Evans had clearly put into the record and the natural lyrical warmth of Harrell, the other front-line player.

The two horns phrase well together on themes throughout *We Will Meet Again*, especially where Schneider is on soprano, and this must have pleased Evans, who had written a good deal of the material. Most of the pieces were there to fit the very personal nature of the album, which alluded to many of the people who had been close to Evans in his life. Thus 'Comrade Conrad', from 1971 and dedicated to a friend who had met a premature death, kicks off the album as a quintet piece. It is followed by a caressing but oddly melancholy ballad, 'Laurie', written for Evans's new girlfriend, Laurie Verchomin; his own solo on this ballad is short but deeply romantic. The other new tune, 'Only Child', is underpinned by a sadness that hints at deeper and more fundamental emotions bordering on grief, so slowly does its rubato-dominated melodic line unfurl. The combination of tender love and loss which threads through the record underlines the dedication to his brother Harry, but here it is perhaps directed more toward his child, Evan, now at some distance due to Evans's estrangement from Nenette.

Older Evans tunes are revisited. 'Five' was first recorded in 1956, while 'Peri's Scope' dates from 1959 and refers to his partner of that time, Peri Cousins. Both pieces are full of hope and creative vigour, sounding as if they are from another life – which in many ways they were. As with the 1977-recorded LP *You Must Believe In Spring*, with its dedications to his long-time partner Ellaine and to Harry Evans, the pianist was here making some candid public pronouncements upon some very personal feelings, old and new. 'We Will Meet Again', performed as a trio outing on *Spring,* is reinterpreted on this new album by Evans alone, in very different personal circumstances now, and its tender line is full of regret. Slotted as the final track on the album, it is a heartbreaking way to end what is clearly a very personal record. The first side of the original vinyl release of *We Will Meet Again* was ended by another solo piano piece, 'For All We Know (We May

Never Meet Again)' by Sam Lewis and Fred Coots, the only non-Evans piece and an even more naked admission of defeat and emotional devastation. *Everybody Digs Bill Evans* back in 1958 had offered the same idea of bookended short solo piano pieces – but the circumstances then allowed them to be filled with hope and spirit. They were songs of innocence and of experience, and Evans, a well-read man, would have been aware of the parallel with William Blake's ideas.

The self-deprecatingly titled 'Bill's Hit Tune' (once more containing a play on words) on *We Will Meet Again* was modelled on Michel Legrand's techniques of marrying harmonic and melodic development, especially through cycles of repetition and variation. It is played unaccompanied by Evans on acoustic piano, then by the quintet (where Evans switches to electric keyboard, a pattern he uses repeatedly on the record). But it remains uneasy and rather leaden, for the melodic fragment that Evans takes for a harmonic tour is of insufficient weight to sustain interest through what is a rather long-winded exposition. Despite the imperfections and flat spots of *We Will Meet Again*, it amounts to a heavyweight emotional experience and is virtually flawless in execution, so the Grammy it won in 1980 should have come as little surprise to Evans and his record company.

These were not the only new pieces that Evans had come up with since the death of his brother. He had also composed a dignified, moving, yet strangely elliptical ballad, 'Letter To Evan', dedicated to the adored son with whom he no longer shared a home. It has a close musical relationship to parts of 'Only Son'. The first surviving rendition of this bittersweet piece comes from a radio-broadcast recording of the trio's September 27th 1979 concert in Buenos Aires, Argentina. Unaccompanied, Evans plays it free from metre, emphasising the intimacy of its emotional message and the deeply personal nature of its creation, managing to combine the apparent contradictions of the bitter and the sweet, the public and the private. Its first phrases recall Debussy-like classical composition techniques – whole-tone scales, parallel 4ths and 5ths – but it develops into another of Evans's show-type tunes, full of sentiment, and could equally have been written by Leonard Bernstein. As a musical document it carries the force of 'Turn Out The Stars' or 'Re: Person I Knew' but addresses different emotions and impulses. Evans was well aware of the difficulties of playing solo. "I would like some day to play more solo," he said at the time. "I don't feel I have a great scope or dimension as a solo pianist because I've never really worked as a solo pianist. But I do *like* to play solo. It's kind of a special feeling of communion and meditation you can't get any other way."[2]

Elsewhere in this remarkable Argentine concert Evans performs a chilling rendition of 'Turn Out The Stars'. The trio combines for a medium-tempo investigation that renews the bleakness and despair at the heart of the piece, with Evans's impatient rushed phrases forcing the trio into distracted and restless probing. For some time Evans had taken to playing this tune as if oblivious to its deeper layers of meaning: that approach has been completely overturned. In the aftermath of his brother's death there is no easy peace to be found here, even in the awful, beautiful flourish of pianistic arabesque at the song's conclusion.

By this time Evans was guiding Johnson and LaBarbera very firmly indeed, their role as accompanists more clearly defined than when Gomez and Zigmund had been with him. It was as if his need to express had grown larger, his compulsion for statement and articulation having outstripped his earlier insistence on continual dialogue and conversation with his peers. In this last trio the spotlight was unquestionably on his artistry. Evans may have brought this about in an entirely unselfconscious way, but it was still true: the urgency he was feeling could only be adequately expressed if he was given the perfect sympathetic platform by his partners from which to do so. Johnson and LaBarbera were from a younger generation than Evans and therefore not his natural peers in the way that LaFaro, Motian, Israels or even Gomez had been. But Evans had chosen well: his new musicians were so intuitive in their listening that they were with him in every nuance and were prepared to follow, whether the tune was a hushed ballad or a pushy mid-tempo swinger. There is no doubt that Evans revelled in the support he was getting. And he was acutely conscious of his own trend toward concentrated effort and extroversion. "With Eddie Gomez I could reach back and pull things out blind that he would know," Evans said, "but it's a little more limited when you change personnel … I suppose we go through periods, and I feel that I'm more outgoing. The last year or so especially I feel like I've been coming into a period of greater expressivity – more outgoing with a little more emotional scope and a little more projection."[3]

It's unfortunate that the recording quality of the Argentine concert tape, while acceptable – and far better than anything on offer in *The Secret Sessions* – is not ideal. The piano is very much to the fore and the bass and drums are at times engulfed by an often very busy Evans. There is also a distinct lack of upper frequencies, so the cymbals and drums are muffled and the bass has a dullness not natural to Johnson's playing. Similarly, there is a lessening of brilliance in the piano's overall sound. A more balanced recording would have given us a rather different perspective on the music produced in Buenos Aires. As it is, one has to make aural adjustments to "re-construct" the sound. But there is little doubt that it was a special night. These sonic problems are largely absent where Evans is unaccompanied, as on 'I Loves You Porgy'. This is an extraordinary performance that rushes from an agonisingly slow, pellucid and poignant statement to an improvised section that is reckless in its haste and abandon. It is impossible to determine at this distance whether this was due to the drugs or his emotional imperatives. The improvisation is spectacular but rather manic; it is certainly not at all appropriate to the overall meaning of the piece. It ends the way it began, with one of Evans's more elaborate double-helix spirals into the instrument's upper register.

'Minha' is performed as a duet with Marc Johnson, the pair sounding more like a Paul Bley duo than at any other time in Evans's career, with Johnson chasing the pianist's capricious musical shadow throughout. 'Someday My Prince Will Come' is the occasion for another carve-up of an old favourite, Evans pushing the tempo from the outset, again almost manic in his pursuit of speed and excitement. Johnson's solo work on this track demonstrates that he had yet to reach the supreme eloquence of Eddie Gomez in his last years with Evans, but his section work is completely at one with piano and drums. LaBarbera goes along with Evans's determination to push and harass the piece to its end; by then it is in tatters, the audience in a state of excitement, and the players exhilarated. Never intended as a hostage to posterity, it doesn't hold up too well now on (unofficial) CD as a recorded performance, but the elation generated is almost tangible: it must have been very exciting to witness.

In contrast to his approach two months later in Paris, Evans's treatment of Tadd Dameron's 'If You Could See Me Now' is affectionate but not particularly respectful, almost as if he is frustrated by the constraints imposed by the delicate balance inherent to the song's melodic and harmonic structure. No such constraints apply to 'Nardis', which starts with a halting, mystical treatment using harmonic devices perhaps absorbed from Debussy's second book of *Preludes*. It then develops into a long, wide-ranging solo-piano ramble through the song's harmonic framework, Evans probing at will into alterations of the voicings which bring out a considerably darker portrait than that initially sketched all those years ago for Cannonball Adderley. This section is full of obsessive, reiterative music, occasionally disturbing in the manner of some Bud Powell performances, seemingly too close to the limits of normal behaviour and making listeners uneasily aware that they are witnessing some private musical ritual: an inner confrontation with personal demons rather than an artist's outward gesture to the larger world.

This is fascinating in its own right and offers a radically different portrait of Evans the musician. This is not the sensitive, reflective musical impressionist whose output might be most likened to a series of watercolours. Here is someone painting in primary colours and with large, urgent, vibrant strokes upon the musical canvas. The opening Evans solo on 'Nardis' lasts just under eight minutes and is some of the fiercest playing of his entire career, with insistent, jabbing left-hand rhythms, reminiscent of McCoy Tyner, and turbulent, frequently jagged and rough-hewn right-hand patterns. Also like McCoy Tyner, he is using the entire span of the keyboard, in contrast to his reliance earlier in his career on a much narrower compass. This in itself opens out his sound and his musical thinking, allowing so many more places for his fingers to go during the construction of a phrase or a pattern of phrases. What is conspicuously absent throughout this assault on 'Nardis' is any resort to Evans's own pet musical devices and clichés: he is pushing into new ground and the excitement is palpable. Sliding finally into a re-statement of the theme, Evans pulls down the level and reins in the torrent of sound. His entry into the tune is the cue for the trio to combine, though piano and drums quickly fall out. Good but unremarkable bass and drum solos follow, bringing the performance to a conclusion after 16 minutes. By then the extraordinary and unexpected unaccompanied piano introduction is already a memory to be treasured in the overall performance.

Evans often said in the last year of his life that he thought his current trio, with Johnson and LaBarbera, had the potential to be the best of his career, and that it was achieving different things to his previous groups. He told Brian Hennessey, "This trio has the greatest potential of all, and I'm also feeling happier about my own playing." He added: "I don't want to belittle any of the earlier trios but sometimes I don't think I was as ready to lead the trio into better music. But now it's moving the same way as the original trio."[4] He may well have felt that this group was following the path of his first, but the context was entirely different. Where the first trio was much more a co-operative outfit, with Scott LaFaro often forcefully influencing the directions they would and would not take, this band was locked to the courses that Evans decided. LaFaro's role was made explicit by pianists Andy LaVerne and Steve Kuhn in 1996 when they discussed a rehearsal tape of the Evans/LaFaro unit. "It seems like Scotty is the one in charge," said LaVerne. "Oh, absolutely," replied Kuhn. "Bill had the greatest respect for Scotty. And Bill being the kind of person he was … with his personal problems and all, if he really respected somebody he could let that person just go with it."[5]

The increased force and authority in Evans's own playing now and his dominance of his trio partners allowed for a unity of purpose. This had been present before, but Evans was shrewd to allow it, given that he was not always able to push forward into new musical areas – hence the becalmed nature of some of his latter-day work. But there were clear new ingredients, uniformly tragic and unwanted, that impelled him to these advances with his final group: the suicide of his brother; his own awareness of his increasingly fragile health; and his decision to allow himself to slide into full-blown cocaine addiction. The effects of cocaine are well documented, and the incredible rush experienced by users can explain some of Evans's more driven, hell-for-leather playing in his last year. He was finding new musical fields to explore and his group were supporting him as never before – but it was all at a terrible personal price. Chick Corea, a long-time admirer of the pianist, wrote about this. "Bill was the first jazz pianist whose fine touch set a standard of silky, velvety piano textures for me," said Corea. "*Sunday At The Village Vanguard* … really opened me up to the possibilities of the piano trio playing other than the straight-ahead bebop approach I had tended toward … On a personal level, Bill's struggle with drugs showed me up close how detrimental to one's physical health and general nutrition taking drugs can be."[6]

Back in Boston in October 1979, the Evans trio performed at Lulu White's club in preparation for another jaunt to Europe prior to the end of the year. Before flying out of the country Evans had to take part in a special concert given at his alma mater, the Southeastern Louisiana University, in early November, designed to finally acknowledge in person his receipt in 1970 of the Distinguished Alumnus Award, the first of its kind from the University. Evans, excited to be back at his alma mater, eagerly showed Johnson and LaBarbera around the campus in the afternoon before the concert. A rather distant and unfocused recording later released of the event provides a ready sense of the trio relaxing and enjoying themselves, with the darker moods of other live performances of the time temporarily swept aside. Evans makes a short introductory remark after the opener, 'Re: Person I Knew', saying: "I won't try to go into what kind of special night this is for me. Suffice to say that at least two of the four years I spent here were two of the happiest years of my life, and I owe a great deal to Southeastern and the faculty."[7] The most consistently enjoyable aspect of this concert is the seamless interplay between the increasingly confident trio, an interplay that would further blossom in the very near future.

Later that November the trio demonstrated to European audiences its collective musical advances. In addition to the usual visits to France, Britain, Germany and the Netherlands, the group went as far south-west as Madrid in Spain where they appeared at the Balboa Jazz Club. Many of the appearances on that tour were broadcast locally and have subsequently turned up on unofficial releases. They demonstrate that the cliché about jazz as a music of the moment is no less applicable to the thoroughly integrated and professional Evans trio of late 1979: the various sets and concerts range from the inspired to the mundane and the mediocre.

Fortunately, one of the inspired concerts, on November 26th at L'espace Pierre Cardin in Paris, was recorded by ORTF and later prepared for release by Elektra Musician, a newly-created jazz division of Warner-Elektra-Atlantic. Helen Keane said, "In the course of Bill Evans's performing career, there were three places he enjoyed playing most outside of the United States: Japan, Brazil and at ORTF in Paris. At the time of this Paris concert, Bill, Marc and Joe had been together for about ten months, during which time Bill had become increasingly enthusiastic and excited about the potential of the group. I believe this inspired performance reflects his enthusiasm and his feelings about the trio he described as 'very much connected to the first trio'."[8]

The Paris Concert Edition One and *Edition Two*, as the LPs would be titled, came from a performance not designed for recording and they were not released during Evans's lifetime (they appeared in 1983 and 1984). But Evans knew about the tapes, was happy for Keane to edit them and would have been satisfied with the results. There was nothing innovative about the repertoire, which was the usual admixture of new and old favourites. 'Letter To Evan' slotted in alongside 'Nardis' and 'Quiet Now', and virtually every phase of his career as a leader was represented. The three men achieved a rare degree of unity in ensemble, accompaniment and solo settings. Marc Johnson's choice of notes is often closer to Chuck Israels than to Scott LaFaro, and his own personality emerges as distinctly separate from those players and from Eddie Gomez. Joe LaBarbera continues to develop the recent methods of Evans drummers toward more assertive and dynamic playing, bringing a greater degree of contrast and pure excitement to a trio which had, in the past, sometimes erred on the side of caution to the point of preciousness.

Evans's own approach continued to develop, although he was still switching between earlier and late incarnations of his very personal style. On *Edition One*'s 'Quiet Now' his recent concern with expression through concentrated means comes to the fore, often through repetition of the theme and harmonies with progressive minor modifications, emphases and displacements. The piece builds considerably through this technique, even in the absence of any particularly propellant drumming. 'Noelle's Theme' is an unaccompanied piano outing, rhapsodic in nature and execution, and cast in a style that Evans might have used at any time in the past 15 or more years. 'My Romance', by contrast, introduces a note of stress which is much more typical of these later performances. It starts, as it had in Buenos Aires, with a solo Evans introduction, and slides into a brisk trio invention which is followed by a drum solo. The exit from this is at double-tempo and flies in a way never documented by the first Evans trio or, indeed, any previous Evans group. These extreme tempos had simply not been touched upon, and Evans gave the credit for this development to LaBarbera. "In the first trio," he said, "we experimented with changes of pace – making a new tempo out of a sub-division of the previous tempo. Now, in 'My Romance', Joe is in charge of things and, after his break, he can take it up or down in pace as he desires."[9]

'I Loves You Porgy', which opened the second side of the original vinyl release of *Edition One*, offers an opportunity to examine Evans's development through his approach to a single song over a long period of time. This and 'My Romance' had been staples of the original trio's nightclub sets, but here 'Porgy' becomes a vehicle for a long and discursive solo investigation in which Evans continually prods and pulls at his material as if impatient to make something new from it. He is unafraid to follow his own musical inclinations and logic as he pursues ideas and motives through the changes, relentlessly re-addressing phrases over a shifting harmonic base – much as Thelonious Monk had been doing for decades and McCoy Tyner was doing at this time in his own high-octane style. "The thing about Bill that I've always felt is that he's one of the few that have maintained a certain continuous line of integrity and performance over the past 20 to 30 years," said pianist Richie Beirach in mid 1980, while Evans was still alive. "He's never really deviated from what he started to do, and he's received a lot of criticism for that. There are other people like that, like McCoy, who just do what they do really well and keep doing it, and grow very slowly, instead of coming out with new things every couple of years. And I really respect Bill for his incredible staying power [in] the long race."[10]

'Up With The Lark' again returns us to the interplay, the broken, short phrasing and the circumscribed ideas of mid-period Evans. While it is a competent performance it is not a memorable one, whereas 'Minha' receives a wholly engaged (and engaging) rhapsodic caress from Evans and Johnson, working faultlessly in tandem. *Edition Two* preserves this balance between old and new, primarily between pensive introspection – as on 'Letter To Evan', a sombre solo piano interpretation in his most romantic manner – and more up-tempo, spirited workouts such as '34 Skidoo' which closed side one of the original LP. The emphasis on *Edition Two* is decidedly darker. Side two opens with 'Laurie', played with great intensity in classic jazz-ballad style and stretching to just a few seconds short of eight minutes. The rest of the side is devoted to the "event" that 'Nardis' had by then become, with Evans shifting the mood, if not the intensity, of his own solo spot. The darkest moments of the version from Buenos Aires may be missing, but Evans still manages to create an intense and substantially new extemporised performance from this old favourite.

In Paris he continued the imperious and authoritative form of the Argentine date, confirming the arrival of his new trio to the outside world. Some six months later Evans would underline how excited he was about the music he was making with his newly perfected group in an interview with Jim Aikin. "You can put three musicians together that you predict will make it work, and it will fall flat on its face," said Evans. "It's very difficult to find the right chemistry. It's almost karmic. And I feel that the trio I have now is karmic, in that the whole thing had to evolve the way it did ... I believe in a steady group. I believe in a group where the people are right for the group, where they believe in the music, and they're responsible, and you stay together. That way, the music grows in ways that you don't even realize."[11] The trio remained in Europe until the week before Christmas 1979, at one point joining up once more with Toots Thielemans, as half of a club set at Laren in the Netherlands was taken up with an enjoyable combination of forces on such favourites as 'Bluesette', 'What Is This Thing Called Love?' and 'The Days Of Wine And Roses'.

Back in America as the year closed, Evans must have been aware of the contrast between his status at home and in the countries he'd just visited. In Europe Evans was lauded as an important and special player in the larger musical world; in the US he mostly functioned as a leading musician on the jazz-club circuit. Published evidence speaks of an unsettled jazz scene in America and of Evans's muted role within it, at least in the minds of those who voted in popularity polls. The *Down Beat* Readers' Poll for 1979 found him managing 15th position – the last entry – in the Hall of Fame listing with just 48 votes, while he failed to appear at all in the Jazz Musician of the Year list, in which Charles Mingus triumphed posthumously after his much-publicised collaboration with Joni Mitchell. Nor did the trio rank anywhere in Jazz Group, which saw Weather Report at the top and The Art Ensemble Of Chicago at number two. In the acoustic piano poll Evans was placed sixth, after Cecil Taylor and just ahead of Monty Alexander, while he tied at tenth in the electric piano list. Undaunted, Evans entered the new decade in typical style, playing club dates in and around New York and planning special events with his manager, though his energy was beginning to falter as the drugs took a greater grip and he began skipping meals.

One of those special events occurred in April 1980, a duet meeting with John Lewis at Harvard University. This took place after a typically sprightly trio set with Johnson and LaBarbera where they tear through 'Someday My Prince Will Come' and Evans displays almost manic intensity on medium-tempo pieces and ballads alike. The set culminates in another compelling 'Nardis' as the pianist quite consciously evokes the styles of Tristano and Powell in particular, using an almost savage energy and rhythmic aggression that few unaccustomed to his late music would credit him with. It is fitting, then, that at points in his improvisation he also invokes the harmonic methods and rhythmic drive of Bela Bartók. This performance particularly struck pianist Marc Coupland, who years later commented, "All of a sudden he's doing this serious harmonic exploration, and all sorts of innovation seems to be happening. Although it was clearly still Bill – maybe because he knew he didn't have a lot of time left – at that point he leapfrogged a lot of pianists and became a vanguard force, musically, for the last couple of years of his life ... To have somebody at the end of his career make some serious musical strides, that's almost unheard of. Guys usually flame out ... [but] all of a sudden he went into overdrive."[12]

After the interval at Harvard, Evans duetted with John Lewis (minus bass and drums) on 'Round Midnight', 'But Not For Me' and 'Billie's Bounce'. Lewis's fertile, condensed but suggestive style proved an effective foil for the more extravagant arabesques from Evans, typical of this last phase of his career. 'Round

Midnight' in particular strikes a good balance, with Lewis's portentous simplicity meshing with Evans's urgent baroque flourishes. Evans's solo on this tune has the impact of a man who is desperate to play as much as is possible in the time allotted, his intensity once again bordering on the manic. On 'But Not For Me' the arrangement allows for a cleverly disguised theme statement from which Lewis emerges as a relaxed, playful soloist. Under Evans's solo Lewis engages in stride passages reminiscent more of George Shearing's approach to the left hand rather than say Teddy Wilson's or James P Johnson's: this performance is more pedestrian, less inspired. Evans's comping for Lewis is curiously overplayed and busy, as if he is trying out the Art Tatum method of accompaniment and simply overwhelming the soloist; his own solo comes at the listener like a bolt out of a gun, so impatient is he to get started.

The final 'Billie's Bounce' is little more than an audience sop, for it is short and contains a bare minimum of distracted improvisation over and above the arrangement. Evans also played on a composition performed by the Harvard Jazz Orchestra that day, a curious and ultimately unsuccessful hybrid of Balinese scales, jazz-tinged classical-orchestra writing and tepid improvisation through a set of variations that seem endless because they are so mundane. The surviving tape shows Evans to be not over-familiar with or over-inspired by the work, and he plays with little of the fire and drive found earlier with his trio and with Lewis.

Just over a month later Evans was once more at the Village Vanguard, moving in on May 27th and finishing up on June 8th 1980. This was the occasion for his last Warner Brothers recording session, on the final four nights of the residency. Evans has left eloquent testimony to his affection for Max Gordon's small but legendary club in Greenwich Village, saying he felt "completely at home" at the Vanguard. "It's a good club for listening," said Evans around this time. "It's a good club for feeling close to the people. Max Gordon and I are old friends. [He] has created an atmosphere of relaxation. Musicians can drop in and out to say hello. It's not a stiff policy where you have to get a pass to get in ... I hope the club goes on forever and ever. They even have the same tables and chairs. I worked there first in '55 and nothing's changed. The only thing that's changed is they put some stuff on the walls."[13]

For Evans it was always a good idea to record at the Vanguard, so he was happy to assist with this exhaustive recording of his current trio's output. The original idea was to release one or perhaps two single records from the stockpile of tapes. Evans and Keane together made a tentative identification of first-choice tracks from the enormous amount of recorded music, but Evans's death would stall their release; in fact, they would have to wait longer than anyone could have guessed at the time. The double-LP-length selection agreed upon by Evans and Keane was issued for the first time over a decade later, and only after a six-CD boxed set had been produced documenting almost a third of the selections recorded over the four nights.

Turn Out The Stars: The Artist's Choice was the "highlights" CD (never released on LP), and it has its problems. Although the tracks were nominated by Evans, there was no final edit made nor sequence chosen before his death, and neither was Helen Keane involved in its eventual production. The decisions fell to Jeff Levenson and Bill Kirchner, with Matt Pierson acting as Executive Producer. What we have on the CD is an approximation of Evans's wishes. LaBarbera remembered Evans's attitude to records and made it clear that there would have been more changes had Evans lived long enough to see these recordings reach the market. "He looked at his records as children," said LaBarbera, "and he always prepared mentally for a recording. He had an idea of how he wanted to be represented, and he wanted the development of the trio to get across ... He believed in total preparation, rather than divine inspiration."[14] Marc Johnson's comments throw further light on what may have emerged on the proposed double LP had it been issued at the time. "We played 'Nardis' at the end of every night," he recalled, "started with 'Re: Person I Knew' every night, [and] played 'My Romance' at the end of the first set. But some things, like 'Polka Dots And Moonbeams' and 'But Not For Me', he just threw in for the first time for the Vanguard date. He was also writing 'Laurie' and the new pieces that we recorded at the Vanguard. In that last year, he was just motivated to create."[15]

The single CD opens with 'Bill's Hit Tune'. It comes across more powerfully than did the studio version, but still has a bothersome, repetitive theme which Evans truncates here by inserting trio improvisation between verses to improve the flow. It is an odd choice with which to begin the record. The set opener for every night, 'Re: Person I Knew', is nowhere to be heard, a fate suffered by 'My Romance', as well as the two "surprise" offerings mentioned by Johnson. 'Laurie' is here, as is 'Nardis', which rightly finishes the programme, but it is difficult to believe that Evans, so proud of his new trio and its rapid development, would have approved of his record company editing out two-thirds of the performance – the bass and drum solos. They had made it on to the records of the award-winning Paris concert, so there is no artistic argument for leaving them out here. Nor is there a problem with time restriction, with around 20 minutes of the resulting CD unfilled: that would easily accommodate any version of 'Nardis' recorded at the Vanguard that summer.

Still, the level of playing, and with it the level of concentration, is very high indeed. Every track contains wonderful moments. 'My Foolish Heart' is tougher and more urgent than before, but does not shed its vulnerability. There is also a beautiful tumbling set of arpeggios toward the end of Evans's solo that seems destined never to end, and the listener hopes it never will, such is its sudden beauty. 'Turn Out The Stars' carries a deal more of the Brahmsian clouds of romanticism in the unaccompanied opening verse before the bass and drums arrive, and Evans continues his newly assertive, no-nonsense, harrying approach to this tune, as if he can grieve no more and no deeper. Like the old New Orleans front lines, they need to play "release" music on the way back from the cemetery.

'Like Someone In Love' recalls many earlier gurus of the piano, including Powell and Rachmaninov, but Evans's mood is predominantly up and pushing in a way that would have been beyond him in the early 1970s when his rhythm was suspect and he was trying to tease new things from old forms. Here he is busy, leading from the front in every musical sense, but deep in the metre being set by bass and drums and comfortable in the swing of the beat. It may well be the drugs talking, a brief high in bloodstream and brain, but the overall effect is cathartic. As 'Two Lonely People' and 'Laurie' go past, one is struck by the fact that Evans chose tunes for this release that are invariably positive. He was avoiding the dark corners and the ruminative as if they had nothing to offer him any more. This was all adrenalin and flow and the future looked good. Only he knew that there was no real future, that his body was going too fast to hold to any tomorrow. With a reasonable pause for 'I Do It For Your Love', we reach 'Nardis'. By this point the piece has become a lengthy investigation, yet here the recording is absurdly truncated, fading out to end the disc. It makes a nonsense for 'Nardis' to be represented this way given its now extended dramatic role in the live set.

It is perhaps instructive to listen to these tracks alongside the 1961 Village Vanguard recordings where freshness and mutual inspiration were dominant. The original trio had then not been together very long; neither had Evans been playing the repertoire into the ground. In the same way that playing with Miles Davis had been pivotal in Evans's career, his first trio was the first full flowering of his own artistic vision, and it happened to coincide with Scott LaFaro's extraordinary purpose and drive, constantly pushing and pulling Evans into new and different impulses and directions. This last trio had a cohesion and mutual interdependence equal to that of the first, even though it was utterly unlike it in character. Now, Evans was pushing everybody else. And while Johnson uses LaFaro as a model – as well as many contemporary bass players – his rhythmic approach is different, and his tone and timbre mark out a bassist growing up in a completely changed world for the jazz musician. A number of bassists had brought new levels of sustain and drive to the double-bass: technical developments on the instrument, as well as their own musical imaginations, meant they could now swap at will between staccato and sustained notes.

LaFaro lived during a time when jazz bassists were generally still using gut strings. This meant that there was less opportunity to produce natural "sustain" for a note – a problem shared by the guitar until amplification gave it a completely new lease of life in the 1940s. His technique was therefore built upon assumptions about the physical nature of his instrument that no longer applied to bassists of Johnson's generation. LaFaro sustained melodic ideas often by using techniques associated with classical acoustic guitarists: rapid note repetition to sustain a melodic curve, especially in the upper registers; occasional plunges into the instrument's lowest registers for dramatic effect; and long diatonic and scalar runs interspersed with well-worked pauses and ostinato patterns, often on asymmetric rhythms. LaFaro's timbre was also much more biting, more conversational, than that produced by later bassists. Steel strings and the discreet use of amplification revolutionised the bassist's role in jazz within a decade of LaFaro's death, as the work of Richard Davis, Eberhard Weber and Miroslav Vitous, among many others, demonstrated. In a sense, and without diminishing Marc Johnson's talent or role, his impact on Evans's work was to make it sound more like a well integrated but orthodox late-1970s piano trio. Drummer Joe LaBarbera was even more influential in this process. The LaFaro trio's drummer had been Paul Motian, a strong individualist who formed his style during the 1950s and based it on earlier models. His playing was imaginative, subtle and capable of great sensitivity, but he could also drive the trio with a spirit that suggested the sort of joyous rhythm associated with Billy Higgins, even though their styles were quite separate.

LaBarbera was a fine drummer and a perfect foil for Evans's late style, but like Johnson he'd grown up in a different generation to Evans and brought a great deal of his admiration for people such as Elvin Jones, Philly Joe Jones and even Tony Williams into the trio. His explosive musical character was right for Evans's increasingly dramatic playing and it had a very marked effect on the trio's distinctive overall sound. Evans was working in a context that was both post-Coltrane Quartet and post-Miles Quintet. Like his old boss Davis he was, in a less pronounced way, playing his usual music but in a markedly different setting. Regardless of the impact that cocaine and other substances may have had on him, he was delivering his message dressed in new clothes, and it was revitalising his art, enabling him to loosen up and push as hard as he dare to fill the stylistic spaces that naturally existed between himself and his younger colleagues. As he stretched in this way Evans discovered a fulfilling new style for the trio as they aimed to meet at some ideal central musical ground in each tune.

Immediate support for these ideas comes as one begins the trek through the six CDs of the boxed set of *Turn Out The Stars*. Derived from all four consecutive recorded nights at the Vanguard, they show the trio breathing together on every piece, working hard to make them succeed, and moving through many different moods and changes of pace – something notably absent from the single CD's highlights. Here is a much more complete picture and one that captures the strange intimacy Evans routinely achieved when recording at this club. There seems to be no track on these CDs where the listener is tempted to think that Evans is simply going through the motions, as he clearly was on so many occasions up to the very end of the 1970s. On CD 4, for example, he and the trio turn in sensitive but emotionally complex versions of 'If You Could See Me Now' and 'Days Of Wine and Roses', but they also tear up 'Bill's Hit Tune', 'Nardis' and 'In Your Own Sweet Way', the latter once again becoming a celebration rather than a dismissal. Evans's own excitement flames like petrol through these performances, his contributions full of adrenalin but perfectly judged and beautifully executed.

CD 1 of the *Turn Out The Stars* box is largely taken up with music from the first night of recording, June 4th, and offers similar repertoire to most Evans live performances of the time – 'Bill's Hit Tune', 'Nardis', 'The Two Lonely People', 'Laurie' and 'My Romance' – mixed with more recent arrivals like the pretty ballad 'Tiffany', and 'Letter To Evan'. The ease and good humour suggest a trio on form and waiting for the spirit to hit them. If the collection is a journey, then this marks the auspicious launch of the ship from the harbour, with everyone expecting richer rewards as the vessel pushes toward its destination. For an example, compare the two takes of 'If You Could See Me Now' on CDs 1 and 4. On 1 the piece is still settling uneasily between a virtuosic Evans treatment and his standard trio-ballad interpretation; two days later, on CD 4, the two approaches are ideally reconciled. Similarly 'Days of Wine and Roses' on CD 2, from June 5th, is lighter, less intense and exuberant than on CD 4 from the following evening. The newer material – 'Tiffany', 'Yet Ne'er Broken' (another Evans anagram hiding a name) and 'Knit For Mary F' – tends to receive broadly similar interpretations, with identifying characteristics developing during the days of recording. Other pieces such as 'Spring Is Here', a tune long in Evans's book, are given workouts that include his originally arranged structure but with a mass of changed details. On such one-offs the other two members of the trio are noticeably less assertive in their contributions, looking to Evans for the lead at all times.

On the last recorded night – Sunday June 8th (taking up CDs 5 and 6) – three sets were put down on tape and the octane level was at a peak. "When the trio lit into its ensemble passages, the impact was not unlike that of a roaring big-band," wrote pianist Harold Danko in his notes for the boxed set. "This exuberant, extroverted and joyful approach extended to most of the material played, with Bill seeming, at times, to be its most youthful member. I can visualise how Bill dropped his hands onto the piano keys to get a full arm weight into his sound. He sat much straighter on this gig, especially during the more demanding tempi, and there was a wonderful, athletic sense to his performances."[16]

This artistic energy is apparent on the very first selection from June 8th, an almost complete re-setting of 'Polka Dots And Moonbeams' which so insidiously slides in the melody, camouflaged by Evans's consistent harmonic reworkings, that it sneaks up on you before you realise it. There is a fecund richness of self-accompaniment and arabesque that Evans works up from a lush harmonic basis. "His classical devices," Danko continued, "were as thoroughly absorbed as his jazz influences. (Rachmaninov comes to mind on these recordings even more than do Chopin, Ravel, and Debussy; perhaps Bill was tapping his own Russian soul.) The result was pure 'Bill Evans'; he had achieved a fully expressive and rhythmic ideal from all the varied elements he had studied."[17]

Ironically, Evans himself felt that the best night of the Vanguard run went unrecorded. He told Ted O'Reilly of *Coda* magazine, "Friday night was quite a good night throughout and, you know, it was all decent, but, sure enough, Saturday night was the night. That was the one we didn't record. That was the peak night. But we got some good stuff on there."[18] Listened to from that perspective, the final two CDs of the *Turn Out The Stars* set do perhaps carry a sense of afterglow – but their very looseness is a highly attractive quality, it being so rare in Evans's output. He is taking chances, pushing himself, thinking hard all the time about what he's doing. It's a joy to be on the adventure with him and the rest of the trio.

Even the medium-fast tempo of 'Turn Out the Stars' after the forbidding opening seems a release following the storm rather than a retreat from deeper responses. 'Quiet Now', by contrast, includes some formidable pyrotechnics from Evans in the unaccompanied opening, leading to a stern reading of this familiar piece. Even 'Emily', a pretty tune with a rather trite emotional message, is finally transformed by Evans into something of real intellectual and emotional depth, making for a portrait of a woman of complex personal riches. The final 'Knit For Mary F' (written by Evans for a friend who often made him beautiful sweaters) harks back to Rachmaninov and Brahms, the music sounding increasingly like an intimate if at times cryptic conversation with the listener. It is a similar story with 'Letter To Evan' before the liveliness of the set-closers, 'A Sleepin' Bee' and 'My Romance'/'Five'. A quick comparison of this 'My Romance' with that recorded by the original trio in 1961 will tell any listener all they need to know about the changes Evans had now passed through by this late stage in his life.

The Italian poet and novelist Cesare Pavese once wrote an essay in which he refers to the concept of creation itself. He says, "One fact must be observed: after a certain silence one proposes to write not a poem but *poems*. One regards the future page as a dangerous exploration of something one will soon know how to tackle … If the adventure has a beginning and an end, it means that the poems composed within it form a bloc and constitute the body of lyric poems of which we have been afraid. It is not easy to realise when such an adventure ends, given the fact that the 'tired' poems, or conclusion poems, are perhaps the finest of the group, and the tedium that accompanies their composition is not great, but different from that which opens a new horizon."[19] Substitute "music" for "poetry" in Pavese's passage and it serves as a useful metaphor not only for the concluding night of Vanguard recordings – and the all too familiar tedium for Evans of yet another piano with out-of-tune notes in the upper registers – but for his whole career. By this stage Evans knew he was running out of time and that this was something of a coda. He was putting such an unrivalled level of effort and concentration into these last recordings that they stand as some of his most enduring music.

Once again, in July and August 1980, Evans crossed the Atlantic, and with his failing health clearly visible to friends and colleagues, he probably guessed it would be his last visit. During this summer tour he appeared in Belgium, Norway, Germany, Italy, Spain, France and, in Britain, at Ronnie Scott's in London. There he was taped unawares, and two CDs from the week's residency later appeared on the Dreyfus label. These two discs are highly variable in quality, with the piano sounding as below par as Evans was physically. Virtually every other concert of the tour was preserved on tape with varying degrees of professionalism, although subsequent releases of any of that material must be counted as bootlegs.

A semi-private appearance on August 15th in Bad Hönningen, billed accurately as Evans's last concert in Germany, is well preserved, the balance between the instruments and the fidelity of the recording itself certainly the equal of the 1979 Paris tapes made by ORTF that would be released on Elektra Musician. The German recording finds Evans coaxing a kaleidoscope of feelings from his 'Letter To Evan', from faltering hesitancy to full-on soliloquy. Next is 'Yet Ne'er Broken' and although it fails to match the concentrated energy of 'Evan' the performance gels well enough. The introduction to 'Laurie' is stiff and poorly articulated, suggesting that Evans was stretching tired fingers further than they wanted to go now, and similar problems plague 'Bill's Hit Tune' on which he is kept afloat by the effortless spring of Johnson and LaBarbera. "He was affected by his physical condition now and then," Johnson later recalled of the tour, "but listening to some of the bootlegs that have been released, I think he was only seriously affected the last month or so, after we had done the Vanguard recordings."[20]

Better things arrive on 'Knit For Mary F' where Evans seems more able to will his hands to the precision demanded by the piece. The mood shifts between grim determination and light swing, but not so violently as to disrupt the overall effectiveness of the music. On 'Your Story' Evans uses a heavy touch worthy of Bud Powell, his fingers seeming to require more from the piano keys than they can deliver. It cannot be described as pretty music. It is passionate and engrossing, with inarticulate struggles going on which listeners can only glimpse and guess at through the insistence of the pianist's urgent message. There are few moments from Evans's career where the music is uncomfortable to listen to, but this is certainly one of them. On 'If You Could See Me Now' Evans offers some of his most clearly-considered, coherent playing of the evening, though he still uses very forceful articulation, and Johnson is particular comes up with some stunning counterpoint to underpin the pianist.

Back in the US at the end of August 1980, Evans and his trio went west, playing in Portland, Oregon, and in Los Angeles, moving at the beginning of September for a week to San Francisco's premier jazz club of the day, Keystone Korner. While in LA Evans attracted the attention of many local musicians, one of whom suggested to Gene Lees that they go to see Evans play. Lees was aware of Evans's cocaine addiction and its disastrous physical effect on his friend, and later recalled the discussion about going to the gig. "'How is he playing?' I said. 'Brilliantly.' 'How does he look?' 'Awful.' 'I don't want to see him … I can't go through that again.'"[21] Lees was not the only one to react in this way; a number of friends felt that Evans was deliberately avoiding hospital treatment for what was by now a critically advanced condition. Pianist Steve Kuhn, for example, felt that Evans "didn't want [it known] what was really going on with the drugs".[22] Marc Johnson was naturally aware of Evans's addiction, but powerless to influence its course. He recalled, "The last week before he died, I remember him telling me how insidious the substance was."[23]

The week at Keystone Korner saw the trio play more than a hundred individual pieces, with many multiple versions of the same tune, all of which were taped by the club's owner, Todd Barkan. Many selections were later released on *Consecration*, an eight-CD boxed set on Alfa Records in Japan, and later used by Timeless Records in Holland who subsequently derived three single CDs from this source. The music across all three of the Timeless discs is consistent with the forceful, energised musician who had been leading his trio around the world with burning conviction that year. His pianistic thinking was continuing to move forward at the same rate as his apparent desire to reach back to the techniques and ideas that had surrounded him when he was a young newcomer to New York. For example, on a version here of 'You And The Night And The Music' there is a stop-time four-bar segment at the end where Evans would normally apply a free-time right-hand flourish to arrest the metre before resolving onto the tonic with bass and drums. This time, however, he powers through the four bars with a perfectly executed in-tempo eighth-note passage that has amazing momentum, the ideas fresh and the excitement high.

This brusqueness does not always work: his up-tempo spin through 'Emily' turns the piece into too much of a throwaway, despite its cute, pianissimo ending. Newer material, such as 'Knit For Mary F' that had been premiered at the Village Vanguard in June, receives more sensitive treatment. Evans begins in full rhapsodic flow, although he is closer here to the abbreviated ritardando and rubato of Art Tatum's ballad approach rather than his own earlier, much richer and more romantic exploitation of time, phrasing and pulse. His solo on this piece is crammed full of ideas, as if he simply doesn't have the patience to wait for them all to present themselves – he just spills them out: over bar lines, twice as fast as they should be, or as asides and embellishments. Any approach seems to do, just so long as the phrase is articulated.

His rhythmic freedom in the opening statement of 'Someday My Prince Will Come' recalls the work of Wynton Kelly in its plasticity of phrasing, the supple ease of note placement, and the variety of note choices, echoing the imagination and excitement that Kelly combined so effortlessly at his peak. The Evans solo on this track is again driving: he takes the lead and pushes ahead with his ideas, enjoying every bar that he is filling with his sound. Similarly on the cute Evans original 'Tiffany' he is relentless in testing and toying with the trinket of a theme, worrying at it until other aspects of its character are revealed. This might seem to be an extension of his displacement theory of 20 years earlier, but was a recent development in his playing (it was heard also in June at the Vanguard and in July at Ronnie Scott's). Evans rarely went in for sustained bouts of variation and paraphrase, where each small substitution or distortion of the original built a larger picture and told a different story. Instead, his normal approach had been to use his comprehensive harmonic knowledge to dress up a largely unconnected group of improvisatory phrases and ideas in as rich a musical cloth as could be devised. Now, here was a potentially major re-evaluation of method by Evans that perhaps only figures so modestly in the overall course of his career because he simply ran out of time to develop it much further.

During these club performances he combines his old and new approaches to improvising on 'Turn Out The Stars'. He uses his old style of broken-up, self-contained phraseology for a while, then suddenly begins to run the phrases into each other, to speed them up and transform them into something completely new. As with earlier renditions that year of a piece once so closely associated with loss, pain and renewal, here 'Stars' is being used virtually as a jamming vehicle, a set of changes on which to get off. More notable still is the unaccompanied introduction to an old Evans favourite, 'My Romance', where his connections back to Tristano, Powell and beyond are spelled out extravagantly. There are yet more nods to Tatum's bewildering technical dexterity when Evans is tossing the time and melody between hands at will, shortly before the bass and drums are brought in for the theme proper, over three minutes into the performance. It is exhilarating to hear him no longer constrained by what he perceives as his own unassailable stylistic boundaries: he is consistently re-defining the areas of piano playing in which he is prepared to operate, but with less control and clear direction than just two months previously. Later in 'My Romance' he hits a groove with Johnson and LaBarbera, using long, multi-noted phrases that could almost be Oscar Peterson if there wasn't such a general absence of blues inflections, though Evans is certainly swinging hard enough for the comparison to stand.

Other moments which give pause for thought include the hasty manner in which he dispatches the theme of 'Letter To Evan', once again impatient to get to the tumultuous soloing at the heart of the thing, the very reason he's playing it that day. 'Gary's Theme' manages to escape such rough treatment, being caressed into life by loving hands and an overflowing heart. Once again Evans is unafraid to try new shapes and patterns in his solo, plunging into double-time right-hand shimmers which, repeated, gain an unearthly beauty. The conclusion to this rendition of McFarland's waltz is almost unbearably poignant, all three musicians moving together as one.

In 2001, after the death of Evans's long-time manager Helen Keane, Fantasy Records released *Last Waltz*, their own eight-CD boxed set on their Milestone label of more music from this Keystone Korner engagement. Comparisons with the Alfa and Timeless releases indicate that the Milestone takes are more alternative performances from the same Keystone run rather than a reissue of the same material (and one source suggests that the split roughly follows the first and second sets of each evening's performance). There are certainly questions to be asked about the consistency and quality of the playing, and Evans would not have approved their release. It is arguable that Keane too had held up their appearance during her lifetime for the same reasons.

Marc Johnson's comments already quoted about Evans's sudden physical decline make it clear that those closest to him day-by-day knew he was near to the edge of physical incapacity. Todd Barkan, the man who recorded the Keystone performances and made them available to the companies that released them over the subsequent years, said: "Whether [Evans] knew death was as close as it was, I have no way of knowing. I doubt he knew it was that close. I don't think he knew he was going to die in ten days, but he knew he was ill and that his liver wasn't functioning very well, and he definitely felt that there were severe limitations on the time he had on Earth. He didn't really think his life had a next stage."[24]

An old friend and associate, Herb Wong, visited Evans backstage during the Keystone residency. "That day was very emotional for both me and him," said Wong. "He had his eyes closed most of the time when he was speaking with me. I know he had been eating literally nothing but junk food, and it saddened me to see him in that particular state. But he seemed to be saying, 'It doesn't matter what state I'm in,' and obviously it didn't matter … He was actually advised to perhaps go into the hospital, but he was very determined, as he put it to me, 'to have the ultimate joy of playing with Joe and Marc'."[25]

The music from Keystone in San Francisco in August 1980 is valedictory in tone when considered alongside the Warners recordings from the Vanguard in June. The repertoire is almost identical, as are the arrangements, but the fire that had illuminated the New York performances is here inverted, as if Evans had to internalise his intensity to feed off his own pleasure in order to keep playing. Wong went on to describe the set of music he heard after leaving Evans backstage to prepare for another Keystone set. "I remember going up and finding a seat on stage right before the public had arrived," said Wong, "and I just sat there and waited to see what was going to happen. I knew that Bill relished doing this and, come hell or high water, he was going to do it … And when he played the set, the music was so charged it was transcendental."[26] Given the circumstances for Wong, this may well be emotion as much as perception speaking. For while the group is recorded beautifully and Evans's piano for the engagement is rich and in tune, adding to the trio's sumptuous sound, it is nonetheless hard to escape the feeling that the inner vitality has been eaten away by now, though the shell is intact. What remains is a fragile type of beauty, acutely poignant because of what we know about the circumstances rather than the music's inherent qualities.

This is not to say Evans plays badly. He is not guilty of crass technical errors or misjudgements, but he is not pushing the envelope the way he had done in midsummer. His most telling moments occur when he lingers over chords or melodies, luxuriating in the sound he is creating in a most untypical way (it would have been more in keeping with Erroll Garner), and there is a version of 'Nardis' where Evans's solo sounds almost in the nature of a farewell (the bass and drum solos are silently edited out of this performance). Some may feel this somehow re-conjures the original trio's ambience, but it seems more realistic to deduce that Evans was playing at the very limits of his physical endurance and that this is all that he was capable of delivering. The amount of time during his improvisations filled by his own pet moves and stock phrases had reached high levels, similar to those of his most jaded days in the 1970s – and this surely says much about his state of mind. These were the final glimmers in his career of what Cesare Pavese referred to in his essay on creativity as the "afterglow".[27]

Evans had just days to live at the conclusion of his Keystone engagement. The group flew back to New York and opened at Fat Tuesday's there on Wednesday September 10th. The trio completed their gig that evening – in fact someone made a very poor-quality private cassette recording of some of the music which inevitably appeared later, edited and sequenced by unknown hands, on various bootlegs. Evans was due back in the following evening but, according to Gene Lees, "Bill was taken with severe stomach pains in his apartment at Fort Lee. Joe [LaBarbera] drove him to … Mount Sinai Hospital and checked him in. Bill died there."[28] Andy LaVerne, hired to play Fat Tuesday's that week on the nights that the Evans trio would take off, remembers the confusion when the pianist was taken ill. He'd planned to go and see Evans playing at the club. "And [then] I got a call to go in on Thursday, and then it was day to day. Everybody was thinking, well, he's just sick but he'll be back tomorrow, [but] he didn't make it, and actually on that Monday he died."[29]

The primary cause of Bill Evans's death, on Monday September 15th 1980, was an unattended bleeding ulcer, but his body was so weakened, his liver in tatters, by years of the wrong drugs, that he had no strength or stamina left with which to fight. People close to him were surprised that he held out as long as he did, especially after his brother Harry's death. According to almost every observer, he was living only for music, and was largely sustained by his involvement in it.

Since Evans's death there has been speculation about the great changes in his playing that so distinguished his last trio and that might have allowed some larger step forward, had he lived another decade or even another five years. Speculation in such circumstances is always futile, of course, but it is perhaps worth remembering that Evans made few rapid spurts of development during his career. It is quite possible that he was forcing the pace precisely because he knew he was running out of time. John Coltrane was faced with a similar personal and musical mountain to climb in his final phase and found a similar solution. We can only be grateful that, in both cases, these gifted artists brought such humility and dedication to their life's work that they made such courageous and musically rewarding decisions. For this we are forever in their debt, and should celebrate the fact.

Bill Evans

Pages 48-53

[1] *Down Beat* December 8th 1960
[2] Booklet notes *The Fantasy Recordings* (Fantasy, 1989)
[3] *Down Beat* October 17th 1968
[4] Marion McPartland radio interview, 1979
[5] Martin Williams, liner notes, *Bill Evans On Riverside* (Riverside 1984)
[6] *Jazz Journal* March 1985
[7] *Down Beat* December 8th 1960
[8] *Down Beat* December 8th 1960
[9] Booklet notes *The Fantasy Recordings* (Fantasy 1989)
[10] *Down Beat* December 8th 1960
[11] *Down Beat* December 8th 1960
[12] *Down Beat* December 8th 1960
[13] Radio interview by Rod Starns, Southeastern University Radio, 1979
[14] Radio interview by Rod Starns, Southeastern University Radio, 1979
[15] Radio interview by Rod Starns, Southeastern University Radio, 1979
[16] CD insert *Homecoming* (Milestone 1999)
[17] Radio interview by Marion McPartland, 1979
[18] Radio interview by Marion McPartland, 1979
[19] *Jazz Journal International* March 1985
[20] CD insert *Homecoming* (Milestone 1999)
[21] *Down Beat* December 8th 1960
[22] Radio interview by Rod Starns, Southeastern University Radio, 1979
[23] *Jazz Journal International* March 1985
[24] Radio interview by Marion McPartland, 1979
[25] Radio interview by Marion McPartland, 1979

Pages 54-61

[1] *Down Beat* March 6th 1957
[2] *Down Beat* March 6th 1957
[3] *Jazz Journal International* March 1985
[4] *Jazz Journal International* October 1987
[5] *Down Beat* November 14th 1957
[6] *Down Beat* October 31st 1957
[7] Booklet notes *Complete Riverside Sessions* (Riverside 1984)
[8] Liner notes *New Jazz Conceptions* (Riverside 1956)
[9] Liner notes *New Jazz Conceptions* (Riverside 1956)
[10] Booklet notes *Complete Riverside Sessions* (Riverside 1984)
[11] *Down Beat* January 23rd 1957
[12] Liner notes *Modern Jazz Concert* (Columbia 1957)
[13] *Down Beat Record Reviews* Volume 3, 1958
[14] Liner notes *A Concert In Jazz* (Verve 1961)
[15] *Down Beat Record Reviews* Volume 3, 1958
[16] Brian Priestley *Mingus* (Quartet 1982)
[17] Liner notes *East Coasting* (Bethlehem 1957)
[18] *Down Beat Record Reviews* Volume 3, 1958
[19] *Down Beat Record Reviews* Volume 3, 1958

Pages 62-69

[1] WKR-FM radio interview 1979 by Bill Gold berg & Eddie Karp, quoted in Ashley Kahn *Kind Of Blue* (Granta 2000)
[2] *Jazz Journal International* March 1985
[3] Miles Davis & Quincy Troupe *Miles* (Simon & Schuster 1989)
[4] Miles Davis & Quincy Troupe *Miles* (Simon & Schuster 1989)
[5] Don DeMichael introductory essay in *Bill Evans Plays* (Richmond Organization 1969)
[6] BBC Radio programme *Along Came Bill* 1990, interview by Brian Hennessey, quoted in Ashley Kahn *Kind Of Blue* (Granta 2000)
[7] Miles Davis & Quincy Troupe *Miles* (Simon & Schuster 1989)
[8] *Jazz Journal International* March 1985
[9] Ian Carr *Miles Davis* (Quartet 1982)
[10] Burt Goldblatt *Newport Jazz Festival - The Illustrated History* (Dial 1977)
[11] *Down Beat* August 7th 1958

[12] *Down Beat* October 2nd 1958
[13] Doug Ramsey *The Secret Sessions* boxed set (Fantasy 1996)
[14] *Jazz Journal International* March 1985
[15] *Jazz Review* December 1958
[16] Miles Davis & Quincy Troupe *Miles* (Simon & Schuster 1989)
[17] Miles Davis & Quincy Troupe *Miles* (Simon & Schuster 1989)
[18] *New York Times* Sept 25th 1977, interview by Paul Wilner, quoted in Ashley Kahn *Kind Of Blue* (Granta 2000)
[19] J.C. Thomas *Chasin' The Trane* (Elm Tree 1976)
[20] *Down Beat* November 22nd 1962

Pages 70-79

[1] *Letter From Evans* Vol 4 No 3
[2] Gene Lees *Complete Fantasy Recordings* (Fantasy 1998)
[3] *Down Beat* December 8th 1960
[4] Liner notes *Chet* (Riverside 1959)
[5] Liner notes *Spring Leaves* (Milestone 1975)
[6] *Down Beat* April 2nd 1959
[7] *Jazz Review* December 1958
[8] Miles Davis & Quincy Troupe *Miles* (Simon & Schuster 1989)
[9] Miles Davis & Quincy Troupe *Miles* (Simon & Schuster 1989)
[10] Miles Davis & Quincy Troupe *Miles* (Simon & Schuster 1989)
[11] *Jazz Journal International* March 1985
[12] *Jazz Journal International* March 1985
[13] Booklet notes *Complete Riverside Recordings* (Riverside 1984)
[14] Liner notes *Kind Of Blue* (Columbia 1959)
[15] Liner notes *Kind Of Blue* (Columbia 1959)
[16] BBC Radio programme *Along Came Bill* 1990, interview by Brian Hennessey, quoted in Ashley Kahn *Kind Of Blue* (Granta 2000)
[17] Insert notes *Tony Scott: At Last!* (32 Jazz, 2000)
[18] *Down Beat* October 15th 1959
[19] *Down Beat* October 15th 1959

Pages 80-91

[1] *Jazz Journal International* March 1985
[2] *Jazz Journal International* March 1985
[3] *Down Beat* June 2nd 1966
[4] *Down Beat* March 9th 1967
[5] Liner notes *Spring Leaves* (Milestone 1975)
[6] *Down Beat* December 8th 1960
[7] *Down Beat* January 7th 1960
[8] Burt Korall, liner notes *Jazz In The Space Age* (Decca 1960)
[9] Liner notes *Jazz In The Space Age* (Decca 1960)
[10] Liner notes *Jazz In The Space Age* (Decca 1960)
[11] *Down Beat* October 22nd 1964
[12] *Down Beat* June 23rd 1960
[13] *Jazz Journal* July 1960
[14] *Jazz Journal* July 1960
[15] *Jazz Journal* July 1960
[16] Liner notes *Spring Leaves* (Milestone 1975)
[17] Liner notes *The Blues And The Abstract Truth* (Impulse! 1961)
[18] *Down Beat* March 30th 1961
[19] *Down Beat* March 30th 1961
[20] *Jazz Journal International* March 1985
[21] *Jazz Journal International* March 1985
[22] Booklet notes *Complete Riverside Recordings* (Riverside 1984)
[23] Liner notes *Spring Leaves* (Milestone 1975)
[24] Booklet notes *Complete Riverside Recordings* (Riverside 1984)
[25] Booklet notes *Complete Riverside Recordings* (Riverside 1984)
[26] *Down Beat* October 11th 1962
[27] *Down Beat* October 11th 1962
[28] *Down Beat* February 25th 1965
[29] Liner notes *Spring Leaves* (Milestone 1975)
[30] Booklet notes *Complete Riverside Recordings*

(Riverside 1984)
[31] *Down Beat* August 17th 1961
[32] Liner notes *Ornette!* (Atlantic 1961)
[33] *Down Beat* August 17th 1961
[34] *Down Beat* November 22nd 1962
[35] Booklet notes *Complete Verve Bill Evans* (Verve 1997)

Pages 92-101

[1] Booklet notes, *Complete Fantasy Recordings* (Fantasy 1989)
[2] *Jazz Journal International* March 1985
[3] Linda Dahl *Stormy Weather* (Quartet 1984)
[4] *Down Beat* November 22nd 1962
[5] *Down Beat* November 22nd 1962
[6] *Down Beat* June 7th 1962
[7] Liner notes, *The Interplay Sessions* (Milestone 1982)
[8] *Down Beat* November 8th 1962
[9] *Down Beat* December 6th 1962
[10] Booklet notes, *Complete Fantasy Recordings* (Fantasy 1989)
[11] *Down Beat* November 22nd 1962
[12] Liner notes, *Undercurrent* (United Artists 1963)
[13] Liner notes, *The Interplay Sessions* (Milestone 1982)
[14] Booklet notes, *Complete Riverside Sessions* (Riverside 1984)
[15] Booklet notes, *Complete Riverside Sessions* (Riverside 1984)

Pages 102-111

[1] Liner notes *Gary McFarland Orchestra* (Verve 1963)
[2] Liner notes *Conversations With Myself* (Verve 1963)
[3] Liner notes *Conversations With Myself* (Verve 1963)
[4] Booklet notes *Complete Verve Bill Evans* (Verve 1997)
[5] Liner notes *Conversations With Myself* (Verve 1963)
[6] *Down Beat* November 5th 1964
[7] *Down Beat* January 2nd 1964
[8] *Down Beat* November 5th 1964
[9] Booklet notes *Complete Verve Bill Evans* (Verve 1997)
[10] Liner notes *At Shelly's Manne-Hole* (Riverside 1963)
[11] Liner notes *At Shelly's Manne-Hole* (Riverside 1963)
[12] Liner notes *At Shelly's Manne-Hole* (Riverside 1963)

Pages 112-119

[1] Liner notes *Complete Fantasy Recordings* (Fantasy 1989)
[2] *Down Beat* October 10th 1963
[3] *Down Beat* September 12th 1963
[4] Booklet notes *Complete Verve Recordings* (Verve 1997)
[5] *Down Beat* August 27th 1964
[6] *Jazz Journal International* March 1985
[7] *Down Beat* April 23rd 1964
[8] *Jazz Journal International* March 1985
[9] Phil Bailey, booklet essay, *Complete Verve Recordings* (Verve 1997)
[10] *Melody Maker* June 20th 1964
[11] *Down Beat* August 13th 1964
[12] Booklet notes *Complete Verve Recordings* (Verve 1997)
[13] *Down Beat* September 24th 1964
[14] *Down Beat* October 8th 1964
[15] *Down Beat* October 22nd 1964
[16] *Down Beat* October 22nd 1964
[17] *Down Beat* October 22nd 1964
[18] *Down Beat* October 22nd 1964
[19] *Down Beat* October 22nd 1964
[20] *Down Beat* October 22nd 1964
[21] Liner notes, Cecil Taylor *Unit Structures* (Blue Note 1966)
[22] *Down Beat* October 21st 1965
[23] *Down Beat* July 16th 1965
[24] *Down Beat* February 25th 1965
[25] *Down Beat* August 12th 1965

Pages 120-131

[1] *Down Beat* February 25th 1965
[2] *Down Beat* August 12th 1965
[3] *Down Beat* June 17th 1965
[4] *Down Beat* June 17th 1965
[5] *Jazz Journal International* March 1985
[6] Liner notes *Bill Evans Trio With Symphony Orchestra* (Verve 1966)
[7] Liner notes *Bill Evans Trio With Symphony Orchestra* (Verve 1966)
[8] Liner notes *Bill Evans Trio With Symphony Orchestra* (Verve 1966)
[9] *Verve Complete Bill Evans Recordings* (Verve 1997)
[10] *Verve Complete Bill Evans Recordings* (Verve 1997)
[11] *Jazz Journal International* March 1985
[12] *Down Beat* January 27th 1966
[13] *Down Beat* February 24th 1966
[14] *Down Beat* April 7th 1966
[15] *Down Beat* April 7th 1966
[16] *Down Beat* April 7th 1966
[17] *Down Beat* April 7th 1966
[18] Liner notes *At Town Hall* (Verve 1966)
[19] *Down Beat* April 7th 1966
[20] *Verve Complete Bill Evans Recordings* (Verve 1997)
[21] *Down Beat* June 2nd 1966
[22] *Jazz Journal* March 1987
[23] *Down Beat* June 2nd 1966
[24] *Verve Complete Bill Evans Recordings* (Verve 1997)
[25] *Jazz Journal International* March 1985
[26] Liner notes *Intermodulation* (Verve 1966)
[27] *Down Beat* May 5th 1966
[28] *Down Beat* April 21st 1966

Pages 132-145

[1] *Down Beat* September 22nd 1966
[2] *Down Beat* September 22nd 1966
[3] Randi Hultin *Born Under The Sign Of Jazz* (Sanctuary 2000)
[4] Randi Hultin *Born Under The Sign Of Jazz* (Sanctuary 2000)
[5] Randi Hultin *Born Under The Sign Of Jazz* (Sanctuary 2000)
[6] *Down Beat* February 9th 1967
[7] *Down Beat* June 15th 1967
[8] Randi Hultin *Born Under The Sign Of Jazz* (Sanctuary 2000)
[9] *Down Beat* August 10th 1967
[10] Burt Goldblatt *Newport Jazz Festival - The Illustrated History* (Dial 1977)
[11] Liner notes *Further Conversations With Myself* (Verve 1967)
[12] *Down Beat* December 14th 1967
[13] *Down Beat* December 14th 1967
[14] *Down Beat* January 25th 1968
[15] *Down Beat* May 2nd 1968
[16] *Down Beat* July 25th 1968
[17] Liner notes *Bill Evans At The Montreux Jazz Festival* (Verve 1968)
[18] *Down Beat* August 8th 1968
[19] *Down Beat* September 19th 1968
[20] Liner notes *Alone* (Verve 1968)
[21] *Down Beat* 17 October 1968
[22] Liner notes *Alone* (Verve 1968)
[23] *Down Beat* September 3rd 1970
[24] *Down Beat* November 9th 1964
[25] *Down Beat* January 23rd 1969
[26] *Down Beat* May 1st 1969
[27] *Down Beat* February 8th 1970
[28] *Jazz Journal International* March 1985
[29] *Down Beat* May 28th and July 23rd 1970
[30] *Down Beat* May 28th 1970
[31] *Down Beat* May 28th 1970
[32] *Down Beat* May 28th 1970
[33] Randi Hultin *Born Under The Sign Of Jazz* (Sanctuary 2000)
[34] Randi Hultin *Born Under The Sign Of Jazz* (Sanctuary 2000)

Pages 146-155

[1] *Jazz Journal International* October 1985
[2] Booklet notes *The Complete Bill Evans On Verve* (Verve 1997)
[3] *Down Beat* March 16th 1971
[4] *Jazz Journal International* March 1987
[5] Randi Hultin *Born Under The Sign Of Jazz* (Sanctuary 2000)
[6] *Down Beat* November 12th 1970
[7] *Down Beat* January 7th 1971
[8] *Down Beat* February 4th 1971
[9] *Down Beat* September 16th 1971
[10] Booklet notes *Bill Evans, Piano Player* (Columbia 1998)
[11] *Jazz Journal International* October 1985
[12] Liner notes *The Bill Evans Album* (Columbia 1971)
[13] *Down Beat* September 16th 1971
[14] Liner notes *The Bill Evans Album* (Columbia 1971)
[15] Booklet notes *Bill Evans, Piano Player* (Columbia 1998)
[16] Liner notes *The Bill Evans Album* (Columbia 1971)
[17] *Down Beat* March 16th 1972
[18] *Down Beat* July 22nd 1971
[19] *Down Beat* September 16th 1971
[20] Liner notes *Living Time* (Columbia 1972)

Pages 156-167

[1] Booklet notes, *Complete Fantasy Recordings* (Fantasy 1989)
[2] *Down Beat* June 21st 1973
[3] Booklet notes, *Complete Fantasy Recordings* (Fantasy 1989)
[4] Liner notes *Symbiosis* (MPS 1974)
[5] Liner notes *Symbiosis* (MPS 1974)
[6] *Jazz Journal International* October 1985
[7] Booklet notes *But Beautiful* (Milestone 1996)
[8] Booklet notes, *Complete Fantasy Recordings* (Fantasy 1989)
[9] Liner notes *Blue In Green: The Concert In Canada* (Milestone 1991)
[10] Booklet notes, *Complete Fantasy Recordings* (Fantasy 1989)
[11] *Jazz Journal International* October 1985
[12] Booklet notes, *Complete Fantasy Recordings* (Fantasy 1989)
[13] *Jazz Journal International* October 1985
[14] *Down Beat* September 9th 1976
[15] *Down Beat* February 24th 1977
[16] *Jazz Journal International* October 1985
[17] *Down Beat* November 20th 1975
[18] *Down Beat* November 20th 1975
[19] Booklet notes, *Complete Fantasy Recordings* (Fantasy 1989)
[20] *Down Beat* April 20th 1978

Pages 168-175

[1] Booklet notes *The Complete Fantasy Recordings* (Fantasy 1989)
[2] *Jazz Journal International* October 1985
[3] Burt Goldblatt *Newport Jazz Festival – The Illustrated History* (Dial 1977)
[4] Booklet notes *The Complete Fantasy Recordings* (Fantasy 1989)
[5] Booklet notes *The Complete Fantasy Recordings* (Fantasy 1989)
[6] *Down Beat* October 1979
[7] Booklet notes *The Complete Bill Evans On Verve* (Verve 1997)
[8] Booklet notes *The Complete Bill Evans On Verve* (Verve 1997)
[9] Radio interview by Marion McPartland, November 1978

Pages 176-183

[1] Radio interview by Marion McPartland, November 1978
[2] *Jazz Journal International* October 1985

[3] Booklet notes *The Complete Bill Evans On Verve* (Verve 1997)
[4] *Down Beat* October 1979
[5] *Jazz Journal International* October 1985
[6] Liner notes *Paris Concert Edition Two* (Elektra Musician 1984)
[7] Radio interview by Marion McPartland, November 1978
[8] Radio interview by Marion McPartland, November 1978
[9] Radio interview by Marion McPartland, November 1978
[10] Liner notes *New Conversations* (Warner Bros 1978)
[11] Liner notes *New Conversations* (Warner Bros 1978)
[12] Liner notes *New Conversations* (Warner Bros 1978)
[13] Liner notes *New Conversations* (Warner Bros 1978)
[14] Liner notes *New Conversations* (Warner Bros 1978)
[15] Radio interview by Marion McPartland, November 1978
[16] *Down Beat* October 1979
[17] *Jazz Journal International* October 1985
[18] *Jazz Journal International* October 1985
[19] Booklet notes *The Complete Bill Evans On Verve* (Verve 1997)
[20] Radio interview by Marion McPartland, November 1978
[21] *Jazz Journal International* March 1987
[22] Insert notes *Turn Out The Stars: The Artist's Choice* (Warner Brothers 1996)
[23] Insert notes *Turn Out The Stars: The Artist's Choice* (Warner Brothers 1996)

Pages 184-199

[1] *Down Beat* October 1979
[2] *Down Beat* October 1979
[3] *Down Beat* October 1979
[4] *Jazz Journal International* October 1985
[5] Booklet notes *The Complete Bill Evans On Verve* (Verve 1997)
[6] Booklet notes *The Complete Bill Evans On Verve* (Verve 1997)
[7] *Homecoming* (Milestone 1999)
[8] Liner notes *The Paris Concert Edition One* (Elektra Musician 1983)
[9] *Contemporary Keyboard* June 1980
[10] *Down Beat* June 1980
[11] *Contemporary Keyboard* June 1980
[12] Booklet notes *The Complete Bill Evans On Verve* (Verve 1997)
[13] *Down Beat* October 1979
[14] Booklet notes, *Turn Out The Stars* boxed set (Warner Bros 1996)
[15] Booklet notes, *Turn Out The Stars* boxed set (Warner Bros 1996)
[16] Booklet notes, *Turn Out The Stars* boxed set (Warner Bros 1996)
[17] Booklet notes, *Turn Out The Stars* boxed set (Warner Bros 1996)
[18] *Coda* February 1985
[19] Cesare Pavese *Concerning Certain Poems Not Yet Written* (Giulio Einaudi/Peter Owen 1962/1969)
[20] Booklet notes, *Turn Out The Stars* boxed set (Warner Bros 1996)
[21] Booklet notes *Complete Fantasy Recordings* (Fantasy 1989)
[22] Booklet notes *The Complete Bill Evans On Verve* (Verve 1997)
[23] Booklet notes, *Turn Out The Stars* boxed set (Warner Bros 1996)
[24] Booklet notes *Complete Fantasy Recordings* (Fantasy 1989)
[25] Booklet notes *The Last Waltz* (Milestone 2000)
[26] Booklet notes *The Last Waltz* (Milestone 2000)
[27] Cesare Pavese *Concerning Certain Poems Not Yet Written* (Giulio Einaudi/Peter Owen 1962/1969)
[28] Booklet notes *Complete Fantasy Recordings* (Fantasy 1989)
[29] Booklet notes *The Complete Bill Evans On Verve* (Verve 1997)

B i l l   E v a n s

This selected discography is split into two sections. Records that Evans made as a leader or co-leader are listed first, with personnel in addition to Evans noted. Records he made as a sideman are overleaf. Both sections are arranged in chronological order of recording. Anything bigger than a tentet is a "large group". There have been many bootleg records available at various times, of varying quality, but this discography concentrates on legitimate issues. Where two original-release catalogue numbers are given, these are mono/stereo versions.

BILL EVANS AS LEADER OR CO-LEADER

New Jazz Conceptions Trio (+T.Kotick/P.Motian). Recorded September 11th/27th **1956**, Reeves studio, New York City. Original release 1957, Riverside RLP 12 223.

Everybody Digs Bill Evans Trio (+S.Jones/P.J.Jones). Recorded December 15th **1958**, Reeves studio, New York City. Original release 1959, Riverside RLP 12 291.

Peace Piece And Other Pieces Trio (+P.Chambers/ P.J.Jones). Recorded January 19th **1959**, Reeves studio, New York City. Original release 1975, Milestone M 47024.

The Ivory Hunters (Bill Evans & Bob Brookmeyer) Quartet (+B.Brookmeyer/P.Heath/C.Kay). Recorded March 12th **1959**, unknown studio, New York City. Original release 1959, United Artists UAL 4004/5004.

Portrait In Jazz Trio (+S.LaFaro/P.Motian). Recorded December 28th **1959**, Reeves studio, New York City. Original release 1960, Riverside RLP 12 315.

Know What I Mean? (Cannonball Adderley with Bill Evans) Quartet (+J.Adderley/P.Heath/C.Kay). Recorded January 27th/February 21st/March 13th **1961**, Bell studio, New York City. Original release 1962, Riverside RLP 433/9433.

Explorations Trio (+S.LaFaro/P.Motian). Recorded February 2nd 1961, Bell studio, New York City. Original release **1961**, Riverside RLP 351.

Sunday At The Village Vanguard Trio (+S.LaFaro/ P.Motian). Recorded June 25th **1961**, Village Vanguard, New York City. Original release 1961, Riverside RLP 376.

Waltz For Debby Trio (+S.LaFaro/P.Motian). Recorded June 25th **1961**, Village Vanguard, New York City. Original release 1962, Riverside RLP 399.

Nirvana (Herbie Mann & The Bill Evans Trio) Quartet (+H.Mann/C.Israels/P.Motian). Recorded December 8th **1961** & May 4th **1962**, Atlantic studio, New York City. Original release 1964, Atlantic SD 1426.

Conception Solo. Recorded April 4th **1962**, Plaza Sound studio, New York City. Original release 1981, Milestone M 47063.

Undercurrent (Evans & Jim Hall) Duo (+J.Hall). Recorded April 24th & May 14th **1962**, Sound Makers studio, New York City. Original release 1962, United Artists UAJ 14003.

Moonbeams Trio (+C.Israels/P.Motian). Recorded May 17th/29th & June 5th **1962**, Sound Makers studio, New York City. Original release 1962, Riverside RLP 428.

How My Heart Sings Trio (+C.Israels/P.Motian). Recorded May 17th/29th & June 5th **1962**, Sound Makers

studio, New York City. Original release 1963, Riverside RLP 473.

Interplay Quintet (+F.Hubbard/J.Hall/P.Heath/P.J.Jones). Recorded July 16th/17th **1962**, Nola's Penthouse studio, New York City. Original release 1963, Riverside RLP 445.

Empathy Trio (+M.Budwig/S.Manne). Recorded August 20th **1962**, unknown studio, New York City. Original release 1962, Verve V6 8497.

The Interplay Sessions Quintet (+Z.Sims/J.Hall/R.Carter/ P.J.Jones). Recorded August 21st/22nd **1962**, Nola's Penthouse studio, New York City. Original release 1982, combined with *Interplay* July sessions, on Milestone M 47066.

The Gary McFarland Orchestra, Special Guest Soloist: Bill Evans Septet (+P.Woods/S.Sinatra/ G.McFarland/J.Hall/ R.Davis/E.Shaughnessy) & strings. Recorded January 24th **1963** (possibly also December **1962**), Webster Hall, New York City. Original release 1963, Verve MGV 8518/V6 8518.

Conversations With Myself Solo. Recorded February 6th/9th/20th **1963**, Webster Hall, New York City. Original release 1963, Verve V6 8526.

Plays The Theme From The VIPs And Other Great Songs Large group & orchestra. Recorded May 6th/summer **1963**, A&R studio/RCA studio/Webster Hall, New York City. Original release 1963, MGM E/SE 4184.

Live At Shelly's Manne-Hole Trio (+C.Israels/L.Bunker). Recorded May 30th/31st **1963**, Shelly's Manne-Hole, Los Angeles. Original release 1963, Riverside RM 487/RS 9487.

Trio '64 Trio (+G.Peacock/P.Motian). Recorded December 18th **1963**, Webster Hall, New York City. Original release 1964, Verve V6 8578.

Stan Getz And Bill Evans (Getz & Evans) Quartet (+S.Getz/E.Jones/R.Davis or R.Carter). Recorded May 5th/6th **1964**, Van Gelder studio, Englewood Cliffs, NJ. Original release 1974, Verve V6 8833.

Trio Live Trio (+C.Israels/L.Bunker). Recorded July 7th/9th **1964**, The Trident Club, Sausalito, CA. Original release 1973, Verve V6 8803.

Waltz For Debby (Bill Evans Trio with Monica Zetterlund) Quartet (+M.Zetterlund/C.Israels/L.Bunker). Recorded August 29th **1964**, AB Europa studio, Stockholm, Sweden. Original release 1964, Philips 6378 508.

Trio '65 Trio (+C.Israels/L.Bunker). Recorded February 3rd **1965**, Van Gelder studio, Englewood Cliffs, New Jersey. Original release 1965, Verve V6 8613.

With Symphony Orchestra Trio (+C.Israels/G.Tate) & strings/woodwind. Recorded September 29th/October 18th/December 16th **1965**, Van Gelder studio, Englewood Cliffs, NJ. Original release 1966, Verve V6 8640.

At Town Hall Volume 1 Trio (+C.Israels/A.Wise). Recorded February 21st **1966**, Town Hall, New York City. Original release 1966, Verve V6 8683.

Intermodulation (Bill Evans & Jim Hall) Duo (+J.Hall). Recorded April 7th/May 10th **1966**, Van Gelder studio, Englewood Cliffs, NJ. Original release 1966, Verve V6 8655.

A Simple Matter Of Conviction Trio (+E.Gomez/
S.Manne). Recorded October 11th **1966**, Van Gelder
studio, Englewood Cliffs, NJ. Original release 1967, Verve
V6 8675.

Further Conversations With Myself Solo. Recorded
August 9th **1967**, Webster Hall, New York City. Original
release 1967, Verve V6 8727.

California Here I Come Trio (+E.Gomez/P.J.Jones).
Recorded August 17th/18th **1967**, Village Vanguard,
New York City. Original release 1984, Verve
VE2 2545.

At The Montreux Jazz Festival Trio (+E.Gomez/
J.DeJohnette). Recorded June 15th **1968**, Casino de
Montreux, Montreux, Switzerland. Original release 1968,
Verve V6 8762.

Alone Solo. Recorded September/October **1968,** Webster
Hall, New York City. Original release 1969, Verve
V6 8792.

What's New Quartet (+J.Steig/E.Gomez/M.Morell).
Recorded January 30th/February 3rd-5th/March 3rd or
11th **1969**, Webster Hall, New York City. Original release
1969, Verve V6 8777.

Jazzhouse Trio (+E.Gomez/M.Morell). Recorded
November 24th **1969**, Jazzhus Montmartre, Copenhagen,
Denmark. Original release 1987, Milestone M 9151.

You're Gonna Hear From Me Trio (+E.Gomez/
M.Morell). Recorded November 24th **1969**, Jazzhus
Montmartre, Copenhagen, Denmark. Original release
1987, Milestone M 9164.

From Left To Right Quartet (+S.Brown/E.Gomez/
M.Morell). Recorded between October **1969** and May
1970, various studios, New York City/San Francisco.
Original release 1970, MGM SE 4723.

Montreux II Trio (+E.Gomez/M.Morell). Recorded June
19th **1970**, Casino de Montreux, Montreux, Switzerland.
Original release 1970, CTI 6004.

Bill Evans, Piano Player Duo (+E.Gomez)/Trio
(+E.Gomez/M.Morell) Recorded November 23rd-24th
(duets) **1970** and May 17th **1971**, Columbia 30th Street
studio, New York City. Original release 1998, Columbia
CK 65361.

The Bill Evans Album Trio (+E.Gomez/M.Morell).
Recorded May 11th/12th/17th/19th/20th & June 9th **1971**,
Columbia 30th Street studio, New York City. Original
release 1971, Columbia C 30855.

Living Time Trio (E.Gomez/M.Morell) & large orchestra.
Recorded May **1972**, Columbia 30th Street studio,
New York City. Original release 1972, Columbia
KC 31490.

The Tokyo Concert Trio (+E.Gomez/M.Morell). Recorded
January 20th **1973**, Yubinchokin Hall, Tokyo, Japan.
Original US release 1974, Fantasy F 9547.

From The Seventies Trio (+E.Gomez/M.Morell)/quintet
(H.Land/K.Burrell/R.Brown/P.J.Jones). Recorded various
dates between November **1973** and May **1977**: Shelly's
Manne-Hole, Los Angeles; Village Vanguard, New York
City; Fantasy studio, Berkeley, CA. Original release 1983,
Fantasy F 9630.

Eloquence Solo/duo (+E.Gomez)/trio (+E.Gomez/
M/Morell). Recorded various dates between November
1973 and December **1975**: Shelly's Manne-Hole, Los
Angeles; Fantasy studio, Berkeley, CA; Casino de
Montreux, Montreux, Switzerland. Original release 1982,
Fantasy F 9618.

Half Moon Bay Trio (+E.Gomez/M.Morell). Recorded
November 4th **1973**, Bach Dancing & Dynamite Society,
Half Moon Bay, CA. Original release 1998, Milestone
MCD 9282 2.

Since We Met Trio (+E.Gomez/M.Morell). Recorded
January 11th/12th **1974**, Village Vanguard, New York
City. Original release 1976, Fantasy F 9501.

Re: Person I Knew Trio (+E.Gomez/M.Morell). Recorded
January 11th/12th **1974**, Village Vanguard, New York
City. Original release 1981, Fantasy F 9608.

Symbiosis Trio (+E.Gomez/M.Morell) & orchestra.
Recorded February 11th/12th/14th **1974**, Columbia
studio, New York City. Original release 1974, MPS 68052.

Blue In Green: The Concert In Canada Trio (+E.Gomez/
M.Morell). Recorded summer **1974**, Carleton University,
Ottawa, Canada; Camp Fortune, Hull, Canada. Original
release 1991, Milestone M 9185.

Featuring Stan Getz: But Beautiful Trio (+E.Gomez/
M.Morell)/quartet (+S.Getz/E.Gomez/M.Morell). Recorded
August 9th/16th **1974**, Singer Conzertzaal, Laren,
Netherlands/ Middleheim, Antwerp, Belgium. Original
release 1996, Milestone MCD 9249 2.

Intuition Duo (+E.Gomez). Recorded November 7th-10th
1974, Fantasy studio, Berkeley, CA. Original release 1975,
Fantasy F 9475.

The Tony Bennett/Bill Evans Album (Bennett/Evans)
Duo (+T.Bennett). Recorded June 10th/13th **1975**, Fantasy
studio, Berkeley, CA. Original release 1975, Fantasy
F 9489.

Montreux III Duo (+E.Gomez). Recorded July 20th
1975, Casino de Montreux, Montreux, Switzerland.
Original release 1976, Fantasy F 9510.

Alone (Again) Solo. Recorded December 16th-18th **1975**,
Fantasy studio, Berkeley, CA. Original release 1977,
Fantasy F 9542.

Quintessence Quintet (+H.Land/K.Burrell/R.Brown/
P.J.Jones). Recorded May **1976**, Fantasy studio, Berkeley,
CA. Original release 1977, Fantasy F 9529.

Together Again (Bennett/Evans) Duo (+T.Bennett).
Recorded September 27th-30th **1976**, unknown studio,
San Francisco. Original release 1977, Improv 7117.

The Paris Concert Trio (+E.Gomez/E.Zigmund).
Recorded November 5th **1976**, Maison de l'ORTF, Paris,
France. Original release 1989, Fantasy FCD 1012.

Crosscurrents Quintet (+L.Konitz/W.Marsh/E.Gomez/
E.Zigmund). Recorded February 28th & March 1st/2nd
1977, Fantasy studio, Berkeley, CA. Original release 1978,
Fantasy F 9568.

I Will Say Goodbye Trio (+E.Gomez/E.Zigmund).
Recorded May 11th-13th **1977**, Fantasy studio, Berkeley,
CA. Original release 1980, on Fantasy F 9593.

Bill Evans

You Must Believe In Spring Trio (+E.Gomez/E.Zigmund). Recorded August 23rd-25th **1977**, Capitol studio, Hollywood, CA. Original release 1981, Warner Bros HS 3504 Y.

New Conversations Solo. Recorded January 26th-28th/ 30th & February 13th-16th **1978**, Columbia 30th Street studio, New York City. Original release 1978, Warner Bros BSK 3177 Y.

Affinity Quintet (+T.Thielemans/L.Schneider/M.Johnson/ E.Zigmund). Recorded October 30th/31st & November 1st/2nd **1978**, Columbia 30th Street studio, New York City. Original release 1979, Warner Bros BSK 3293 Y.

We Will Meet Again Quintet (T.Harrell/L.Schneider/ M.Johnson/ J.LaBarbera). Recorded August 6th-9th **1979**, Columbia 30th Street studio, New York City. Original release 1980, Warner Bros HS 3411Y.

The Paris Concert: Edition One Trio (+M.Johnson/ J.LaBarbera). Recorded November 26th **1979**, Espace Pierre Cardin, Paris, France. Original release 1983, Elektra Musician 1 60164 D.

The Paris Concert: Edition Two Trio (+M.Johnson/ J.LaBarbera). Recorded November 26th **1979**, L'espace Pierre Cardin, Paris, France. Original release 1984, Elektra Musician 1 60311 D.

Letter To Evan Trio (+Johnson/LaBarbera). Recorded July 21st **1980**, Ronnie Scott's club, London, England. Original release 1993, Dreyfus 191 064 2.

Turn Out The Stars: The Artist's Choice Trio (+M.Johnson/J.LaBarbera). Recorded June 4th-8th **1980**, Village Vanguard, New York City. Original release 1996, Warner Bros 946425 2.

Turn Out The Stars: The Final Village Vanguard Recordings, June 1980 Trio (+M.Johnson/J.LaBarbera). Recorded June 4th-8th **1980**, Village Vanguard, New York City. Original six-CD release 1996, Warner Bros 945925 2.

Turn Out The Stars Trio (+Johnson/LaBarbera). Recorded August 2nd **1980**, Ronnie Scott's, London, England. Original release 1993, Dreyfus 191 063 2.

Consecration Trio (+M.Johnson/J.LaBarbera). Recorded August 31st -September 7th **1980**, Keystone Korner, San Francisco. Original eight-CD release 1990, Alfa Jazz R26168.

The Last Waltz: The Final Recordings, Keystone Korner, September 1980 Trio (+M.Johnson/J.LaBarbera). Recorded August 31st -September 7th **1980**, Keystone Korner, San Francisco. Original eight-CD release 2000, Milestone 4430 2.

MAJOR COLLECTIONS

The Complete Riverside Recordings Twelve CDs; **1956 to 1963**. Original release 1984, Riverside R 018.

The Complete Bill Evans On Verve Eighteen CDs; **1957 to 1969**. Original release 1996, Verve 527 953-2.

The Complete Fantasy Recordings Nine CDs; **1973 to 1977**. Original release 1989, Fantasy 9FCD 1012 2.

The Secret Sessions Eight CDs; recordings made semi-officially from **1966 to 1975** at The Village Vanguard, New York City. Original release 1996, Milestone 8MCD 4421 2.

BILL EVANS AS SIDEMAN

Dick Garcia *A Message From Dick Garcia*. Quartet. Recorded **1955**, unknown studio, New York City. Original release 1955, Dawn DLP 1106.

Lucy Reed *The Singin' Reed*. Quintet. Recorded August 13th-15th **1955**, unknown studio, New York City. Original release 1955, on Fantasy 3 212.

George Russell *Jazz Workshop*. Sextet ("Smalltet"). Recorded March 31st/October 17th/December 21st **1956**, Webster Hall, New York City. Original release 1957, RCA Victor LPM 1372.

Tony Scott *The Touch Of Tony Scott*. Large group. Recorded July 2nd/3rd/5th/6th **1956**, Webster Hall, New York. Original release 1956, RCA Victor LPM 1353.

Don Elliott/Bill Evans *Tenderly*. Duo. Rehearsals recorded **1956-57**, Elliott's house, Connecticut. Original release 2001, Milestone MCD 93172.

Tony Scott *The Complete Tony Scott*. Large group. Recorded December 11th/13th/14th **1956** & February 6th **1957**, Webster Hall, New York. Original release 1957, RCA Victor LPM 1452.

Various *Modern Jazz Concert*. Large group. Recorded June 10th/18th/20th **1957**, Columbia 30th Street studio, New York City. Original release 1957, Columbia WL 127.

Joe Puma *Jazz*. Quartet. Recorded summer **1957**, unknown studio, New York City. Original release 1957, Jubilee JLP 1070.

Charles Mingus *East Coasting*. Sextet. Recorded August 6th **1957**, unknown studio, New York City. Original release 1957, Bethlehem BTM 6814.

Jimmy Knepper *A Swinging Introduction*. Quintet. Recorded September **1957**, unknown studio, New York City. Original release 1958, Bethlehem BCP 77.

Sahib Shihab *Jazz Sahib*. Sextet. Recorded November 7th **1957**, unknown studio, Hackensack, NJ. Original release 1958, Savoy MGM 12124.

Tony Scott *The Modern Art Of Jazz*. Quartet/sextet/ septet. Recorded November 16th **1957**, unknown studio, New York City. Original release 1958, Seeco CELP 425.

Prestige All Stars *Roots*. Sextet. Recorded December 6th **1957**, Rudy Van Gelder studio, Hackensack, NJ. Original release 1958, Prestige 8202.

Eddie Costa *Guys And Dolls Like Vibes*. Quartet. Recorded January 15th-17th **1958**, unknown studio, New York City. Original release 1958, Coral CRL 57230.

Don Elliott *The Mello Sound Of Don Elliott*. Septet & choir. Recorded February 10th/11th **1958**, unknown studio, New York City. Original release 1958, Decca DL 9208.

Helen Merrill with Bobby Jaspar *The Nearness Of You*. Sextet. Recorded February 21st **1958**, unknown studio, New York City. Original release 1958, EmArcy MG 36134.

Hal McKusick *Cross Section Saxes*. Quintet. Recorded March 25th/28th & April 7th **1958**, unknown studio, New York City. Original release 1958, Decca DL 9209.

Miles Davis *1958 Miles*. Quintet/sextet. Recorded May 26th **1958**, Columbia 30th Street studios, New York City. Original release 1959, Columbia 467918 2.

Michel Legrand *Legrand Jazz*. Large group. Recorded June 25th **1958**, Columbia 30th Street studio, New York City. Original release 1959, Columbia CL 1250.

Cannonball Adderley *Portrait Of Cannonball*. Quintet. Recorded July 1st **1958**, Reeves studio, New York City. Original release 1958, Riverside 12 269.

Miles Davis *Miles Davis & Thelonious Monk At Newport*. Sextet. Recorded (Davis) July 3rd **1958**, Freebody Park, Newport, RI. Original release 1964, Columbia CL 2178.

Cannonball Adderley *Jump For Joy*. Sextet & strings. Recorded August 20th/21st **1958**, Fine studio, New York City. Original release 1958, Mercury MG 20530.

Miles Davis *Jazz At The Plaza*. Sextet. Recorded September 9th **1958**, Plaza Hotel, New York City. Original release 1973, Columbia C 32470.

Art Farmer *Modern Art*. Quintet. Recorded September 10th/11th/14th **1958**, Nola's Penthouse studio, New York City. Original release 1959, United Artists UAL 4007/5007.

George Russell *New York, NY*. Large group. Recorded September 12th/November 24th **1958** & March 24th **1959**, unknown studio, New York City. Original release 1959, Decca DL 7 9216.

Chet Baker *Chet*. Sextet/quartet. Recorded December 30th **1958** & January 19th **1959**, Reeves studio, New York City. Original release 1959, Riverside RLP 12 299/1135.

Bill Potts/Porgy & Bess All-Stars *The Jazz Soul Of Porgy And Bess*. Large group. Recorded January 13th-15th **1959**, Webster Hall, New York City. Original release 1960, United Artists UAL4043/UAS 4032.

Lee Konitz *Live At The Half Note*. Quintet. Recorded February 24th/March 3rd **1959**, Half Note Cafe, New York City. Original release 1995, Verve 521 659 2.

Miles Davis *Kind Of Blue*. Sextet/quintet. Recorded March 2nd/April 22nd 1959, Columbia 30th Street studio, New York City. Original release 1959, Columbia CL 1355/CS 8163.

George Russell *Jazz In The Space Age*. Large group. Recorded May & August 1st **1960**, unknown studio, New York City. Original release 1960, Decca DL 7 9219.

Lee Konitz & Jimmy Giuffre *Lee Konitz Meets Jimmy Giuffre*. Octet. Recorded May 12th/13th **1959**, unknown studio, New York City. Original release 1960, Verve MGV 8335/MGVS 6073.

Teo Macero *Something New Something Borrowed*. Octet. Recorded May 15th **1959**, probably Columbia studio, New York City. Original release 1959, Columbia CL 1388/CS 8183.

John Lewis *Odds Against Tomorrow*. Large group. Recorded July 16th/17th/20th **1959**, unknown studio, New York City. Original release 1959, United Artists UAL 4061/UAS 5061.

Chet Baker *Plays The Best Of Lerner & Loewe*. Septet. Recorded July 21st/22nd **1959**, Reeves studio, New York City. Original release 1959, Riverside RLP 12 307/1152.

Tony Scott *Golden Moments*. Quartet. Recorded August 1st/9th **1959**, The Showplace, New York City. Original release 1976, Muse MR 5230.

Lee Konitz *You And Lee*. Tentet. Recorded October 29th **1959**, unknown studio, New York City. Original release 1960, Verve MGV 8362/MGVS 6131.

Frank Minion *The Soft Land Of Make Believe*. Quartet. Recorded January **1960**, unknown studio, New York City. Original release 1960, Bethlehem BCP 6052.

Donald Byrd & Pepper Adams *The Soul Of Jazz Percussion*. Sextet. Recorded spring **1960**, unknown studio, New York City. Original release 1960, Warwick W 5003 ST.

Kai Winding & JJ Johnson *The Great Kai & JJ, Brand New, Swinging Together Again*. Quintet. Recorded October 3rd/November 2nd/4th/8th **1960**, unknown studio, New York City. Original release 1961, Impulse! A1/A(S)1.

Kai Winding *The Incredible Kai Winding Trombones*. Septet. Recorded December 13th **1960**, unknown studio, New York City. Original release 1961, Impulse! A3/A(S)3.

Gunther Schuller Orchestra *Jazz Abstractions*. Sextet/octet/nonet/tentet & strings. Recorded December 20th **1960**, unknown studio, New York City. Original release 1961, Atlantic SD 1365.

Oliver Nelson *The Blues And The Abstract Truth*. Septet. Recorded February 23rd **1961**, Van Gelder studio, Englewood Cliffs, NJ. Original release 1961, on Impulse! A5/A(S)5.

Mark Murphy & Ernie Wilkins *Rah*. Large group. Recorded October 16th **1961**, Plaza studio, New York City. Original release 1962, Riverside RLP 395/9395.

Dave Pike *Pike's Peak*. Quartet. Recorded February 6th **1962**, unknown studio, New York City. Original release 1962, Epic LA 16025/SLA 17025.

Tadd Dameron *The Magic Touch*. Large group. Recorded February 27th/March 9th/April 16th **1962**, Plaza studio, New York City. Original release 1962, Riverside RLP 419/9419.

Benny Golson *Pop + Jazz = Swing*. Sextet & orchestra. Recorded April **1962**, unknown studio, New York City. Original release 1962, Audio Fidelity AFLP 1978.

Bill Evans

An *italic* item in the index indicates an Evans album title, unless an artist is given (in brackets) or the item is described as a soundtrack, TV show etc. An *italic* page number indicates an illustration.

ACKNOWLEDGEMENTS

Author's thanks

This project was started a number of years ago through the encouragement of three people. Steve Voce, Richard Palmer and Barry McRae in their very different ways guided me to the subject and helped me at various problematic stages. They may be surprised to learn it, but I am grateful for their generosity, good humour and resourcefulness. Bill Evans enthusiast Mike Sage also helped with some knotty research problems.

At the sharp end, a number of people were models of courtesy, faith and resilience in pursuit of that elusive record, tape, book and magazine. Terri Hinte of Fantasy Records (US) deserves a major vote of thanks. Becky Stevenson and Julie Alison at Universal Jazz (UK) both went to great lengths. Sharon Kelly and Adam Sieff at Sony Jazz (UK) both helped me about the Columbia years. Florence Halfon at Warner Bros (UK) tried hard to help with the latter-day Evans releases at a time when little of it was current in the catalogue. Over and above this was the unfailing help provided by Peter Fincham and his brilliant staff at Mole Jazz, London, across every area of arcane research I could come up with.

My grateful thanks to my publisher and editor, Tony Bacon, his partner Nigel Osborne, Sally Stockwell, and all the team at Backbeat. Also thanks to Peter Symes for invaluable picture research.

Last, a note on chronology. The first draft of this book was completed at the same time as the publication of Peter Pettinger's study of Bill Evans, How My Heart Sings. Thus I was not able to avail myself of its qualities during my research and writing – but I used it as a valuable authenticator and sounding-board when I came to the final editing of the text. So I only reinvented the wheel once.

I dedicate this book to my family, whose presence constantly reminds me that the final thing to emerge from Pandora's Box was hope.

Picture Credits

Photographs were supplied by the following (number indicates page; source in *italics*): **Cover** *Jan Persson*; **2** *Jan Persson*; **9** *Steve Schapiro*; **16** *Steve Schapiro*; **18/19** all pictures by *Don Hunstein/Sony*; **20** *Robert W Parent*; **21** top *Robert W Parent*; **21** centre right *Ray Avery Jazz Archives*; **22/23** all pictures *Steve Schapiro*; **24/25** all pictures *Steve Schapiro*; **26** main picture *Steve Schapiro*; **28** picture centre left and main picture *Lee Tanner*; **29** main picture *Ray Avery Jazz Archives*; **30/31** all pictures *Jan Persson*; **32/33** main picture and below right *Jan Persson*; **34/35** all pictures *Jan Persson*; **36** main picture *Ray Avery Jazz Archives*; **37** *Val Wilmer*; **38** top *Lee Tanner*; **38/39** main picture *Jan Persson*; **39** top *Jan Persson*; **40** all main pictures *Jak Kilby*; **41** both pictures *Jan Persson*; **42** top left *Ray Avery Jazz Archives*; **43** main picture *Val Wilmer*; **44/45** main picture *Ray Avery Jazz Archives*; **46/47** all main pictures *Jacques Hvistendahl*; **49** *Lee Tanner*; **55** *Lee Tanner*; **63** *Don Hunstein/Sony*; **71** *Robert W Parent*; **81** *Steve Schapiro*; **93** *Steve Schapiro*; **103** *Jan Persson*; **113** *Ray Avery Jazz Archives*; **121** *Jan Persson*; **133** *Jan Persson*; **147** *Jan Persson*; **157** *Ray Avery Jazz Archives*; **169** *Lee Tanner*; **177** *Jacques Hvistendahl*; **185** *Jacques Hvistendahl*.

Other illustrated items including LP sleeves, CD inserts and magazines are from the collections of Stan Britt, Ted Hatch, Per Husby, *Jazz Journal International*, Keith Shadwick, Peter Symes, and The National Jazz Foundation Archive.

The publishers would also like to thank: Brian Hennessy; David Nathan (National Jazz Foundation Archive); Jim Roberts.

"A day will come when a tranquil glance will bring order and unity into the arduous chaos which starts tomorrow."
Cesare Pavese, *Concerning Certain Poems Not Yet Written*